Parole, Pardon, Pass and
Amnesty Documents
of the Civil War

Parole, Pardon, Pass and Amnesty Documents of the Civil War

An Illustrated History

John Martin Davis, Jr., and
George B. Tremmel

Foreword by Lawrence S. Rowland

McFarland & Company, Inc., Publishers
Jefferson, North Carolina, and London

Acknowledgments

The major source of the illustrations used in the book is the collection of coauthor Marty Davis. The authors also would like to recognize contributions of images from North Carolina collectors Ed Jones of Archdale and Dr. Charles Knupp of Greenville; Tennessee collector Tom Carson of Chattanooga; and Gary Doster of Athens, Georgia. We also note, with our gratitude, the contributions of Lea Kemp, archivist, and her assistant, Natalie Batten, Intern, of the Rochester (NY) Museum and Science Center.

LIBRARY OF CONGRESS CATALOGUING-IN-PUBLICATION DATA

Davis, John Martin, Jr. 1944–
Parole, pardon, pass and amnesty documents of the Civil War : an illustrated history / John Martin Davis, Jr., and George B. Tremmel ; foreword by Lawrence S. Rowland.
p. cm.
Includes bibliographical references and index.

ISBN 978-0-7864-7441-7
softcover : acid free paper ∞

1. United States—History—Civil War, 1861–1865—Law and legislation—Sources. 2. United States—History—Civil War, 1861–1865—Prisoners and prisons—Legal status, laws, etc.—Sources. 3. United States—History—Civil War, 1861–1865—Claims—Sources. I. Tremmel, George B., 1942– II. Title.
KF7221.D38 2013   973.7'1—dc23   2013030620

BRITISH LIBRARY CATALOGUING DATA ARE AVAILABLE

© 2014 John Martin Davis, Jr., and George B. Tremmel. All rights reserved

No part of this book may be reproduced or transmitted in any form or by any means, electronic or mechanical, including photocopying or recording, or by any information storage and retrieval system, without permission in writing from the publisher.

On the cover: *clockwise* Jefferson Davis Bail Bond; Administering the Oath of Allegiance to Confederate Prisoners, *Frank Leslie's Illustrated Newspaper*, December 1864; 20th OVM Regiment Blank Pass and Oath; *background* iStockphoto/Thinkstock

Manufactured in the United States of America

McFarland & Company, Inc., Publishers
Box 611, Jefferson, North Carolina 28640
www.mcfarlandpub.com

Contents

Acknowledgments iv
Foreword by Lawrence S. Rowland 1
Preface 3
Introduction 5

1. Treason   9
2. Promises of Loyalty   14
3. Passes and Paroles   24
4. Presidential Pardons   49
5. Prisoner Oaths   71
6. Paroles on Surrender   92
7. Postwar Amnesty   110

Introduction to the Appendices 139
Appendix 1: Paroles 140
Appendix 2: Passes 146
Appendix 3: Pardons 161
Appendix 4: Promises of Loyalty 166
Notes 185
Bibliography 187
Index 189

Foreword

by Lawrence S. Rowland

The only known quote to survive from the iconic barbarian warlord Attila the Hun is "Never tell the truth if a lie will suit your purposes as well." The reason this quote has survived in popular literature is because it separates civilized values from barbaric values. One of the hallmarks of civilized behavior is to tell the truth. This value has been enshrined in Western civilization for three thousand years since Moses revealed it to be the Commandment of God's covenant with the Israelites: "Thou shalt not bear false witness." Since then, Greek and Roman legislators turned it into legal dogma. Sworn oaths have been the standard for legal testimony. Written and signed contracts have been the cement of business transactions. The popular phrase for describing a man of honor in Western civilization is "'His word is his bond." In times of political stress and turmoil, oaths of loyalty and promises of behavior have been commonly used to try to bring order and peace. Breaking of sworn oaths and promises has been considered capital offenses since Roman times.

The greatest political stress the American Republic has ever endured was the Civil War and it resulted in the most deadly and destructive turmoil in the nation's history. Naturally, loyalty oaths became standard for all sides. This was not new. Sworn oaths were required for pardons and paroles in the Revolutionary War. In South Carolina, Col. Isaac Hayne was paroled by the occupying British forces on a promise not to take up arms against the occupiers. When he attempted to raise volunteers to join Col. Francis Marion and Col. William Harden's guerrilla bands, "'the Swamp Foxes," he was captured and hanged in Charleston in retaliation for the American execution of the British spy and Benedict Arnold conspirator, Major John Andre.

When the first political crisis of the Civil War era, the Nullification Crisis of 1828–1833, erupted, South Carolina required a controversial "Test Oath" from militia officers and many public officials which essentially compelled the officials to swear primary allegiance to the state. The South Carolina attorney general who defended the Test Oath in court was Robert Barnwell Rhett. He later became South Carolina's "Father of Secession" and, next to John C. Calhoun, the most influential and famous South Carolina politician of the antebellum era. When South Carolina seceded, one of their foremost justifications was that the national government had broken the signed contractual agreements in the Constitution of the United States. This position was adopted by all the seceding Confederate States. The next four years saw a titanic clash of loyalties, sworn and otherwise. Probably no period of American history has witnessed more conflicting and opposing oaths, promises, pardons and paroles than the Civil War.

This work is an illustrative sample of these numerous and sometimes curious documents with authoritative explanations for the circumstances and history of each. Naturally, a larger number of these documents come from the Border States where the loyalties were more fluid and the military situation was constantly changing. This book is a treasure for collectors and enthusiasts of Civil War history. It is also a window into the tortured moral choices, legal expediencies and military necessities of the greatest political crisis in United States history.

Lawrence S. Rowland is a distinguished history professor emeritus at the University of South Carolina–Beaufort.

Preface

Searching, collecting and researching consumed well over a decade prior to preparing this work. Countless incidents of assistance, direction and correction fail recollection. Associates, librarians, archivists, and kindred collectors are all owed a debt of gratitude. Special thanks is due Arkansas dealer Howard Norton who patiently listened to detailed descriptions of specific items needed to illustrate the Civil War signs of paroles, pardons and oaths of loyalty. Early in the quest, the staff of the Georgia Historical Society opened their cabinets, boxes and folders, some undisturbed for years, to an inquisitive lawyer from Texas. The archives were a treasure trove of wonder and questions. Now deceased, historian Jack Jackson of Austin, while en route to Dallas airport, shared his own family's experiences and the required registration. Later, he forwarded copies of his family records that encouraged further Texas enquiries. Without his persistent encouragement, this project would have been concluded as only another comprehensive research study of another retired professional with a disposition towards history. Special mention is due Mary Bones, Curator of the Museum of the Big Bend, who transcribed the initial manuscript to print and made numerous well-needed edits.

—*Marty Davis*

This is my fourth book on little studied topics of Civil War history. It also continues the collaboration with friend and fellow author, Marty Davis, who co-authored "Confederate Treasury Certificates," published in 2009. Unlike my previous works, this book is not about Confederate financial history. Presented, here, is the story of the history and documents of the paroles, passes, pardons and promises of loyalty used by both sides of the War. In my, somewhat biased opinion, this history gives an interesting insight into the politics, culture and battlefield realities present during the conduct of the war. I hope you agree.

—*George Tremmel*

A Note on Illustrations

All illustrations in this work have been resized to varying degrees to allow placement in the text. None of the illustrated documents appear in actual size.

Numbering Convention: Illustrations are identified by a catalog numbering scheme developed by George Tremmel. The identification key uses a two letter abbreviation for the *state/*

district where the document was issued followed by a five digit code. The first digit indicates the *type* of document:

        1 — Parole
        2 — Pass
        3 — Pardon
        4 — Promise of Loyalty
        5 — Miscellaneous Document

The next two digits show the *year* of issue during the 1800s: 61, 62, 63, etc.
The last two digits are the *sequence number* for a specific state, type, and year.

For example, the illustration numbered "DC-2.64.01" indicates that the illustration is from the District of Columbia, is a pass document, was issued in 1864 and has sequence number 01.

Introduction

During civil unrest, American political notions swing between the "bell-curve" extremes of tyrants and traitors. Domestic rebellions highlight differences. During peacetime, most citizens accept that a sovereign's purpose is to protect them from enemies, both foreign and domestic. Rebellion threatens government's right to continue, whether elected or anointed. Medieval monarchs were viewed as God's appointed rulers of their land, but by the eighteenth century many questioned the divine right of kings. To that point, Thomas Jefferson had emblazoned across his personal seal: "Rebellion to tyrants and obedience to God."[1]

The essence of rebellion is disloyalty to the government in power. Civil War is a nation's final resort after the failure of the political system in place. Consequently, the most direct return to normalcy after an insurrection is the predominance of loyalty to the government in office. After the American Civil War ended with the defeat of the Confederate States, a process of rehabilitation was installed that lasted for decades. Today, that process can be seen in places such as South Africa where is it is described as "truth and reconciliation." Historically, sovereigns have dealt with traitors in one of three ways: death, banishment and pardon. The initial response to a rebellion often was execution of the insurgents, in the hope of crushing an uprising before it spreads with swift and firm action. Banishment was reserved, normally, for high-profile leaders of a rebellion where the risk of martyrdom could be counterproductive. Accompanying the exile of a traitor was the confiscation of property and titles. If the rebellion is widely supported by the people, the sanctions of death or exile are often too extreme and costly to the society as a whole. In that case, forgiveness and clemency are more in line with future tranquility.

The individual clemency granted by a sovereign to a treacherous citizen is termed a pardon. Few examples of execution of traitors, and even fewer of exile, are known during the American Civil War. President Abraham Lincoln liberally forgave both condemned traitors and captured Rebels. Early on, disloyal political prisoners were paroled on their word of honor as gentlemen not to do harm against the United States and to be loyal to the Constitution, laws and government. After the war began, Rebel soldiers were paroled until duly exchanged under the rules of war, if they kept their word not to combat the United States. Late in the war, full pardons were offered to those willing to return to the state of full citizenship in the United States. To qualify for clemency, the traitor had to request forgiveness and admit his acts of disloyalty. Essential to this process was some consensus as to the meaning of disloyalty.

"Death to Traitors" has been the American reaction to disloyalty since Independence.

However, the crime of treason is more specific than a general betrayal of a cause or trust — treason is a charge reserved for subjects that betray a sovereign by giving aid and support to an enemy during war. Being the highest of capital crimes, only a sovereign can pardon a traitor. A repentant traitor can request clemency and, if deemed worthy, might be pardoned. The pardon process normally includes a recitation of all acts of treason and a sincere pledge before God to remain forever loyal. Once pardoned, if ever again disloyal, the traitor would face the gallows.

Both the feudal church and state demanded fealty of all subjects. *Fidelitas*, faithful duty, was sanctioned by both canon and common law, and violations were severely punished. Consequently, treason and heresy were criminal and sinful, punishable by death. Fidelity was proclaimed in public and sealed by oath given in the name of the Almighty. A subsequent breach of this sacred pledge of allegiance was damnable and treasonable. Breaking an official oath was also a felony, and remains so today.

Nineteenth-century Americans valued the dissent allowed by free speech and press. Both were essential to a vibrant democracy and assured by the Bill of Rights. By the midpoint of the 19th century, most citizens had accepted the idea that the Union was inviolate and domestic threats to the Union could only be tolerated within limits. Punishment of treason, like the Magna Charta right, habeas corpus, was essential to the Union and both were mentioned in the United States Constitution. Although the true nature of treason eluded lawmakers, few had sympathy for traitors. After the Revolution, American Royalists were arrested, their estates confiscated and families deported. The conundrum for the young republic was to define the difference between punishable treason and domestic dissent. Civil disobedience with violence clouded the distinction between acts of protest and acts of disloyalty.

After the Civil War began, few were enlightened enough to recall the observation of Thomas Jefferson that "a little rebellion now and then is a good thing and as necessary in the political world as storms in the physical." After South Carolina seceded and government property was seized, Washington predictably imposed restrictions on speech, assembly and travel. Citizens were required to produce a properly signed and registered pass, if questioned. Anyone requesting a license or other privilege was required to give a loyalty oath. Those believed to be dangerous and disloyal were confined in political prisons under the control of the State Department. Further, the constitutional method of challenging unlawful detention, the writ of habeas corpus, was suspended. In Border States and near military forts and naval shipyards, martial law was imposed that superseded judiciary review of executive-branch actions.[2]

Initially, efforts to subdue rebellion were focused along the Mason-Dixon line. Consequently, a growing number of political prisoners were being held in old forts along the northeastern seaboard. Eventually, most detainees were paroled after giving their solemn oath to be loyal and peaceful. Within a year, the parole process was formalized and the War Department assumed responsibility. Later, captive Confederate officers were paroled on their word of honor not to wage war until properly exchanged. Presidential pardons became common at this time. The first general amnesty was offered near the end of 1863. That process included an oath of loyalty, registration and the demonstration of genuine sincerity. If pardoned, former Rebel soldiers could relocate to a Union state and be employed by the government. On the other hand, Federal army deserters, although forgiven if they voluntarily returned to their regiment, had to continue their army enlistment term. Ironically, more Union deserters were executed than Rebel traitors by the federal government.

Amnesty qualifications became more strenuous as the war came to an end. Upon surrender, Rebel enlisted troops were given safeguards and allowed to return home. Rebel officers and civilian planters were viewed with suspicion. Consequently, their rehabilitation process was slow and conditional. While President Andrew Johnson issued a series of amnesty proclamations, Congress seized the reconstruction process. "Ironclad" oaths, assuring the oath taker's past and future loyalty, became the standard requirement for public service. In the end, President Lincoln's broad clemency to former Rebels was replaced with a retributive process.

The "field test" of paroles and loyalty oaths was in the crucial Border States. Essential to maintaining the Union, initially, was the president's appreciation of the blended politics of states such as Maryland, Missouri, Kentucky and Indiana. Other states, including Delaware, western Virginia, Indiana and Ohio, had strong factions in support of policies more in line with South Carolina and Louisiana than Massachusetts and Vermont. The evolution of the policies of the Lincoln administration is most clearly seen in the subtle, but forward movement toward emancipation and reconstruction as developed in the states of Maryland and Missouri. For example, arrests of state prisoners, suspension of habeas corpus and release on parole first occurred in these two states. The words of the loyalty oaths required for passes, paroles and pardons grew over time from a few simple lines to several paragraphs. Conditions were added and qualifications modified. The Border States more closely reflected the national conscience than the proponents of radical Republicanism in the country's abolitionist northeastern region.

The proper punishment of the Rebels was long debated. Articulation of the radical position was well presented by future president James A. Garfield. As a representative from Ohio, the former Union major general, on January 28, 1864, argued that, as enemies of the state, Rebels should have their property confiscated and be exiled. Historically, confiscation was enacted by all but one of the 13 original colonies against Tories in arms against the new republic — such were the rights of belligerents under the laws of war. In a speech delivered in the U.S. House of Representatives on June 28, 1864, Garfield suggested that traitors be driven from the soil "as God and his angels drove Satan and his host from Heaven. He was not too merciful to be just, and to hurl down in chains and everlasting darkness the 'traitor angel' who first broke peace in Heaven and rebelled against Him." The burden of proof, he argued in Congress, should be placed upon the Rebels to establish by "holy writ" that they were worthy of trust.

The "Era of the Oath" continued until the end of the century, but with declining conditions and restrictions. Remnants remain today in the honors rendered to the national flag. The Pledge of Allegiance is an offspring of oaths dating back to the Civil War. Although today the words are more symbolic than legally binding, during times of national crisis, affronts to the flag ceremony engender strong emotion. Seldom charged, treason remains a capital felony.

Our legal heritage includes the British libel and sedition laws as existed at the time of Independence. Threats toward our flag, Constitution and government ignite responses as ferocious today as during the Revolution or Rebellion. Courts remain cautious in their response to civil dissenters and political protestors. More are familiar with Thomas Jefferson's warning that "the unsuccessful struggles against tyranny have been the chief martyrs of treason laws in all countries."[3]

1

Treason

The nagging legal issue surrounding the Civil War was treason and its consequences. Under Article III, Section 3, of the Constitution, treason was simply defined as "levying War against [the United States], or in adhering to their Enemies, giving them Aid and Comfort." The only punishment was death by hanging. "Death to Traitors" was the catch phrase toward disloyal citizens during the Revolution (Fig. 1). One complication was that only a person owing allegiance to the United States could be charged with treason. If one was a foreign national, he could not be a traitor to the flag. That ambiguity was never resolved and the associated legal uncertainties contributed to an uneven political response to the Rebellion.

By an act of Congress dated April 30, 1790, signed by President George Washington, death by hanging was the punishment for treason. The Sedition Act of July 14, 1798, added

(Fig. 1) Union patriotic envelope. E. Cogan, Philadelphia, c. 1862. 3¼ × 5¾ inches (sheet size measurements). (PA-5.62.01)

the high misdemeanor of conspiracy and insurrection as lesser forms of disloyalty. A fine of $5,000 or five years in prison was provided for the two new offenses. A foreign national could be charged for spying, also a capital offense, but never treason. Most accused of wartime disloyalty stood before a military tribunal rather than a civilian court. Habeas corpus, a jury of peers and judicial reviews were not available after martial law was declared.

Under English common law, a conviction of treason resulted in loss of life, honor and forfeiture of estates. The Constitution provided that "no attainder of Treason shall work corruption of Blood, or Forfeiture except during the life of the Person attainted." State statutes also punished treason. For instance, the abolitionist John Brown was charged, convicted and executed for treason under the laws of the State of Virginia for his 1859 attack on the U.S. Arsenal at Harpers Ferry. There are other felonies related to treason: *Misprision of treason* is the crime of concealment of treason; *sedition* is inciting insurrection or causing civil unrest; and *spying* is espionage against the government on behalf of a foreign government. None of these crimes, however, had the moral disgrace associated with being labeled a traitor against the nation.

Federal officials were quick to warn government contractors to stay clear of actions the administration considered acts of treason. During the early months of 1861, Secretary of State William H. Seward cautioned shipowners not to transfer vessels to the states threatening to secede. An official with the New York and Virginia Steamship Company was approached by the governor of Virginia in hopes of acquiring the coastal steamers *Yorktown* and *Jamestown*. Secretary Seward knew that Virginia had already seized the two vessels after threats of secession. A company executive inquired if his company could sell the two ships to Virginia. In no uncertain terms, the secretary advised that it would be construed as giving aid and comfort to an enemy of the United States if his company were to transfer ownership to known enemies. Further, he added, such a sale would be considered an act of treason and all involved would be so charged and suffer the corresponding prosecution and penalties.[1]

To label a rebel a traitor is not the same as the standard required for an indictment of treason in federal court. The distinction arose during the grand jury session in New York on April 27, 1861. Federal judge Samuel R. Betts of the district court instructed the grand jury that the crime of misprision of treason only required that a citizen had failed to make known to the proper authorities acts harmful to the government by known enemies of the United States. This case involved persons in New York Harbor helping to build, man, fit and supply vessels to be used as privateers against ships flagged as United States vessels. The judge ruled it was not necessary to have evidence that the person charged was in fact at war with the United States. In another privateer case Judge Nelson, of the United States Circuit Court of New York, instructed that the words alone, oral, written or printed, however treasonable, seditious or criminal, in themselves, do not constitute an overt act of treason within the definition of the crime. Although the words may be evidence of intent to commit the overt act of treason, by themselves, they would not support an indictment.[2]

The most familiar show of national loyalty is the Pledge of Allegiance. This oath was neither a product of the Constitution nor Congress. Christian educator Francis Bellamy created the pledge, often recited by school children, in 1892 to celebrate the 400th anniversary of the arrival of Christopher Columbus to America. First published in the *Youth's Companion* magazine, the oath was amended in 1954 with the addition of the words "under God" at the suggestion of President Dwight D. Eisenhower. Although the Civil War has been described as the "Era of the Oath," not until World War II was the Pledge of Allegiance universally required.[3]

An oath is more than a mere promise or pledge. Oaths are given with solemn ceremony to signify their truthfulness before God and man. When memorialized in writing a statement of fact becomes an affidavit. To utter a false oath or affidavit is perjury, punishable by the law. Standard oath language is "I do solemnly swear or affirm … so help me God." Under the Constitution, Article II, Section 8, the president swears to faithfully execute the duties of his office to the best of his ability and to preserve, protect and defend the Constitution. Members of Congress and federal officials make similar promises. Commissioned officers do the same. Every Union officer was required to take a new oath after the Confederate States of America declared independence. The so-called "ironclad" oath of loyalty became law on July 2, 1862. Afterward every person appointed to any federal office of honor or profit had to subscribe to an oath of loyalty.

Soon after Fort Sumter fell, in the spring of 1861, "disloyal" citizens were arrested and held as political prisoners in forts in New York, Washington, Boston and Baltimore. At the time, the capital was the most vulnerable city in the nation since most Washington residents were Southern in their sympathies.

After the initial threat of Secessionist invasion subsided, the president offered paroles to political prisoners if future loyalty could be assured. A parolee could be released if he promised not to aid the enemy or do other harm to the United States. A simple statement of loyalty was all that was required. As time went on, greater assurance was demanded. Oaths became the universal solvent to captured civilian traitors. Over the course of the war, Lincoln's clemency grew to include paroles, pardons and general amnesty simply for sworn pledges of loyalty. Under the so-called "10 percent plan" seceded states could rejoin the Union without prejudice if 10 percent of the voters agreed to remain loyal during the war. Army deserters escaped firing squads by returning and swearing oaths of allegiance. At war's end, surrendered Confederate soldiers were given paroles and safeguards home if only they promised to cease the Rebellion. After peace, presidential pardons were abundant.

Sworn and subscribed oaths of loyalty were issued in every state of the Union through the end of the century. The overly generous granting of pardons almost forced President Andrew Johnson from office. After his impeachment acquittal, Congress created its own brand of loyalty. Restoration of voting and other civil rights depended on congressional forgiveness. The U.S. Supreme Court also was involved. Loyalty, and the proof thereof, was crucial, in the view of Congress, to the survival of the Union during postwar Reconstruction. Actual loyalty was more elusive than a mere promise. National allegiance remains an issue today, be it the Pledge of Allegiance, military funerals or honors to the flag. Flag desecration is as emotional today as during the Civil War.

The most overt act of disloyalty is the swearing of allegiance to another sovereign. The citizens of South Carolina did just that, immediately after their state seceded late in 1860. The enlistment contract into the army of the State of South Carolina was clear evidence of disloyalty to the United States (Fig. 2). By March of 1861, similar pledges were required of all soldiers of the Army of the Confederate States of America. That summer civilian employees across the South gave oaths if they wished to continue as customs officials and post-office agents for the new government (Fig. 3). These oaths required allegiance to the Confederate Constitution and a promise to defend it against all enemies. Confederate soldiers also promised to obey orders of the president of the Confederate States of America according to the Rules and Articles of War. All these oaths were acts of treason against the United States after a state of war existed.

To offset the open display of Americans' taking oaths of allegiance to another sovereign,

(Fig. 2) Confederate Army enlistment contract. Castle Pinckney, SC, March 30, 1861. 9½ × 8 inches. (SC-5.61.01)

the U.S. government required all army and naval officers to retake their oaths of loyalty given when they were first commissioned. The second oaths of office came after April 27, 1861. Army regulations were republished August 19, 1861, wherein Article XL, Paragraph 935, required every recruiting officer to administer the following oath to every new recruit or reenlisting soldier:

> I [Name] do solemnly swear (or affirm) that I will bear true allegiance to the United States of America, and that I will serve them honestly and faithfully against all their enemies or oppressors

whatsoever, and observe and obey the orders of the President of the United States and the orders of the officers appointed over me, according to the rules and articles of the government of the armies of the United States.

Death to traitors proved to be more a threat than a promise. Hundreds of political prisoners were jailed, but few executed. Even when political prisoners were transferred from the State to the War Department, military commissions were reluctant to execute private citizens. Capital punishment imposed by a court-martial was reserved for desertion rather than treason. A Union deserter named Private Johnson became the first execution of the war. Almost three hundred federal executions followed. The average time between court-martial sentencing and death was less than a month. Notably, only seven cases included the charge of treason. All treason charges were ancillary to serious crimes, such as murder or desertion. Of those executed, more than half were either foreign born or members of black regiments. Sons of respected, native-born, white families were normally spared, no matter their politics.

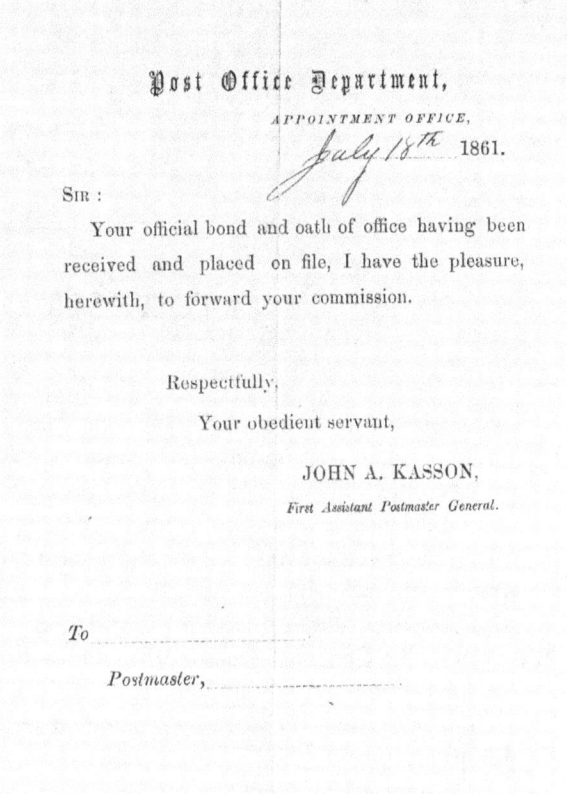

(Fig. 3) Confederate. Transmittal form for postal commission and acknowledgment of receipt of bond and oath. July 18, 1861. 8 × 5 inches. (VA-5.61.02)

During the last year of the war, President Lincoln reversed all death sentences imposed by courts-martial. A Union deserter more likely would suffer death for unauthorized absence than a Rebel for treason. Such was the ambiguity of civil war.

President Lincoln's clemency began with paroles and pardons and continued with a general amnesty. After Lincoln's assassination, President Andrew Johnson continued with his own amnesty of May 29, 1865. Allegiance, registration and sincerity were Johnson's primary requirements. Presidential pardons, if required and deemed worthy, were available to those denied amnesty. Johnson ultimately issued four proclamations of amnesty. The last was on Christmas Day 1868, but only applied to a dozen individuals. Included were Jefferson Davis and Robert E. Lee; however, by then Congress had assumed control of the Reconstruction process. This soon was followed by President Johnson's impeachment trial and adoption of the 14th Amendment. Full restoration of citizenship to every former Rebel did not occur until June 8, 1898, nine years after Jefferson Davis's death. Davis never again held public or elective office. The era of the oath did not end until the turn of the 20th century.

2

Promises of Loyalty

A simple definition of treason is the betrayal of one's sovereign to an enemy. The word is from the Latin for "giving up" or *traditio*. Derived from Judas Iscariot's handing over Jesus Christ to the Romans, the Latin term *traditorem* became traitor in English. Treason was considered the most loathsome of all mortal crimes and biblical sins. Dante Alighieri in his *Divine Comedy* reserved the lowest level of purgatory for traitors. No wonder, both the church and America's founding fathers in the U.S. Constitution reserved the severest punishment for traitors. To redeem a traitor both man's and God's forgiveness were essential. Only solemn oaths, sworn before God, could remove the taint of disloyalty to those praying for forgiveness. Since breaking an oath was more apparent than disloyalty, people were more often punished for perjury than treason. Oaths, therefore, had serious legal consequences if broken as an act of disloyalty.

Even before the Civil War was officially recognized, elected officials and appointed administrators began to resign in protest of the election of President Lincoln. Secretary of War John B. Floyd resigned December 29, 1860, before Lincoln's inauguration. A Washington, D.C., grand jury, in January 1861, indicted Floyd for conspiracy and maladministration of office. In July, nine United States senators representing Virginia, North Carolina, Texas, Arkansas and Tennessee were expelled. On August 16, President Lincoln proclaimed the seceding states to be in a condition of insurrection. Senator John C. Breckinridge was expelled December 4, 1861, followed by Senator Jesse D. Bright of Indiana, on February 5, 1862. These high-profile defections underscored the fragility of the Union. Treachery, traitors and conspiracies were at the forefront of weekly headlines. Consequently, both the public and Congress demanded action in response to all acts of disloyalty, whether actual or suspected.

President Abraham Lincoln always was reluctant to punish citizen "traitors" to the fullest extent of the law. To him, death seemed too severe for only extreme political expressions. The treason law as modified July 31, 1861, provided an alternative sentence of five years' imprisonment and a $5,000 fine in lieu of death. Congress later enacted a confiscation act to punish those Rebels whose property was used for "insurrectionary purposes." The President also blockaded southern ports to deprive Rebels of the benefits of foreign commerce. Blockades, typically, are acts of war against a foreign enemy, while port closures are imposed during civil unrest. Distinctions between protests and treason always confounded lawmakers. Economic sanctions were more palatable to a nation unsure of the legal consequences of secession and rebellion.

To control riots and violent disobedience, the federal government imposed harsh controls. Martial law was declared in Baltimore by General Benjamin Butler, Department of Annapolis, on May 14, 1861, and then in Alexandria, Virginia. That August, General John Frémont imposed martial rule in Saint Louis, Missouri, for all of the Western Department. By fall, 175 people were being held as political prisoners at Fort Lafayette, in New York Harbor, of which only half were southerners. The balance were from Border States, the North and 14 foreigner countries. By November, a third of the prisoners were released after giving promises of good behavior.

While martial law and travel restrictions had a chilling effect along the border to would-be protestors, the ultimate control of disloyal citizens was confinement in political prisons. Illegal arrests were normally reviewed through the writ of habeas corpus. Specifically, the "Suspension Clause" of the Constitution, Article I, Section 7, provides that the privilege of habeas corpus shall not be suspended, unless in cases of rebellion or invasion as the public safety may require it. President Lincoln enjoined a Maryland circuit court that questioned his suspension of the writ of habeas corpus in *Ex Parte Merryman*. Chief Justice Roger B. Taney decreed the order illegal, but Lincoln persisted in his order to "to preserve public safety." Later the secretary of state warned detainees in Fort Lafayette, in December 1861, that legal action by political prisoners would be considered a factor before granting their release. Habeas corpus continued to trouble the administration. Not until after the Civil War did the U.S. Supreme Court hold that the suspension of the writ of habeas corpus was unconstitutional if civilian courts were open.[1]

The administration appreciated the *in terrorem* effect of arresting and confining suspected conspirators and other disloyal citizens in political prisons without charges. Keeping Southern sympathizers locked up without counsel, charges or even a trial had an immediate cooling effect on dissent and protest. Treason trials were long, complicated, costly and highly unpredictable in outcome. After a short stay in an uncomfortable state prison, most middle-aged dissidents were willing to sign a promise not to misbehave in the future. Some, after a more extended period of confinement, even agreed to publicly swear their allegiance to the Union. A release of the dissident after assuring good conduct and allegiance was usually seen as an act of clemency by the administration. Political trials seldom had a good or foreseeable outcome.

The secretary of state next created the United States Passport Office to control travel. After August 18, 1861, all persons entering or leaving the United States had to have a current passport issued by the State Department. Application required evidence of good character and loyalty plus payment of a three dollar fee. The most active passport office was at the port of New York, located on Broadway. Delays between application and issuance could be extremely long, depending on military exigencies and official indifference. Passport officials were always watchful for army deserters and Rebel sympathizers, and slowed passport issuance during times of military alert.

The travel-pass system was first imposed in Washington, Georgetown and Alexandria. By September of 1862, all military personnel, except general officers, were required to have a pass approved by a division commander. The military governor initially was responsible for regulating civilian passes in areas under martial law. Travel purpose and full identification were required. A directive from the commanding officer for the defenses of Washington, published in General Order No. 2, September 10, 1862, allowed division commanders to delegate that responsibility to a staff officer. Signature samples of issuers were used to verify proper authority. Checkpoint guards compared passes with authorized signature facsimiles.

In addition to passports, civilians were required to carry local passes if moving beyond

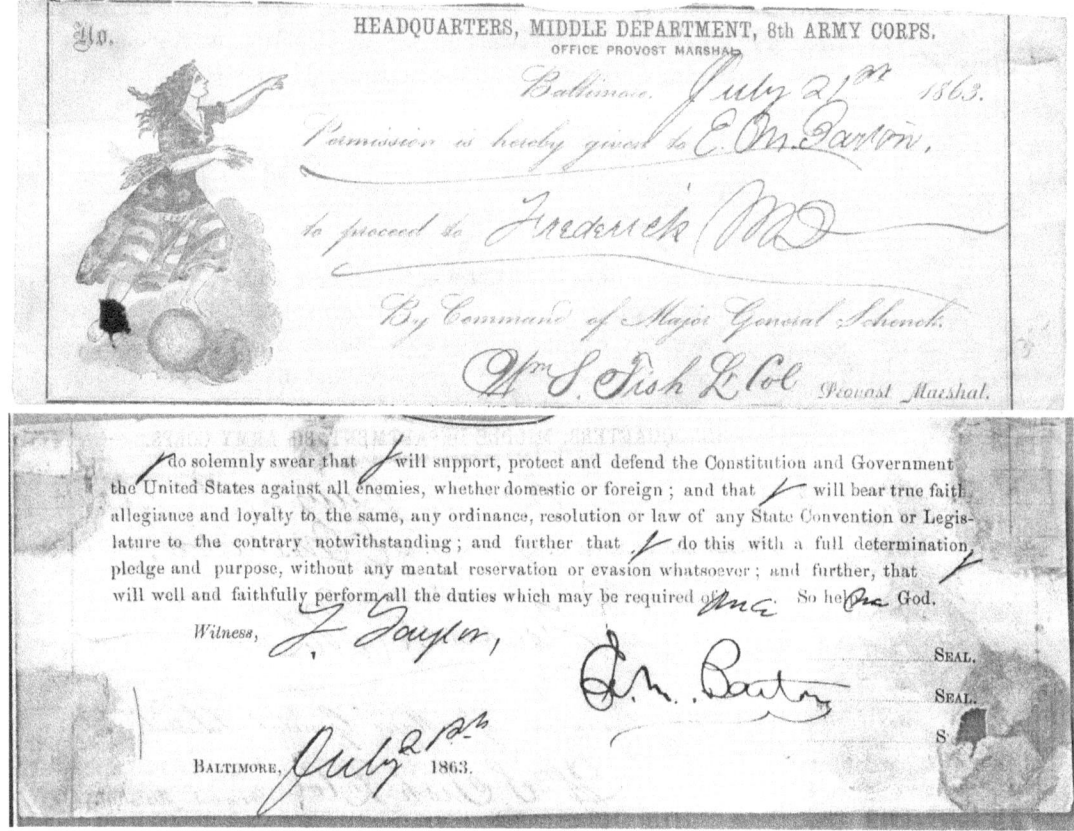

(Fig. 4) Pass issued by Office of Provost Marshal, Middle Department, 8th Army Corps. Baltimore. On reverse, oath to "support, protect and defend the Constitution and Government of the United States." July 21, 1863. 3 × 8 inches. (MD-2.63.01)

the limits of the Federal lines. Loyalty oaths were required prior to the issuance of passes. Oaths usually were recorded in a separate ledger. By 1863 the process was formalized, complete with standard forms and district general orders (Fig. 4). Under an Act of Congress, dated March 3, 1863, the Provost Marshal General's Bureau was established to curb desertions and capture spies, with the pass system as the primary control. The law provided that violators would be tried by military tribunal. Travel was considered a privilege, and passes were awarded only to the loyal and well-behaved citizens. Brigadier General James B. Fry of Illinois served as provost marshal general until the post was discontinued on August 28, 1866.

Military pass procedures as published by the Department of the South, at Hilton Head Island, South Carolina, in the *Free South*, Beaufort, South Carolina, on November 19, 1864, were typical. All civilians traveling within that department were required to have a pass on their person at all times while military personnel needed only orders or leave papers. Passes were issued for exit but not return. Travelers reported to the provost marshal upon arrival with evidence of a current oath of allegiance. The provost marshal would administer and record the new oath of allegiance if necessary. All travelers had to prove they were traveling under competent authority, held valid papers and had legitimate business in the department. Passes were of limited duration, never exceeding a month, and could be suspended or cancelled at any time for any reason.[2]

Unique to men in uniform were the rules of military order and discipline as dispensed by military court-martial. Military justice was separate and distinct from martial law, which is the control of civilian populations during a declared state of emergency. A more comprehensive form of military control was rule by a military governor appointed by the president. Consequently, state and local governments were suspended during a military governorship. Further, martial law replaced criminal courts, while provost police replaced civilian authority during the time of emergency. No appeal of decisions by military commanders during martial law was possible. At their discretion, military governors could restore some civilian offices if conditions permitted. Finally, habeas corpus and appeals through the judiciary were not available during military rule.

During martial rule peace rallies could be considered disloyal assemblies. A number of northern presses were closed and editors jailed during declared states of emergency. Some in Congress went so far as to claim that any person not in full support of the war with a full "heart and soul" was disloyal. To that end, Congress requested the secretary of the treasury to compile a list of his employees not considered truly loyal. Later, a special House committee investigated disloyalty within all government departments.

Late in the summer of 1861, Representative John F. Potter, of Wisconsin, chaired the House committee that investigated federal employees who refused to take the new oath of allegiance. That modified oath added the language "to support the Constitution of the United States," a sworn promise of fidelity to the Union notwithstanding "any ordinance, resolution, or law if any State Convention to the contrary." By the end of the year, the Potter Loyalty Committee identified three hundred civil servants suspected of disloyalty. All either resigned or were terminated. "Negro" employees, minors and women were specifically exempted from having to take an oath. To the dismay of the State Department, foreign nationals initially were forced to take the oath. After formal protests from their governments such oaths were discontinued.[3]

Congress and the president soon realized that an all-volunteer army was insufficient to quash the insurrection. National conscription became law September 24, 1862. Even during volunteer enlistments, war protests were common. After the draft, resistance increased. Marshals were instructed by the attorney general to arrest any person disrupting recruitment by action, speech or writings. Deputy marshals could take necessary measures, free of court oversight. After arrest, offenders could be tried before Military Commissions, beyond the jurisdiction of federal or state courts. Additionally, habeas corpus was suspended for cases involving national conscription.

Custody of political or "State" prisoners was transferred to the War Department early in 1862. A special commission would decide if continued incarceration was necessary. The commission, composed of General John A. Dix and Judge Edward Pierpont, determined that most political prisoners could be released. The president, on February 14, 1862, offered pardons to most "State" prisoners if they promised to render no aid or comfort to enemies of the United States (Fig. 5). Any political prisoner considered a danger to the public safety was excluded from clemency. The presidential parole required prisoners to give a signed sworn oath, but there was no standard format. Often a provision was added that if the prisoner violated his parole, death would follow.

Prisoners were soon released from the Old Capitol Prison at Washington, Fort McHenry in Baltimore, Fort Warren in Boston Harbor and the largest number from Fort Lafayette, New York. Generally, early paroles only stipulated "not to render any aid or comfort to the enemy in hostility to the United States." The standardized oath later read:

> Richmond April 18, 1862
>
> I the Undersigned, a citizen of the United States and now a political prisoner in the Confederate States, do hereby solemnly pledge my word of honor that I will not by arms, information or otherwise during the existing hostilities between the United States and the Confederate States of America, aid or abet the enemies of the said Confederate States, or any of them in any form or manner whatsoever until released or exchanged. And I further pledge my word of honor that at the expiration of thirty days from this date, viz: Eighteenth day of April 1862, unless I secure the release of A. E. Smith now a prisoner in the United States, I will return to the city of Richmond Va and report to Genl Jno H Winder.
>
> Wm Ayres
>
> Teste
> Wm Smith

(Fig. 5) Parole of civilian U.S. political prisoner, Richmond, April 18, 1862. (VA-4.62.01)

I do solemnly swear (or affirm) that I will support, protect and defend the Constitution and Government of the United States against all enemies, whether domestic or foreign and I will bear true faith, allegiance and loyalty to the same, any ordinance resolution or law of any state convention or legislature to the contrary notwithstanding; and further, that I do this with a full determination, pledge and purpose without any mental reservation or evasion, whatsoever, So Help Me God.

Congress, on July 2, 1862, made essential an oath of loyalty for all government officials, employees and agents. The so-called "ironclad" oath provided:

That hereafter every person ... appointed to any office of honor or profit under the Government of the United States, ... in the ... military, ... departments of the public service, excepting the President of the United States, shall, before entering upon the duties of such office, and before being entitled to any of the salary or other emoluments thereof, take and subscribe to the following oath or affirmation: "I, A. B., do solemnly swear (or affirm) that I have never voluntarily borne arms against the United States, since I have been a citizen thereof; that I have voluntarily given no aid, countenance, counsel, or encouragement to persons engaged in armed hostility thereto; that I have neither sought nor accepted nor attempted to exercise the functions of any office whatever under any authority or pretended authority in hostility to the United States; that I have not yielded a voluntary support to any pretended government, authority, power or constitution within the United States; hostile or inimical thereto. And I do further swear (or affirm) that, to the best of my knowledge and ability, I will support and defend the Constitution of the United States against all enemies, foreign and domestic; that I will bear true faith and allegiance to the same; that I take this obligation freely, without any mental reservation or purpose of evasion; and that I will well and faithfully discharge the duties of the office on which I am about to enter, so help me God"; which said oath, so taken and signed shall be preserved among the files of the ... Department to which the said office may appertain. And any person who shall falsely take the oath shall be guilty of perjury, and on conviction, in addition to the penalties now prescribed for that offense, shall be deprived of his office and rendered incapable forever after of holding any office or place under the United States.

Although the "ironclad" oath covered federal employees, agents and officials, it soon became almost universal. No one could receive federal payments without filing an oath. Some objected, especially in the Border States, claiming that a requirement of past loyalty was an ex post facto law, prohibited by the Constitution. Even congressmen complained that the oath imposed an additional qualification for congressional office, that of past loyalty. Wartime necessity prevailed. Consequently, dissenters along with those who were disloyal were purged from the federal rolls.

On July 17, 1862, Congress revisited the crime of treason and its lesser included offenses. The penalties for conspiracy to overthrow the government were doubled to ten years imprisonment and/or a $10,000 fine. The confiscation of estates owned by Rebels was ameliorated by Section 13 of the act, which allowed the president to extend pardons and amnesty to disloyal citizens if expedient for the public welfare. Executive pardon was provided by the Constitution, but amnesty was not mentioned. A *pardon* is individual forgiveness and exoneration from punishment. An *amnesty* is a pardon offered in general to all that fall within a forgiven class of offenders.

On September 24, 1862, the president declared that any person discouraging enlistment or resisting the draft would be deemed guilty "per se" of a "disloyal practice," subject to trial by military tribunal beyond the protection of habeas corpus and trial by jury. In the words of the time, such behavior was outside the "wheels of justice" as practiced in the centers of commerce during peacetime. For such culprits, the provost marshal acted as a "sieve through which the worthy alone may pass, and the vile are retained by the meshes." "Bayonets will not brook law's delay" against traitors as noted by one northern editor. When apprehended, a draft dodger was usually given the choice of enlisting or facing a military tribunal.[4]

The transfer of political prisoners to the custody of the War Department simplified imposition of martial law. On August 8, 1862, the secretary of war directed all marshals and local police to arrest and imprison any person engaged in any disloyal act, speech or writing. Additional disloyal acts included impeding army enlistments and the vague charge of "giving aid or comfort to the enemy." Essential to the far-reaching effect of this order was that determining disloyalty was left to the personal discretion of the police officer. To spur action, local officials were readily reimbursed for the cost of the arrests. Upon arrest, disloyal citizens were subjected to charges before a military commission and considered political prisoners. As such they had no rights for a writ of habeas corpus, review by a civilian court or trial by a civilian jury. Often those charged with interfering with army enlistments were allowed to volunteer to enlist after which the sentence of the military commission was vacated.

The midterm election of 1862 surprisingly revealed to Congress that the public was more concerned with the loss of freedom than they were with prosecuting draft dodgers. Accordingly, after the national election, the secretary of war was directed to release prisoners held on charges of opposing the draft or giving aid to the enemy, unless a threat to public safety. Rebels also were offered freedom if they promised not to render aid to enemies of the United States. Parolees could either remain and be subject to strict surveillance or move south where they were to remain during the war. Excluded from release was anyone serving court-imposed punishments or those awaiting trial. This was the first of several general releases ordered by President Lincoln.

The president, in his sole discretion, could remove sanctions imposed on those accused of treason and disloyalty, whether charged or not. Owners of confiscated or abandoned assets, if pardoned, were allowed to file claims for property. The practical purpose of such clemency was to empty political prisons, saving costs and manpower. The policy fit into Lincoln's "carrot and stick" approach aimed at encouraging disloyal citizens to return to the Union. Paroles were not pardons, only a type of release. Technically, only an officer or gentleman was allowed to give a "parole of honor" because, according to Victorian standards of behavior, "gentlemen" would keep their word. Private soldiers were released after an officer affirmed they could be trusted to maintain good behavior. Occasionally, because of haste or oversight, "paroles of honor" were sometimes issued to enlisted prisoners. Such fine distinctions of wording were dropped in the western commands.

President Lincoln suspended the writ of habeas corpus nationwide by proclamation on September 15, 1863. The order covered all prisoners held by federal officials, military and naval authorities. That included prisoners of war, political prisoners, spies, aiders and abettors of the enemy and army deserters. Previously, suspension of habeas corpus had been declared for specified geographic areas. The order did not apply to minors, who were wards of the court. All held afterward could be tried by military commission or special courts-martial. At military tribunals, normal rules of evidence, recordings of the proceedings and judicial appeals did not apply. Presidential clemency and pardon were the only forms of relief an accused convicted at a military tribunal could request.

On March 3, 1863, Congress authorized the president to suspend the writ of habeas corpus if, in his judgment, such was necessary for public safety. The solicitor general of the War Department gave guidance to commanders in cases involving arrest or desertion. If state courts issued a writ of habeas corpus questioning the arrest of a draft dodger or deserter, Circular No. 36, dated July 1, 1863, from the provost marshal general's office instructed the manner in which military officials were to respond. First and foremost, all writs had to be answered promptly, with respect, and in writing. The response had to identify the arrested person held by military authorities. (Note that to deliver the confined deserter or draft dodger would not be consistent with the duty of the provost marshal.) Additionally, in the response the facts of the case had to be detailed. The court was to be advised that it could appeal to either the U.S. Supreme Court or in some manner it deemed just. After the advising opinion, on September 15, the president suspended the writ of habeas corpus nationwide. Later, military officials were directed to release underage deserters if their minority status was legal and established.[5]

While the imposition of martial law and the suspension of habeas corpus was expected in Rebel territory, and tolerated in states sympathizing with the South, such as Maryland and Missouri, the actions were a different matter in the loyal states. The heavy hand of martial law and the terror of political prisons were little tolerated in the North. The press and public opinion split according to political positions regarding the war. State courts questioned the legality of the president's proclamations regarding martial law and the suspension of the writ of habeas corpus. In Indiana, a civilian, licensed, liquid-liquor dealer, Joseph Griffin, was arrested and imprisoned for violating the provost marshal's order prohibiting the sale of spirits to enlisted soldiers. Griffin, through his friends, eventually charged the arresting military officer, Captain Frank Wilcox, for illegal arrest and false imprisonment. The Indiana Supreme Court, on appeal, sided with civilian Griffin and ordered him released. The court in Indiana ruled that while civilian courts were open and civil authority had not been expelled by force, no person who was not a member of the armed forces could be punished by the military under martial laws. Martial law, the court noted, is temporary as long as an actual or impending enemy force renders it a necessity for the military. Ultimately, the U.S. Supreme Court did not consider the question until after the war.[6]

Soon after that decision, the president declared martial law for the country. By 1864, military commissions were established across the nation. Especially targeted were "disloyal" newspaper editors, not only in Saint Louis and Baltimore but also in the loyal states of Maine, New Jersey, New York, Ohio and Indiana. The commercial paper *Journal of Commerce*, of New York, published an article containing 18 columns of the names of private citizens who had been arrested by military authorities. The editor was unable to determine the nature of the alleged offenses for which they were arrested. All were held without the benefit of charges, a grand jury indictment or confrontation of witnesses. None were accused of any military connection or offense. Also, the civil courts were open. In the border state of Missouri, Congressman William A. Hall was arrested by a provost and confined to a Saint Louis prison for uttering words against the president. Most arrests occurred in Kentucky, according to the editor, in the month of August. Disloyal organizations, such as the Sons of Liberty, American Knights, and Knights of the Bush, were targeted. Louisville's city officials, the state's lieutenant governor and many private citizens were detained. A few were banished to Richmond, Virginia. About 40 members of disloyal organizations were escorted under guard to the state border.[7]

The number of military arrests of civilians held as political prisoners was never released during the war. After the war, the provost marshal general published a list of political arrests from June 1861 to January 1866. The compilations, admittedly not complete, contained 38,000 names of civilians arrested by military provost officers. The list included 6,500 prisoners of war and about 2,500 deserters and "bounty jumpers." The government only identified 4,500 as state or political prisoners. Not until May 1, 1865, did the secretary of war, upon instruction from the president, remit all sentences awarded by military tribunals during the war. Not until seven months later, on December 1, 1865, did President Andrew Johnson restore the writ of habeas corpus in all states except Virginia, Kentucky, Tennessee, North Carolina, South Carolina, Georgia, Florida, Alabama, Mississippi, Louisiana, Oklahoma, Texas, the District of Columbia and the territories of New Mexico and Arizona.[8]

American presidents on three occasions prior to the Civil War had issued general amnesties: Washington in 1795; Adams in 1800; and Madison in 1815. President Lincoln in his December 8, 1863, "Message to Congress" disclosed a plan of amnesty whereby states in rebellion could be restored to the Union if a process were followed. Congress had already implied such authority when it authorized clemency under Section 13 of the Confiscation Act for those who "resume their allegiance to the United States and inaugurate loyal governments." The political motive fostering amnesty was to undermine the Rebellion by reducing the number of its supporters. Sanctuary was offered to pardoned Rebels wishing to remain within the Federal lines. For border populations, clemency was tempting both to Rebel deserters and idle civilians.

Not until after the war ended did the attorney general of the United States issue an opinion covering the source, scope and purpose of presidential pardons. The attorney general, in an opinion dated May 1, 1865, examined for President Johnson his power to grant pardons under Article II, Section 2, Clause 1, of the U.S. Constitution. In the text of the Confiscation Act passed by Congress July 17, 1862, the president was authorized to extend to Rebels pardons and "amnesty" with some exceptions, as he may deem expedient for the public welfare. Neither pardon nor amnesty was defined by the Constitution nor Congress. Under the common law, an individual pardon was a remission of guilt. On the other hand, amnesty was a general pardon granted to a class rather than to a single person. Both were acts of "oblivion or forgetfulness" given in mercy and grace. The attorney general stated that the purpose of amnesty was to sooth and heal the malignant passions that may linger after insurrection or rebellion. Both required the recipient to confess guilt, actual or imputed, proved or uncharged. A pardon could be partial and conditional. Neither a pardon nor amnesty could be conditional on anything illegal or immoral, and both must be consistent with the grant of clemency. A person must request clemency, be it in the form of a pardon or amnesty, and state truthfully the acts for which he wanted to be forgiven. If the statement of facts was false, or if fraud was used to secure the grant of clemency, the pardon or amnesty was void. A pardon was not a license or indulgence to commit an act of treason or disloyalty in the future. If the person secured a pardon or amnesty by fraud and falsehood, not only was he not forgiven, he also added the crime of perjury to his charges.[9]

A painful consequence of the refusal of the federal government to recognize the Confederacy as a legitimate government was the reluctance to conduct prisoner of war exchanges. As the number of Union prisoners grew in 1861, Congress, on December 11, requested the president pursue "systematic measures for the exchange of prisoners." In Missouri, General John Frémont negotiated informal exchanges with Confederate general Sterling Price away from Washington oversight. Other field negotiated releases were motivated by humanitarian rather than political concerns. Battlefield releases usually involved only individuals, often injured, rather than general prisoner exchanges. Such trades continued through the summer of 1862. Not surprisingly, delays in prisoner releases angered affected families who complained to their respective elected officials.

After the successful but costly victory at Antietam on September 17, 1862, President Lincoln announced his intent to emancipate slaves in the Rebel territory by the end of the year. This release of slaves followed a prisoner exchange cartel (a formal agreement) negotiated July 22, 1862, between Union general John A. Dix and Confederate general D. H. Hill. The cartel incorporated a scale of rank equivalency standard for exchanged captives. That August, three thousand Union prisoners were returned for an equivalent number of Rebels at the designated exchange point of Aiken Landing, Virginia. Prisoner counts again spiked after the Battles of Vicksburg and Gettysburg in July 1863. Later that year, President Jefferson Davis threatened to suspend the parole of Union officers in retaliation for actions by General Benjamin Butler while occupying New Orleans. Cartels were suspended and did not resume until the later part of 1864.

Despite President Lincoln's refusal to recognize the seceding states as a foreign combatant, he directed Union soldiers to treat Rebels under the rules of war. On April 24, 1863, War Office General Order No. 100, styled "Instructions for the Government of Armies of the United States in the Field," established military guidelines for treating enemy prisoners. The "Articles of War" were based on the teachings of the German-American political philosopher Francis Lieber who advocated the humane treatment of both civilian populations and prisoners of war. The killing of captives and the use of poison or torture were all forbidden. The 101 articles were read monthly to Union troops and subscribed to by all Union officers. The articles were part of the oath of allegiance taken upon enlistment. Violations of the articles were punishable by court-martial. Adherence to the articles absolved soldiers from criminal responsibility for all felonies (i.e., homicide, arson and kidnapping) committed during war.

Article 81 of the Rules of War forbade corresponding with or aiding the enemy. If a soldier were charged with this offense he could suffer death or such other punishment a court-martial or military commission might direct. Civilians as well as soldiers could be charged under this article. During occupation, disloyal citizens maintaining contact with Rebels were at risk. A *prima facie* presumption was that all locals in hostile zones were enemies. Any person during time of war found lurking around a Federal post, fortification or encampment could be brought before a general court-martial or military commission for spying, under Article 82, and face death penalty charges. In actuality, deserters were executed by both sides far more often than spies or traitors.

3

Passes and Paroles

After Fort Sumter fell in April 1861, President Lincoln requested that loyal states provide 75,000 volunteers to augment the country's regular army. Governors from three Border States — Kentucky, Missouri and Tennessee — declined his request claiming neutrality. Congress was called into emergency session after Border States forbade Federal troop movements within their jurisdictions. Three days after the troop call-up, the president proclaimed a blockade of southern ports that initially affected seven states. A week later, Virginia and North Carolina were added to the closure order.

Fear spread in the nation's capital. Spies were arrested in Washington's Virginia and Maryland suburbs while Rebels watched Federal defensive positions from across the Potomac. Washington residents realized how vulnerable they were, especially after plans were revealed of an upcoming attack on the navy yard at Norfolk and army arsenal at Harper's Ferry.

The Washington of 1860 was a modest southern town of 75,000 residents. Only Fort Washington, south of town, protected the city. After railroad bridges were burned in Maryland, Brigadier General Benjamin F. Butler took control of Annapolis and Baltimore. Travel was tightly controlled and passes required the recipient to vow on his "word of honor that he is and will be ever loyal to the United States." All were warned that the penalty for breaking that promise "will be Death"[1]

Strong Southern support throughout Maryland was the first test of the newly elected president's resolve to sustain the Union. Even before the inauguration, rumors spread that there would be a riot should Lincoln appear in the streets of Baltimore. The pro–Southern city marshal, George P. Kane, on January 16, 1861, assured officials there was no need to worry if Lincoln scheduled a procession through the city as part of the festivities around the inauguration on March 4. Kane wrote that the rumors were wholly without foundation, and assured planners that the people of Baltimore were law-abiding citizens. During the prior inauguration of President Buchanan, some street ruffians had insulted the president. Marshal Kane stated that those disruptors were members of fanatical clubs that no longer existed in his city.[2]

Problems, feared prior to the presidential inauguration, did not occur until after Lincoln was in office. On August 19, 1861, a troop train conveying members of the sixth Massachusetts Regiment traveling from Philadelphia arrived at Camden Station in Baltimore. Outside the station was a crowd of several thousand, including many Southern sympathizers. Upon leaving the station, the troops were in formation when gunfire erupted at the corner of South and Pratt Streets. After order was restored, three soldiers and 11 citizens were dead. Soon thereafter, railroad bridges were burned, leading to the suspension of train service. Federal troops under General Benjamin Butler took charge of the situation, declaring martial law and donning weapons. Rail service resumed May 16. Provost police arrested Marshal Kane who was confined at Fort McHenry. On July 1, members of the Baltimore police commission joined Marshal Kane, as well as the mayor of the city, at Fort McHenry. To that group were added several members of the Maryland legislature who were lobbying for passage of a secession ordinance. In July, all the political prisoners were transferred to the military prison in New York Harbor, at Fort Lafayette.[3]

General Nathaniel P. Banks assumed command of the Department of Annapolis, including the city of Baltimore, after his recent transfer to Fortress Monroe, Virginia. General Banks appointed John B. Kenly of the First Regiment of Maryland Volunteers as his provost marshal. Provost Kenly oversaw all policing of the city of Baltimore. As such, he published the martial rules governing all citizens while civil authority was suspended. After arresting the objecting public officials, all other city personnel were warned that if all martial orders were not complied with, offenders would be arrested and replaced with loyal men. The notice, according to the order, was necessary to save the city from anarchy. General Banks reinforced his provost's words declaring all such actions were "to prevent secret, violent, and treasonable combinations of disloyal men against the government of the United States." The swift arrest of nine members of the Maryland House of Delegates, the state printer, the city marshal, mayor and city police commissioner served as a clear example that the military authorities were not afraid to detain disloyal citizens at the slightest provocation, regardless of their political influence.[4]

The Maryland political prisoners joined almost two hundred other citizens unwilling to take the oath of allegiance to the law and government of the United States. Half were from Border States, and the majority of those confined at Fort Lafayette were from Maryland. The first political prisoners were E. S. Ruggles of Fredericksburg, Virginia, and Purcell M. Quillan of Charleston, South Carolina, both imprisoned on July 20, 1861. Because the facility at Fort Lafayette was controlled by the State Department, prisoners were officially logged in as "state" prisoners to distinguish them from civil or military prisoners. The routine for "booking" a "state" prisoner usually began with an order from Washington to arrest and confine a suspected disloyalist — no charges were required. U.S. marshals, assisted by military or civilian police, then made the arrest. The prisoners were first taken to Fort Hamilton prison, on the mainland, before being taken by boat to Fort Lafayette in New York Harbor, where a Lieutenant Wood took them into custody. The prisoner's papers, baggage and person would be searched prior to being processed and taken to a gun embrasure, where he would be confined with seven or eight other prisoners. The dark space was lighted only by a small porthole. Inside the enclosure were straw mattresses on iron beds, blankets, pillows, sheets and basins of only saltwater for washing and sanitation. Laundry was scarce. Daily meals consisted of a morning breakfast of salt pork, bread and milk-sweetened hickory water. The tin-plate dinner was either rice or bean soup, along with a piece of pork or beef and a portion of bread. Only a slice of bread and a cup of hickory water were served for supper. Fresh water was always in short supply. Prisoners were allowed to write letters, subject to censorship, by the light of a single candle. Lights out was at nine. All mail was opened, read, and only if approved, delivered. Political prisoners were permitted few visitors and securing attorney representation was difficult. The first group of political prisoners was transferred to Fort Warren in Boston Harbor during October 1861 — a larger facility with a capacity closer to one thousand inmates. The mayor of Washington, D.C., James G. Berret, was already at Fort Warren when the Maryland officials were transferred.[5]

Late in 1861, the Maryland Committee of the Militia contacted Massachusetts governor John A. Andrew concerning three state volunteer soldiers killed during the April riots in Baltimore. Families were contacted in Lowell and Lawrence through their respective mayors by Governor Andrew. The Maryland House of Delegates appropriated $7,000 to compensate the soldiers' families who had died or were wounded. Governor Andrew later wrote that the past could not be forgotten, but it could be forgiven. He added that the "martyrs of Baltimore" had cemented an eternal union of sympathy between the sister states of Maryland and Massachusetts. That same week, in December, the Maryland legislature assured Washington that it was forever Union and would always forbid any participation in the suicidal rebellion in support of secession. The legislature, to expedite solidarity and loyalty, expressed its understanding of the extraordinary measures necessary to crush disloyal actions during the first half of the year. Martial law initially was accepted with little complaint.[6]

The president, on April 27, 1861, had suspended the writ of habeas corpus in all regions adjoining the military railroad line between Washington, D.C., and Philadelphia. The pass system was strictly enforced. On July 2, the president extended the military line from Washington to New York City (Fig. 6).

The Department of New Mexico headquartered in Santa Fe announced in August that the writ of habeas corpus was suspended "to guard against the treasonable designs of persons disloyal to the Government." Officers were cautioned not to annoy "peaceable and well disposed citizens," but to concentrate on "covert acts" endangering the public safety. On October 14, the president extended the suspension of habeas corpus northward to Bangor, Maine. Release was obtained by swearing a loyalty oath and being paroled. The oath taker promised not to

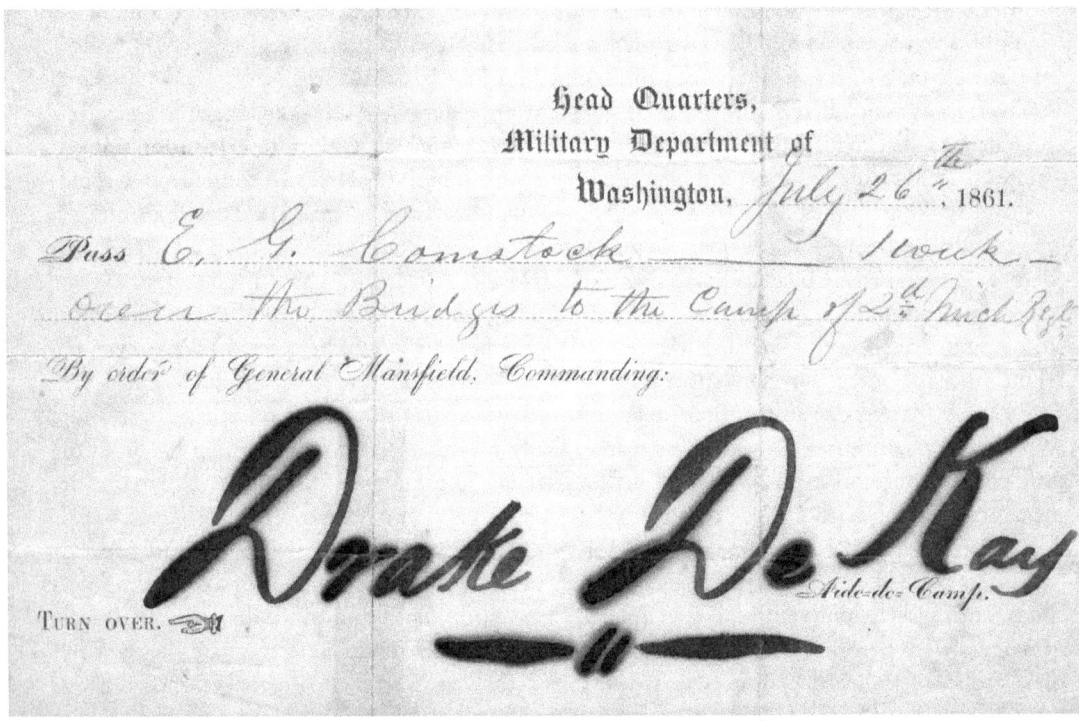

(Fig. 6) Pass issued by Military Department of Washington. On reverse, warning that "the penalty will be death" if "found in arms against the Union." July 26, 1861. 5 × 8 inches. (DC-2.61.01)

openly or covertly commit any act of hostility against the government of the United States. Group paroles, although not standard, sometimes were administered.[7]

Seventy-five "prisoners of state" filed a "memorial" (a true copy of an original document) detailing their arrest and conditions of confinement on George's Island at Fort Warren in Boston Harbor. The writers of the *in perpetuam reimemoriam* included James Mason of Virginia and John Slidell of Louisiana. Both had been taken from aboard the British mail steamer *Trent* on November 8, 1861. Other protesters included the governor of Kentucky, Charles S. Morehead, and several army and naval officers who had resigned their commissions in support of the Rebels. Some were captured by secret agents in northern metropolitan centers. Most detainees were released after a year. The State Department's standard oath for paroles began with a promise to "support, protect and defend the Constitution." Another paragraph provided that the subscriber would not "enter any of the States in insurrection" nor "hold any correspondence whatever with persons residing in those States" without the permission of the secretary of state.[8]

The Saint Louis federal arsenal was ideally situated on the Mississippi River for the warehouse of military arms for the western forts. On April 20, 1861, a Missouri militia company seized the arsenal. Two weeks later, in extra session, the Missouri legislature passed a military bill requiring all members of the state militia to take an oath of loyalty to the state. With money appropriated from school funds, the governor formed militia companies that soon encamped in Saint Louis at Camp Jackson. Captain Nathaniel Lyon, U.S. Army, with a small force of regular and home guards captured Camp Jackson on May 10. The Union forces held fast despite strong Rebel support from Arkansas and Texas. In July, Major General John C. Frémont was given command of the Western Department, including all states and territories west of the Mississippi, plus Illinois. At a convention in July, Missouri state offices held by Rebels were declared vacant. Special elections were called.

When General Frémont arrived in Saint Louis on July 25, funds and forces were depleted. He acquired arms and men through his own resources. Troops were paid an enlistment bonus from $300,000 held at the Saint Louis subtreasury. That August, General Lyon pursued the Rebels into Springfield before engaging them at Wilson's Creek. The Federals won the battle but General Lyon lost his life. Afterward, Union forces regrouped in Springfield while Rebel troops moved southeast. Northern Missouri was disorganized. Federal troops soon withdrew from Springfield, returning to Saint Louis where martial law was declared on August 14. Soon after, Secessionist newspapers were suspended and travel restrictions imposed (Fig. 7).

A Saint Louis military commission convicted Rebel lieutenant Joseph Aubuchon of treason on September 5, 1861. His prison sentence was suspended by General Frémont in General Order No. 12, Western Department, Saint Louis, on September 16, 1861. In an act of leniency, the Rebel was allowed to go home. On a broader scale, the Saint Louis provost marshal permitted Rebel residents to leave the city if each gave their "word of honor that he is and will be ever loyal to the United States." "If ever ... found in arms against the Union, or in any way aiding her enemy, the penalty will be Death," was the warning all received before departing.

The Third Missouri Convention convened in Jefferson City on October 10, 1861. In addition to cutting the number and salaries of state employees, the assembly adopted a "Convention Oath" that required attorneys to swear allegiance to the Union in order to practice law. All that refused were effectively disbarred. Soon other professions were added (Fig. 8).

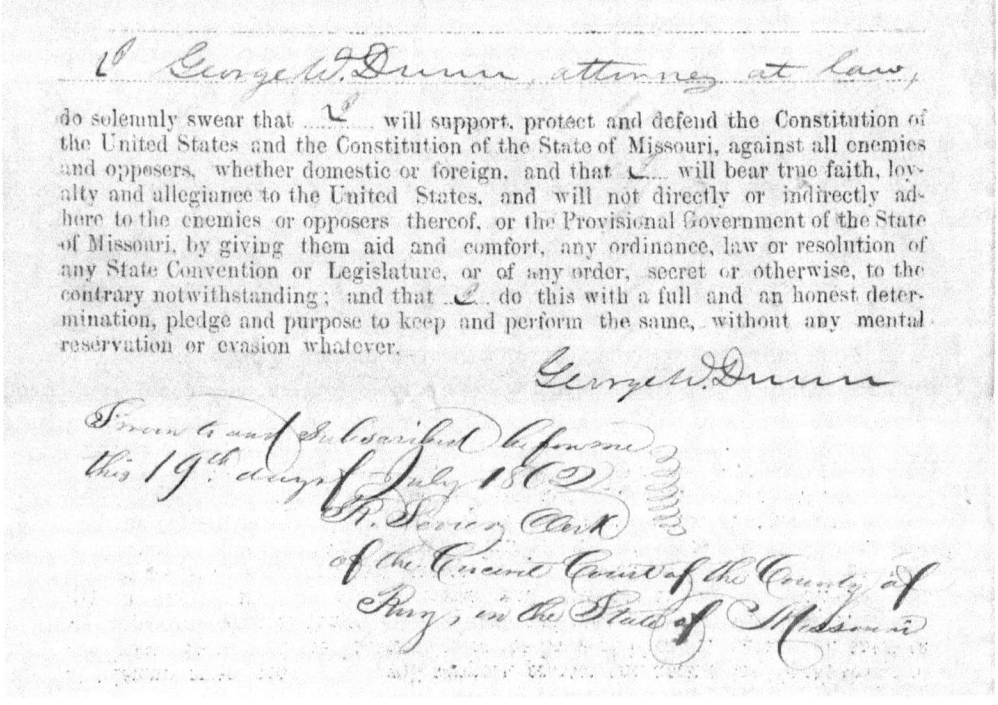

(Fig. 7) Pass issued by provost marshal, 19th Regiment Missouri Volunteers. Saint Louis. On reverse warning of death penalty if found in arms against United States. October 23, 1861. 5 × 8 inches. (MO-2.61.02)

(Fig. 8) Convention oath of attorney, required to practice law in Missouri. July 19, 1862. 8½ × 8 inches. (MO-4.62.01)

To protect commerce along the Mississippi River, Brigadier General Samuel R. Curtis, commander of the Saint Louis District, on December 6, 1861, provided in General Order No. 5, that all captains of transportation and shippers must take an oath (Fig. 9). The order required the taker to swear the following:

> I solemnly swear that I will bear true allegiance to the United States and support and sustain the Constitution and laws thereof; that I will maintain the national sovereignty paramount to that of all State, county, or confederate power; that I will discourage, discountenance, and forever oppose secession, Rebellion and disintegration of the Federal Union; that I disclaim and denounce all faith and fellowship with the so-called Confederate States and Confederate armies and pledge my honor, my property and my life to the sacred performance of this my solemn oath of allegiance to the Government of the United States.

On December 2, 1861, President Lincoln authorized the commander of the Department of Missouri to suspend the writ of habeas corpus during martial law. General Order No. 34, Department of Missouri, December 18, 1861, issued in compliance with the president's directive, provided for commissions to hear cases of persons charged with aiding the enemy and destroying bridges, roads and buildings. Further, the commissions could condemn property owned by disloyal citizens under General Order No. 13, Department of Missouri, Saint Louis, December 14, 1861.

Beginning in January 1862, Missouri newspapers had to submit articles to the Provost Marshal's office prior to distribution. Any newspaper failing to comply could be closed. After a series of disloyal acts, members of the Saint Louis Mercantile Library Association and Chamber of Commerce gave loyalty oaths in order to remain open. The order also prevented businesses from displaying Rebel flags or banners. On February 3, all members of the faculty and

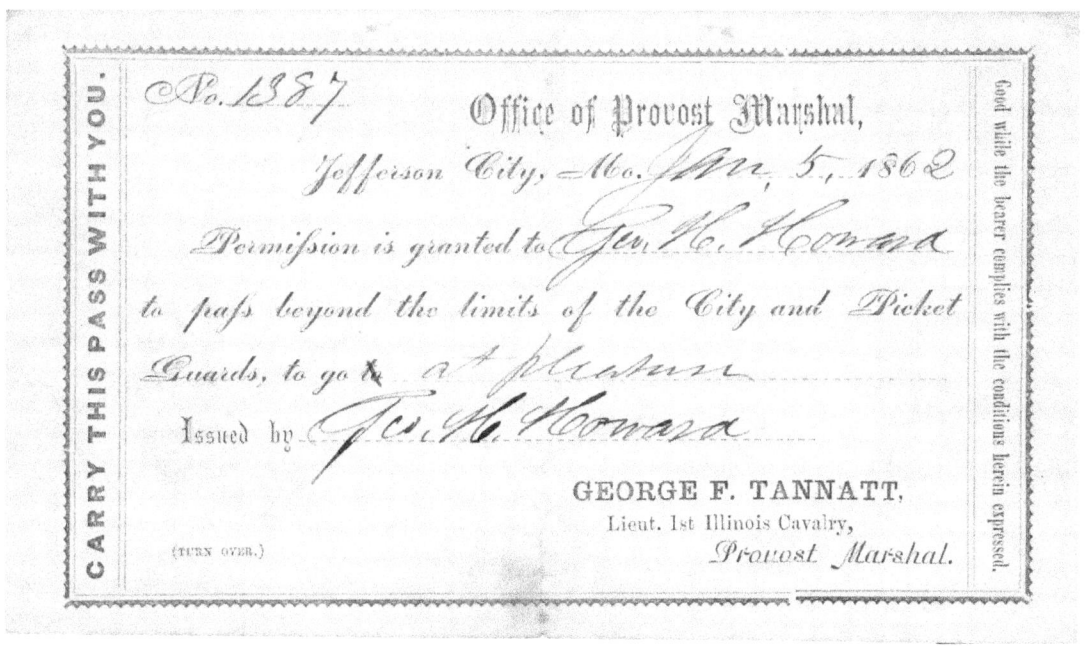

(Fig. 9) Pass issued with oath of allegiance (Dept. of MO. G. O. No. 13) for commerce on the Mississippi River. Subscriber promised to preserve the Union and discourage the Rebellion. Jefferson City, Missouri. January 5, 1862. 3¾ × 6¼ inches. (MO-2.62.01)

administration of the University of Missouri at Saint Louis were required to give loyalty oaths to remain on campus.

After the Battle of Pea Ridge, on March 8, 1862, organized Confederate action in Missouri ceased, but irregular raids continued. The next state convention opened in Jefferson City in June. At the assembly, an expansion of the "Convention Oath" covered all teachers, ministers and bankers, as well as future voters in state elections (Fig. 10). The convention attempted, but failed, to abolish slavery, much to the displeasure of Washington officials who remained suspicious of the border state's genuine loyalty.

As a result of the increased guerrilla activity, a number of Saint Louis citizens and their families were arrested and escorted beyond the protection of the Federal lines. Individuals could only take $200 with them, while families were allowed a maximum of $1,000. The balance of their assets was appropriated by state authorities for the benefit of wounded soldiers. Exiles were given a "safeguard" that protected them from arrest or molestation until beyond the Federal lines. If they took the oath of allegiance, as required by the Missouri Convention,

CONVENTION OATH.

I, _____ do solemnly swear, that I will support, protect and defend the Constitution of the United States, and the Constitution of the State of Missouri, against all enemies and opposers, whether domestic or foreign; that I will bear true faith, loyalty, and allegiance to the United States, and will not, directly or indirectly, adhere to the enemies or opposers thereof, or of the Provisional Government of the State of Missouri, by giving them aid and comfort, any ordinance, law, or resolution of any State Convention or Legislature, or of any order or organization, secret or otherwise, to the contrary notwithstanding; and that I do this with a full and honest determination, pledge and purpose to keep and perform the same, without any mental reservation or evasion whatever: So help me God.

State of Missouri,
County of

(Fig. 10) Convention oath to support provisional government of Missouri, ca. 1862. 10 × 8 inches. (MO-4.62.03)

(Fig. 11) United States safeguard. Lexington, Missouri. April 9, 1862. 10 × 8 inches. (MO-5.62.01)

and posted a bond assuring good behavior, they could remain, but they still were subject to strict surveillance (Fig. 11).

Disloyal citizens were sent to the Saint Louis arsenal. In August 1862, the assistant adjutant general, Western Department, Saint Louis, informed all commands to cease charging dissidents with offenses "too trivial in character." He explained that imprisonment was costly, and "if entertaining secession feelings constitutes a grave offense, one sufficient to imprison a man, the Government would have two-thirds of the State to feed at its expense." The provost marshal general still required oaths from disloyal persons in arms against the government, with a $1,000 bond to assure good behavior.

Because of the continuing threats of rebel guerrillas in the southern and western border areas of Missouri, strict martial law remained in effect during 1862. The raiders destroyed thousands of dollars of private property belonging to Missouri citizens. The department commander authorized bonds of assurance to levy a tax against wealthy dissenters to help compensate for losses sustained by citizens as a result of the guerrilla raids. The graduated assessment, if not paid, increased the tax an additional 25 percent as a penalty against the disloyal property owners. If the tax and penalty remained unpaid, the disloyalist was declared an enemy and sent outside the Federal lines. His property would be seized to support families of the sick and wounded. After Rebel raiders kidnapped and murdered an elderly gentleman known for his loyalty in Palmyra, the Union commander, General Schofield, executed ten Rebel prisoners, chosen by lot, in retaliation that October. The Missouri state elections were scheduled for November, but the question of emancipation was deferred until the next session.[9]

Rebel raids spilled over into western Kansas. A guerrilla band led by Colonel William Quantrill attacked Lawrence, Kansas, on August 21, 1863. Homes, businesses and public buildings were plundered and burned, and more than two hundred civilians were killed. Within a week, Union general Thomas Ewing, issued General Order No. 11 for the district from Kansas City. His directive forced all residents of Bates, Vernon, Jackson, and Cass Counties to leave their farms in Missouri within 15 days, to deny the raiders safe haven across the border. If the exiled residents could prove their loyalty, they were permitted to resettle near a military station near their homes and draw government rations for their families. Disloyal citizens had to leave the district. Abandoned stores and farms would be destroyed. Loyal citizens could file claims for compensation. Lastly, a "no man's zone" was created in Missouri to deny both Rebel marauders and Union Jayhawkers access to plunder.[10]

The next region for concerted Federal effort was western Virginia, more Union, rural, and with fewer slaves than Tidewater Virginia. Western Virginia early separated itself from the Richmond government. The mayor of Wheeling refused to comply with Governor John Letcher's order of April 20, 1861, to seize the U.S. customhouse, post office and other federal property. By then, the arsenal at Harper's Ferry had been burned and abandoned by Federal troops. In May, Major General George B. McClellan, U.S.A., took command of the Department of Ohio, including western Virginia.

From his headquarters in Cincinnati, General McClellan on May 26, 1861, issued a "Proclamation to the Union Men of Western Virginia." The proclamation informed residents that the Union army would cross the Ohio River "to restore peace and confidence, to protect the majesty of the law, and to rescue our brothers from the grasp of armed traitors." He noted that the government had abstained from sending troops into their state until the "free expression of opinion" through a free election was complete. By remaining with the Union, he expected "the loyal men of Western Virginia" to organize, arm and protect themselves. Union forces soon occupied Grafton in western Virginia, but Rebel raids continued. McClellan declared that guerrillas would be treated as public enemies rather than prisoners of war. Arms control was imposed.[11]

Not surprisingly, western Virginia stood firmly loyal in contrast to the planter-dominated Tidewater. Slavery was only a small part of western Virginia's economy. On June 11, 1861, representatives of 40 counties met in Wheeling to declare support for the Union and rejection of the Richmond secession ordinance of February 13, 1861. Two days later a separatist provisional government, led by Lieutenant Governor Frank Pierpont began swearing in new officials to support the U.S. Constitution, United States and its government. Within days, Virginia governor John Letcher made a plea for all true Virginians to gather at Hopkinsville armed and ready to free western Virginia from "the traitor in the midst of you." Despite Governor Letcher's call to arms, the people of western Virginia assembled to form a government on July 2 (Fig. 12).[12]

On August 20, 1861, the commanding general of the Army of Occupation, Brigadier General W. S. Rosecrans, in Clarksburg, Virginia, issued a proclamation to "Loyal Citizens." After a series of attacks on "peaceful citizens, unarmed travelers and single soldiers," he requested all loyal citizens to "put a stop to neighborhood and private wars." He reminded them that the state had a constitution and laws. To eliminate further harm, he directed that "each town and district choose five of its most reliable and energetic citizens" to form a committee of public safety to work with civic and military authorities for peace and good order.[13]

Problems continued for the western Virginia occupation army. Brigadier General B. F. Kelley in command of the Upper Potomac, in October, 1861, ordered all disloyal citizens to lay down their arms, return home and take an oath of allegiance. All that complied were promised pardons with full protection. Fewer restrictions were imposed on business and travel permit holders who behaved. General Kelley's order "effecting great good among the people" was noted in Washington. By the end of the year, Union forces occupied Raleigh County, the point of entry into Kentucky. Rebel communications between the central and western portions of the state were severed, and matters improved for the occupation forces.[14]

On March 29, 1862, Major General Frémont took command of the "Mountain Department" consisting of western Virginia, eastern Kentucky and East Tennessee. His campaign plans to engage General Stonewall Jackson's forces in the Shenandoah Valley never occurred. At his own request, General Frémont was relieved of duty on June 26. Subsequently, the "Mountain District" was reorganized and the new command encompassed all of northern Virginia. A new defensive plan for West Virginia was implemented.

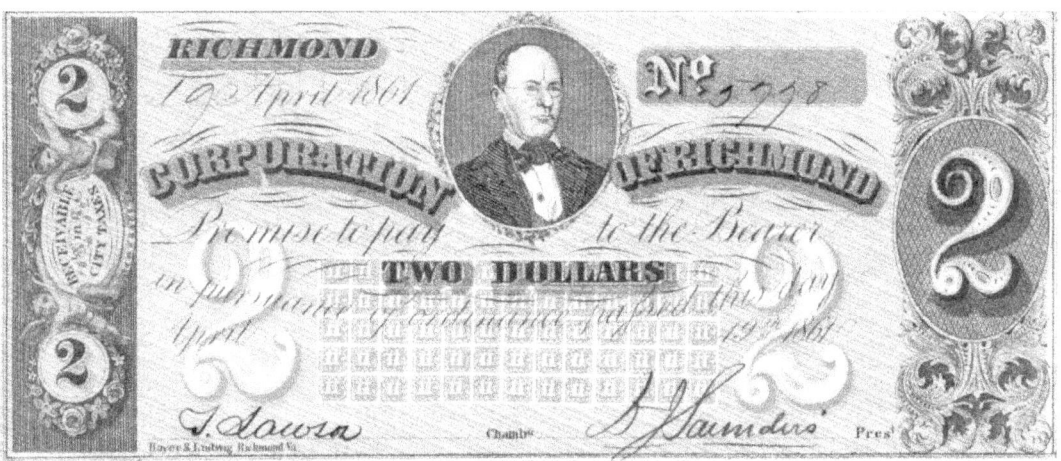

(Fig. 12) Virginia governer John Letcher's portrait on $2 Corporation of Richmond currency. 1861 (Tremmel No.: VA-R3)

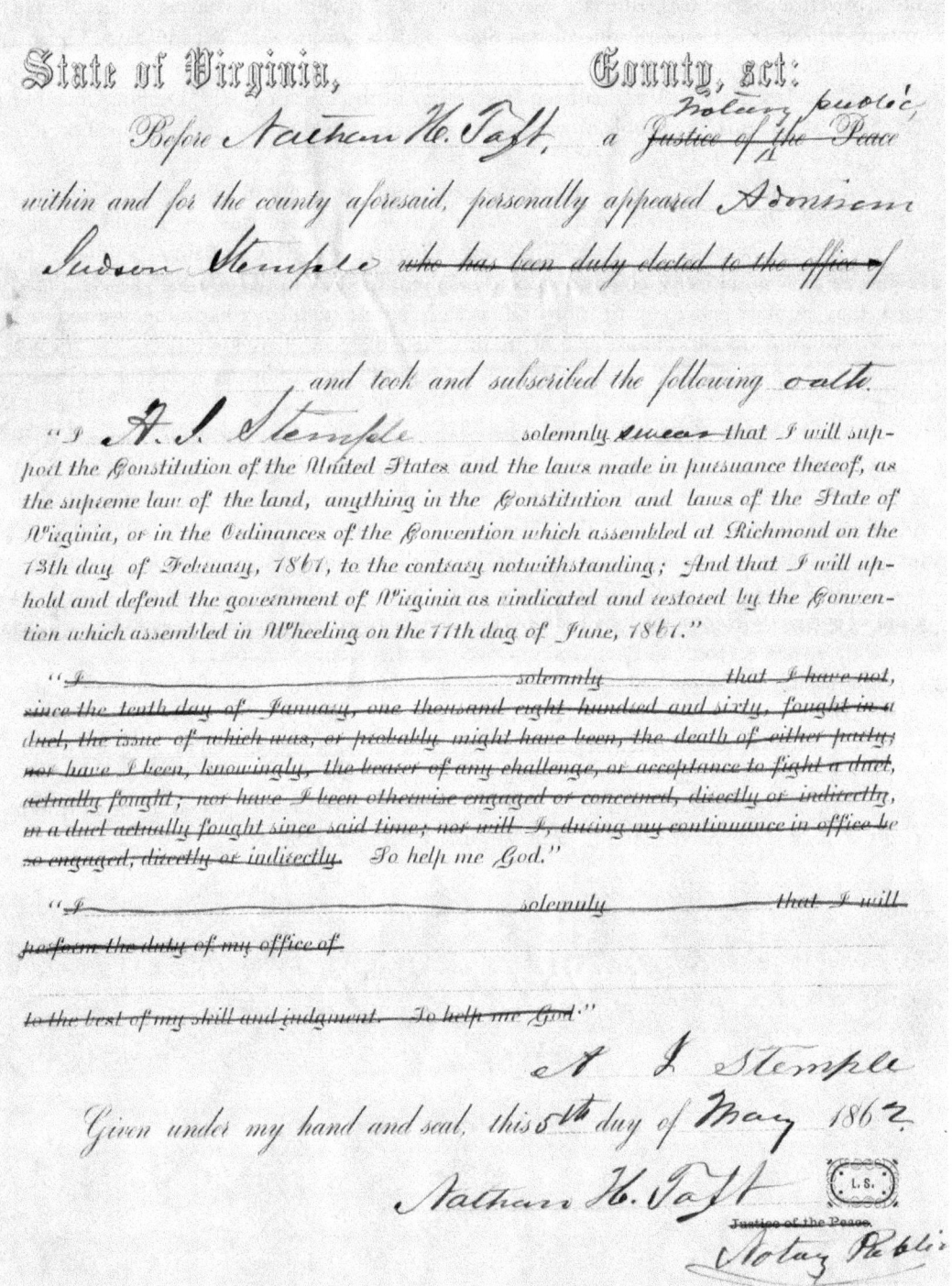

(Fig. 13) Convention oath to defend government assembled in Wheeling on June 11, 1861. (West) Virginia. May 5, 1862. 10 × 7½ inches. (VA-4.62.04)

The loyalty oaths used in western Virginia were interesting in several unique aspects. The signer promised, as usual, to support the United States Constitution and the laws of Virginia, except the ordinance of the Secession Convention at Richmond assembled February 13, 1861. The signer also promised to "uphold and defend the government of Virginia as restored by the Convention assembled in Wheeling on the 11th day of June, 1861." A novel assertion required that each citizen proclaim that he had not participated in a duel since 1860 (Fig. 13). The oath process began in earnest in May 1862, prior to the statehood vote for West Virginia.

Congress, on December 31, 1862, admitted West Virginia to the Union as the 35th state. The new state consisted of 48 counties located west of the Alleghany Mountains, with a population of 349,000, entitling it to three members in Congress and one judicial district. The new state capital was Wheeling, with a port of delivery for customs purposes at Parkersburg. Loyal eastern Virginians relocated there after taking oaths required of all newcomers (Fig. 14). West Virginia participated in the next national election.

Another strategic border state was Kentucky, which was claimed by both sides. Confederates held Bowling Green the first year, while Union troops from Ohio occupied Louisville. Although both armies stated they would respect Kentucky's neutrality, each warned if the other was not expelled, martial law would be enforced. Despite its claim of neutrality, Kentucky was contested ground.[15]

Several Border States called for a convention for the latter part of May 1861, to determine a collective decision concerning secession. Kentucky selected delegates to attend, two-thirds

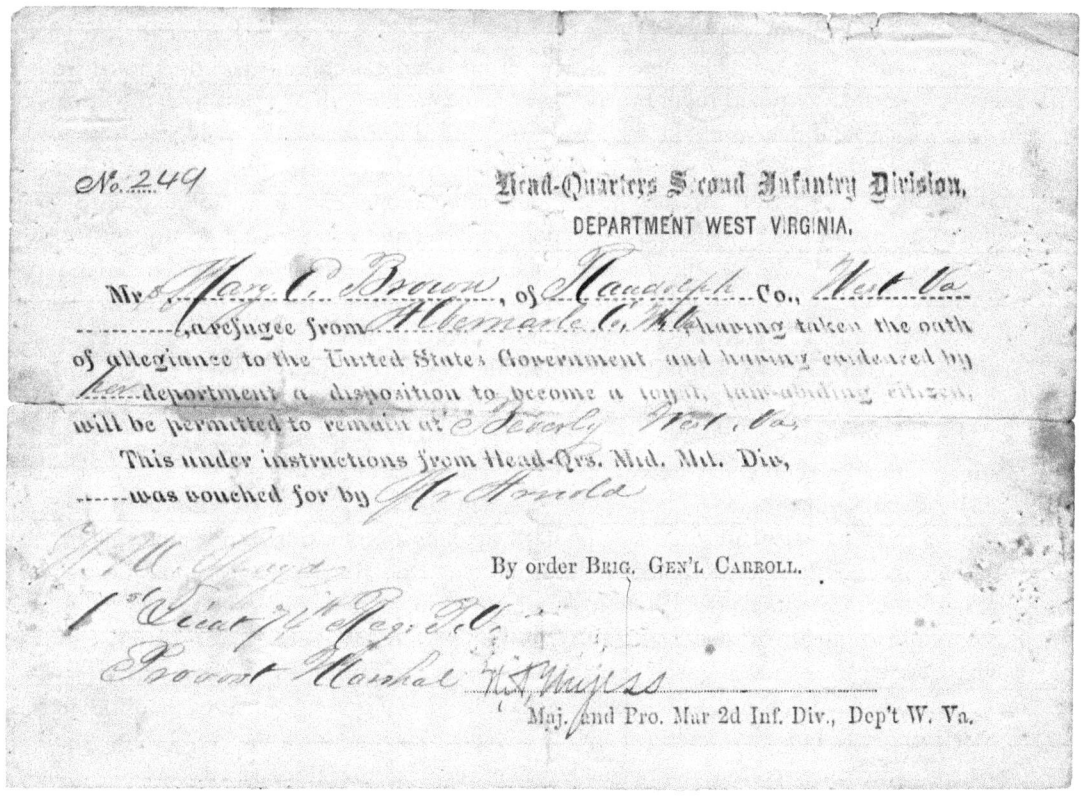

(Fig. 14) Refugee oath, Beverly County, West Virginia, [ND]. 6 × 7¾ inches. (WV-4.65.01)

of whom were Union men, as was the convention chairman, Kentucky senator John J. Crittenden. On May 27, the border convention was called to order in Frankfurt. Only delegates from Missouri joined the Kentucky representatives. The convention accomplished little other than a consensus that the two states preferred to remain neutral. After adjournment, the governor of Kentucky, Beriah Magoffin, while somewhat sympathetic to the South, nevertheless, made an address offering his state's resolve to remain loyal to the flag, the Union and the Constitution of the United States. Kentucky's representatives in Congress were, in the majority, loyal Democrats. By late summer, Tennessee, which had approved an ordinance of secession on June 8, 1861, declared an embargo on the shipment of goods into Kentucky. Despite the official position of neutrality, Kentucky men began to volunteer for service in both the Union and Confederate armies. Forces began to gather in preparation for invasion from the surrounding states, both Union and Rebel.[16]

The initial Union defense of Louisville, Kentucky, was the responsibility of General Robert A. Anderson, of Fort Sumter fame. By the fall of 1861, Anderson realized Lexington, Franklin and Louisville would soon be lost to Rebel forces. To make matters worse, Anderson became ill. The commander of the Department of Ohio, General Ormsby M. Mitchel, warned Washington that if Kentucky was not more fully occupied by Union forces, the entire state would be lost. Mitchel lacked sufficient troops for such an occupation. In response, the governor of Ohio sent eight state regiments, newly formed after the War Department accelerated the officer-commissioning and troop-mustering process. With the additional troops, General Mitchel, a Kentucky native, crossed the Cumberland Gap and invaded East Tennessee in late fall 1861.[17]

General J. T. Boyle was next placed in charge of the U.S. forces in Kentucky. After his arrival on June 9, 1862, he instructed all within his district who had recently arrived from Rebel-held territory to report to his provost marshal to take the oath of loyalty and, if necessary, post a security bond that would be forfeited if they failed to conduct themselves accordingly. Oaths were administered at Louisville by Colonel Henry Dent, in Bowling Green by Colonel S. D. Bruce, by Major L. P. Brocket in Lexington and Colonel Silas R. J. Noble in Paducah. Each respondent was to bring evidence of good character and names of supporting witnesses to the passport office. Those who violated the oath could be considered public enemies and sent to prison in Louisville prior to departure to the political prison at Camp Chase, Ohio. All were warned to moderate their language and actions so as not to excite the public. Any citizens suspected of aiding, harboring or concealing guerrillas or failing to report such would be brought before a military tribunal. Communities considered disloyal would be assessed for damages committed by Rebel raiders in order to compensate losses sustained by loyal citizens. Standing military commissions were prepared to hear all cases involving disloyal citizens.[18]

Although Kentucky was no longer claiming neutrality and remained within the Union, a considerable number of its citizens supported the Confederate cause both financially and with manpower. During the special session of the state legislature in August 1862, Governor Magoffin condemned the invasion of his state by Colonel John Hunt Morgan's "Partisan Rangers." To moderate the other side, the governor went on to apologize for the imposition of martial law by the federal government and the arrests of political prisoners. After recommending immediate peace and settlement of the war, Magoffin resigned. Speaker of the state senate James F. Robinson was elected by the lawmakers to complete the remaining term of office. Next, to bring about a speedy conclusion of the rebellion, the divided legislature considered a proposal of gradual slave emancipation with partial compensation. This was soundly defeated. Soon thereafter, Confederate troops forced the legislature to adjourn, leave Lexington and reconvene in Louisville. State records and archives were also moved prior to the invasion.[19]

In February 1862, General U. S. Grant captured the Confederate forts of Fort Henry and Donelson, near the Tennessee-Kentucky border, and opened the Tennessee and Cumberland Rivers to Union gunboats. Grant moved toward Nashville and General Ormbsy Mitchel occupied Bowling Green on February 15, 1862. By August Mitchel had entered Alabama and captured Huntsville, gaining control of the rail lines back to Nashville. Because Rebel sentiments were so strong in Alabama, he refrained from using oaths as part of his occupation. Instead citizens, in return for passes and favors, could "pledge" not to engage in warfare. A "peaceable citizen" certificate promised rewards to a citizen who would stop violence and provide information for public safety. After his success, Mitchel was summoned to Washington and given command of the Department of the South in South Carolina. Mitchel's approach also got the attention of Alabama's Confederate officials. Subsequent pledges in Rebel counties required "true allegiance" from local officials, down to the level of justice of the peace (Fig. 15).

General Mitchel's gentle approach to occupation, for a time, helped him to open the rail lines in Alabama between Stephenson, Bridgeport, Florence, Tuscumbia and Decatur back to Nashville. His provosts, from command headquarters at Huntsville, prepared lists of citizens, divided between friendly, neutral and Rebel. The latter were instructed to disclose all stores, such as fodder, corn and forge, and livestock. If any of the identified Rebel sympathizers failed to comply, they were subject to banishment and confiscation of their property. If they submitted the requested inventory listing, the families were allowed to remain on their farms, continue to draw on their stores for personal consumption and remain unmolested as long as they maintained good behavior. Whenever General Mitchel's quartermaster needed stores, he would draw upon the listed items, but only a tithe at a time. If the identified dissenters later agreed to sign a "peaceable citizen" pledge, other privileges would be forthcoming.[20]

The fall of Forts Henry and Donelson to General Grant forced the Rebels to abandon Bowling Green, Kentucky, and regroup in Nashville. President Davis declared martial law for East Tennessee on April 8, 1862. General Grant earlier had declared martial law for West Tennessee, on February 22. The Union army now controlled traffic down the Mississippi River between Saint Louis and Memphis.

During this time, President Lincoln appointed Senator Andrew Johnson military governor of Tennessee, headquartered in Nashville, with the rank of brigadier general of volunteers. Johnson, accompanied by other Washington officials, arrived in Nashville on March 12, 1862, to organize his office. The Nashville mayor earlier had surrendered the city to General Buell on February 25. The mayor, city council and most municipal officials, after meeting with Governor Johnson, voted 16 to 1 against taking the oath of allegiance offered by the Provost. After a short cooling-off period, on March 29, the group of recalcitrant city officials was arrested. The governor appointed replacements to work with his deputies. Subsequently, all members of the board of education, teachers and minor officials were allowed to take the oath or resign. Several newspaper editors and leading businessmen joined the mayor in prison for disloyal acts. By July 13, a list, of more than seven hundred leading residents who had taken the oath was published in a local newspaper. Loyal merchants and tradesmen reopened their businesses. Wealthy citizens were assessed between $50 and $300 for the public relief of abandoned Rebel wives, children and widows under protection declared August 18 and December 13. Pass regulations were in place and functioning by September 10. After guerrilla raiders threatened the city's outskirts, tighter military controls were enforced.[21]

The Nashville federal court reopened in May 1862. By midmonth, Judge John Catron

The State of Alabama,
MONTGOMERY COUNTY.

I, B. Eliasberg, do solemnly swear that I will bear true allegiance to, observe and support the Constitution of the CONFEDERATE STATES OF AMERICA, and that I will serve them honestly and faithfully against all their enemies or opposers whatsoever.

Subscribed and sworn to before me, this 8th day of April, 1862.

J. H. Nettle, J.P.   B. Eliasberg

(Fig. 15) Confederate pledge of "true allegiance." Montgomery, Alabama. April 2, 1862. 8 × 8 inches. (AL-4.62.03)

instructed the grand jury, convened to consider cases of treason, "to ferret out all those aiding and abetting the guerrillas raiding parties attacking local residents." The day after the charge to the grand jury, former governor Neil S. Brown and members of the Tennessee Secessionist Party were charged with treason and arrested. The group was soon discharged after giving oaths of allegiance; ultimately, the criminal charges were dismissed. For the next month, a large number of residents were arrested for using seditious language. Most were released after posting a security bond of $1,000 and promising good behavior. On June 17, six Nashville ministers refused to take the oath offered by the governor in his office. After waiting ten days all but one were arrested and sent to prison. The sixth minister was simply confined to his home because of poor health and advanced age. The next day the headmaster of the Nashville female boarding school and the superintendent of the state lunatic asylum joined the preachers in jail. Later, recalcitrant citizens were exiled beyond the safety of the Union lines for their disloyalty. By November, a large number of merchants had taken the oath and were released from prison.[22]

By December, Governor Johnson had established regional commissions to administer oaths to residents of towns recently occupied by Major General W. S. Rosecrans and his men in the Department of the Cumberland. Commissioners only considered the character of noncombatants. Some were required to post security bonds to support compliance to their loyalty obligations. Some in Murfreesboro were unwilling to take the oath. On March 8, 1863, all were given ten days to change their minds or be prepared to be exiled south of the Union lines. The group was permitted to take away noncontraband personal effects. Those banished were warned that if they were recaptured in town without permission, they would be considered enemy spies and suffer the consequences.[23]

The residents of Union-occupied Winchester, Tennessee, were given the opportunity, under Department of the Cumberland, General Order No. 175, of March 28, 1863, to become "peaceable

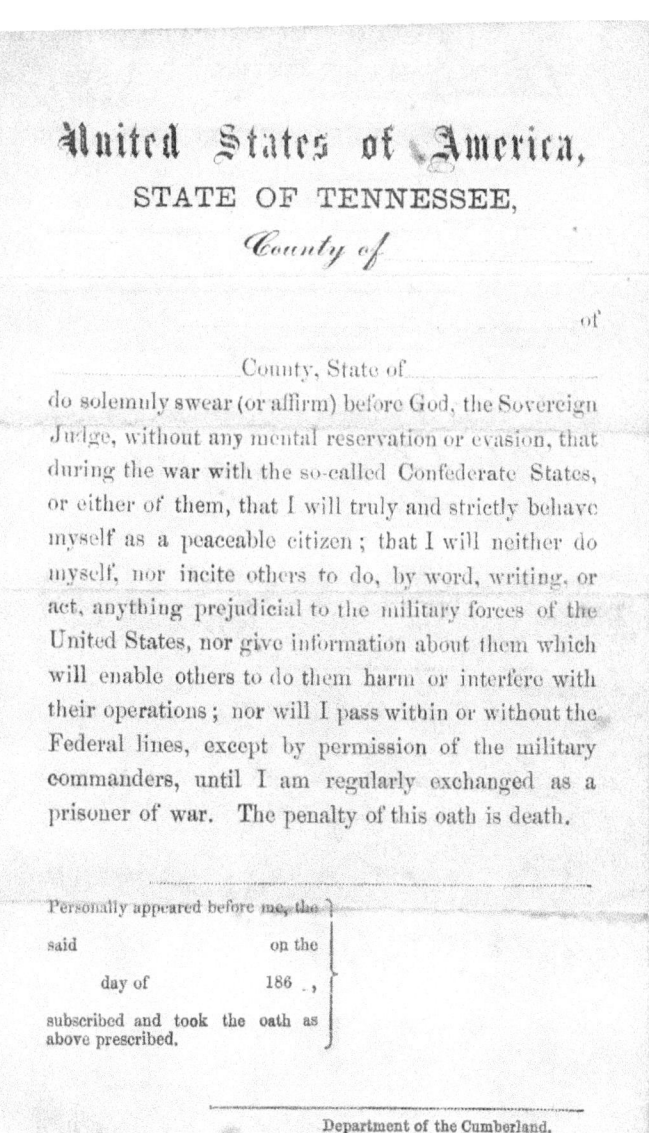

(Fig. 16) "Peaceable Citizen" oath, Department of Cumberland, for prisoner of war. Tennessee, ca. 1862. 7 × 4¼ inches. (TN-4.62.02)

citizens" by posting a bond and remaining loyal to the Union. Recalcitrant civilians unwilling to become "peaceable" were escorted beyond the safety of the occupied lines. Only if sincere and true could a citizen be entitled to the benefits of being "peaceable." These certificates were executed in duplicate and filed in a register with the associated bonds (Fig. 16).

Governor Johnson announced that after a sufficient number of citizens had taken the oath of allegiance, military rule would be relaxed. In his first "Address to the People," Governor Johnson offered amnesty to any peaceful citizen willing to recognize the supremacy of the federal constitution and federal laws. The offer was refused by the Nashville mayor and city council members after which they were made political prisoners. Later, the state's former governor, judges and bank cashiers were arrested. The press was suppressed. Disloyal clergy were not exempt, and any who preached "treason" from the pulpit were sanctioned. The Confederates held fast in East Tennessee until September 1863. The Union military governor's influence and power barely extended beyond Nashville.

After Union troops occupied Tennessee and Kentucky, martial law was imposed. As a consequence, the provost marshal required merchants and businessmen to take a special oath of allegiance and post a security bond before reopening. Such was the case in Cynthiana, Kentucky, in February 1863, after the 118th Ohio Volunteer Infantry cleared the town of Rebels (Fig. 17).

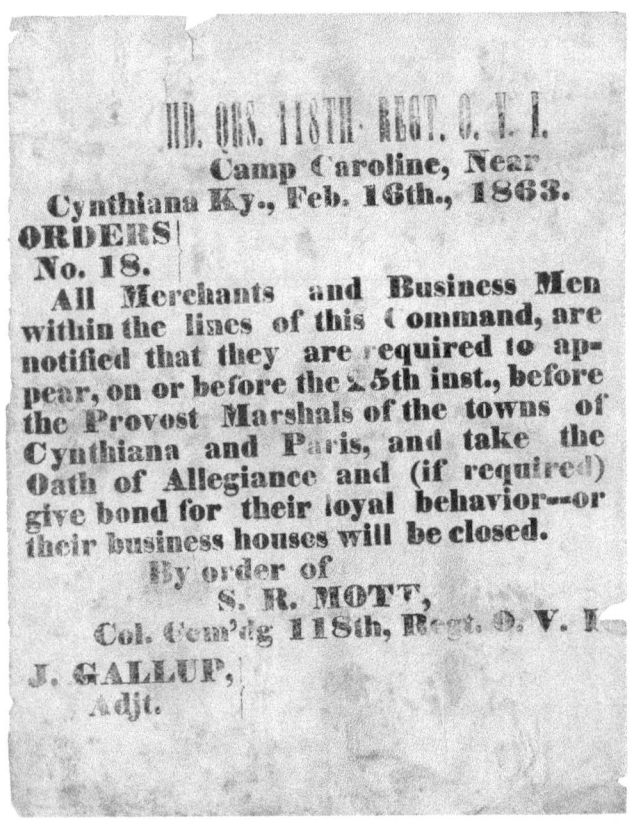

(Fig. 17) Broadside Order No. 18, Hd. Qrs. 118th Regt. O.V.I. requiring Oaths by business houses. Camp Caroline, Cynthiana, Kentucky. February 16, 1863. 8 × 7 inches. (KY-5.63.01)

On June 6, 1862, the commander of the U.S. ram *Switzerland*, Capt. Charles Elliet, Jr., was pleased to inform the secretary of war that the city of Memphis had surrendered and that the United States flag again flew above the customshouse and court buildings. Within a week, post offices were delivering mail and commerce resumed. The provost marshall enforced General U. S. Grant's General Order No. 8, dated June 20, 1862, requiring the board of aldermen, mayor, recorder and other leading officials to take the oath of allegiance within three days or be considered traitors subject to arrest. By July 10, all families of rebel soldiers or officials were ordered beyond the Union lines within five days. Six days later, Grant's successor in Memphis offered oaths to all male residents. About 1,300 were reported to have complied, but about 500 left the city to join their families below Memphis. River commerce between Memphis and northern landings, such as Cairo, resumed. After a number of vessels were fired upon by

Rebel shore batteries in September, General William T. Sherman ordered, in retaliation, ten disloyal Memphis families to be exiled for every shot fired at a Union vessel. Thirty Rebel families were reported banished. Outside the city, in the rural outskirts, raids occurred daily.[24]

In Memphis, loyalty requirements were again announced by the 16th Army Corps, General Order No. 65, in May 1863. Citizens were given 20 days to declare if they were loyal or an enemy of the United States. The order applied to men and women alike, and bonds were required "for the faithful keeping of the terms of the oath." The Memphis oath introduced a promise to "defend and support the said United States against all enemies foreign and domestic and especially against the rebellious league known as the Confederate States of America." Every adult not taking the oath was deemed an enemy of the United States and subject to penalties. The order reminded residents they had enjoyed a year of federal protection and now must decide whether or not to be loyal. Giving aid to the Rebels constituted a capital offense, as all were warned. Finally, registration as enemies exposed assets to confiscation.[25]

President Lincoln, by proclamation dated September 22, 1862, stated that the purpose of the war was to restore the law of the land to the seceded states, including federal elections. Following the president's remarks, Governor Johnson announced on December 29, an election would be held for selection of members to Congress from the ninth and tenth Congressional Districts of Tennessee. To vote, citizens had to prove loyalty. Rebel raids on election day prevented the polls from opening. Not until the military Departments of Tennessee, Cumberland and Ohio were combined under the command of General U. S. Grant did Tennessee become sufficiently safe to hold elections. The Rebel's occupation of Tennessee did not lessen until after the Union victories of Lookout Mountain and Missionary Ridge in November 1863.

The administration of Union oaths, courts and elections proceeded slowly after Rebel territory came under Federal control. During the first year of the war, only remote island outposts in Key West, Port Royal and Cape Hatteras remained isolated Union enclaves. Military rule in occupied zones required strong control and vigilance. In the Border States, at least, some of the population was loyal. Security and benefits were temporary, and if Union forces withdrew, Rebel troops and loyalties returned.

Key West, although deep within Rebel territory, was always Union occupied. On September 6, 1861, the commanding officer of the U.S. troops of Key West, Florida, issued his General Order No. 82 that provided that any citizen of the island and his family refusing to take the oath of allegiance to the United States must leave. Similar warnings were made within Federal enclaves along the coastal waters of Virginia and the Carolinas after Union troops captured coastal fortifications.[26]

Thirty loyal citizens at Hatteras Inlet, North Carolina, outside Fort Clark, agreed as a group to remain within the protective line of Union forces. The sworn document executed in Hyde County on August 30, 1862, assured the commanding officer of the Ninth Regiment of New York Volunteers that all would bear "true allegiance" to the United States of America. They also promised to keep the commander informed of any enemy approach and assist in the defense of the fort. This was important because Hatteras Inlet controlled Albemarle Sound, a key approach to Fort Monroe. However, little Union progress was made beyond the united Union line. The Federal commander at Hatteras Inlet accepted Carolina recruits into the Union army after volunteers were given loyalty oaths. This modest force of loyal North Carolina soldiers provided the Union a propaganda success.[27]

A joint amphibious task force captured the Rebel forts at Port Royal Sound, South Carolina, on November 7, 1861, securing an anchorage and staging area for the future assaults on

Savannah and Charleston. Martial rule was immediately imposed in the Beaufort District. Initially the order had little consequence because all local residents, except slaves, had escaped to the mainland in advance of the Federal landings. Since the zone was occupied by Union personnel, loyalty oaths were delayed, although a rigid pass system for newcomers was installed. Effective May 10, 1861, nationwide, all officers of the Union army and navy had to give a new oath of allegiance. Enlisted men swore an oath at the time of their enlistment, so all free men at Port Royal had already sworn their loyalty before the occupation.

In time, as more civilians from the north and relocating refugees entered the Department of the South, more loyalty oaths became necessary. Beginning the second week of September 1862, General David Hunter, the departmental commander, required the following oath from all civilian employees:

> I _____ of _____ by occupation a _____ do solemnly swear that I will bear true allegiance to the United States of America, and will support and sustain the Constitution and laws thereof; that I have voluntarily given no aid, counsel, countenance, or encouragement to persons engaged in armed hostility thereto; that I will discourage, discountenance and forever oppose all secession, Rebellion, and disintegration of the Federal Union; that I will uphold the authority of the Federal Government as against the authority of the so-called Confederate States, or any other state or sovereignty whatever, and do hereby pledge my honor, my property and my life for the due observance of this my solemn oath of allegiance.[28]

The Department of the Gulf was created at New Orleans on March 21, 1862, and General Benjamin Butler was appointed its commanding general. The Stars and Stripes flew over the New Orleans mint on April 27. General Butler occupied the city two days later. He remained until December 10, after which Major General Nathaniel Banks assumed command. Butler's departure came two days after President Jefferson Davis condemned "Beast Butler" for horrible insults to the ladies of New Orleans and his abusive exercise of martial rule. In retaliation, President Davis halted future prisoner exchanges. Butler's military occupation was the first widespread exercise of military rule in a completely hostile territory. Although his methods were firm, remarkably, he quickly resumed civilian services and commerce despite a recalcitrant population.

The imposition of martial law in New Orleans was much different than that imposed in Baltimore and Saint Louis. Butler's General Order No. 15, May 1, 1862, warned his own disembarking troops that "amid the temptations and inducements of a large city, all plundering of public or private property, by any person or persons, is hereby forbidden, under the severest penalties." After controlling his own soldiers, he focused on the Rebels. These controls were broad in scope, such as the following:

- Displays of Rebel flags and emblems were forbidden.
- Public property, arms and funds were confiscated.
- Publications were censored.
- Businesses had to register.
- Churches were warned to conduct services of "profound peace."
- Public houses, saloons, and inns were licensed.
- Local police and courts were suspended.
- Public gatherings, speeches and assemblies were prohibited.
- For murder of any soldier, the assassin would be immediately punished and buildings at the murder scene destroyed.
- Confederate bonds and currency were withdrawn from circulation.
- Martial rule would last indefinitely.

General Butler convened a military commission of five officers to hear cases involving high crimes and misdemeanors punishable by death or long prison terms. Rules of evidence were "relaxed," records were brief and findings not subject to appeal — a process similar to a court martial. Those convicted of martial-law violations could face death, as announced in General Order No. 23 of May 2, 1862.

All New Orleans residents understood that if they expected to receive "favor, protection, privilege, passport, or to have money paid to them," compliance with military rules was necessary. On June 10, Butler issued General Order No. 41, requiring all military, civil, judicial, executive and legislative state officials to take the oath of allegiance "in order to remain in office" (Fig. 18).

Butler stated in the preamble to his order that "this oath will not be, as it has never been, forced upon any." Under a later General Order (No. 76) a citizen either had to take the oath or declare himself a friendly foreign national or be classed an "Enemy of the United States." Such a designation subjected the "Enemy" to confiscation of property and expulsion from the safety of the Federal lines (Fig.19).

Further, General Butler enforced all laws of the United States with vigor. Those willing to take the oath of allegiance would be protected, but Rebels would be treated accordingly. Order and peace were ultimately restored after William Mumford was hanged on June 7, 1862, for hauling down the American flag at the United States Mint.

The registration directive (General Order No. 41) required foreigners to give a pledge in order to remain in New Orleans under protection of the military. Such foreign registration ceased after President Lincoln directed that friendly nationals did not have to comply. The State Department had also protested Butler's order. Butler took this action against foreigners after a British official turned firearms, money and uniforms over to Confederate officials prior to the occupation. By August, almost twelve thousand residents had registered with the Provost Office. In December, loyal citizens in the first and second district of Louisiana were allowed to vote for representatives to the United States Congress. General Butler was pleased, referencing the first paragraph of General Order 41, that taking the oath was simply stating, "I am an American citizen, the highest title known." By the end of the year, hundreds of parcels of real estate belonging to "Registered Enemies" of the United States were in possession of the special agent of the Treasury Department, Benjamin Flanders, the future Reconstruction governor of Louisiana (Fig. 20).

After Major General Nathaniel P. Banks assumed command of New Orleans, a number of residents who had been declared "public enemies," wished to remove the taint of that designation in order to resume business and save their assets from seizure. General Banks's General Order No. 9, of January 12, 1863, allowed those already designated "public enemies" to erase that disgrace by taking the oath of allegiance. The original time limit for coming forward was extended if the applicant convinced the provost marshal that there was a valid reason for missing the original deadline, other than stubbornness.[29]

Early oaths of loyalty, used to release citizens from political prisons, contained language that some in the Border States felt might subject them to confiscation of assets behind enemy lines. Also, for many of the released political prisoners who were returned south some of the words used in the oath reflected loyalty to the Union and were contrary to the Confederate Constitution. A few complained that if such words were modified, so they would not be subject to arrest or seizure by Confederate authorities, they would freely pledge good behavior in the future. On December 13, 1862, the judge advocate of the army, L. C. Turner, instructed the commander of the political prison at Fort Hamilton to discharge in the future anyone

Headquarters Department of the Gulf,
New Orleans, June 10, 1862.

GENERAL ORDERS No. 41.

The Constitution and laws of the United States require that all military, civil, judicial, executive and legislative officers of the United States, and of the several States, shall take an oath to support the Constitution and laws. If a person desires to serve the United States, or to receive special profit from a protection from the United States, he should take upon himself the corresponding obligations. This oath will not be, as it has never been, forced upon any. It is too sacred an obligation, too exalted in its tenure, and brings with it too many benefits and privileges, to be profaned by unwilling lip service. It enables its recipient to say, "I am an American citizen," the highest title known, save that of him who can say with St. Paul, "I was free born," and have never renounced that freedom.

Judges, justices, sheriffs, attorneys, notaries and all officers of the law whatever, and all persons who have ever been, or who have ever claimed to be, citizens of the United States in this Department, who therefore exercise any office, hold any place of trust or calling whatever, which calls for the doing of any legal act whatever, or for the doing of any act, judicial or administrative, which shall or may affect any other person than the actor, must take and subscribe the following oath: "I do solemnly swear (or affirm) that I will bear true faith and allegiance to the United States of America, and will support the Constitution thereof." All acts, doings, deeds, instruments, records or certificates, certified or attested by, and transactions done, performed or made by any of the persons above described, from and after the 15th day of June inst., who shall not have taken and subscribed such oath, are void and of no effect.

It having become necessary, in the judgment of the Commanding General, as a "public exigency," to distinguish those who are well disposed toward the Government of the United States, from those who still hold allegiance to the Confederate States, and ample time having been given to all citizens for reflection upon this subject, and full protection to person and property of every law-abiding citizen having been afforded, according to the terms of the proclamation of May 1st:

Be it further ordered, That all persons ever heretofore citizens of the United States, asking or receiving any favor, protection, privilege, passport, or to have money paid them, property, or other valuable thing whatever delivered to them, or any benefit of the power of the United States extended to them, except protection from personal violence, must take and subscribe the oath above specified, before

(Fig. 18) Above and opposite: General Order No. 41, Department of the Gulf Oath. New Orleans. June 10, 1862. 5 × 8 inches. (LA-5.62.03)

2

their request can be heard, or any act done in their favor by any officer of the United States, within this Department. And for this purpose all persons shall be deemed to have been citizens of the United States who shall have been residents therein for the space of five years and upward, and if foreign born, shall not have claimed and received a protection of their Government, duly signed and registered by the proper officer, more than sixty days previous to the publication of this order.

It having come to the knowledge of the Commanding General that many persons resident within this Department have heretofore been aiding rebellion by furnishing arms and munitions of war, running the blockade, giving information, concealing property, and abetting, by other ways, the so-called Confederate States, in violation of the laws of neutrality imposed upon them by their Sovereigns, as well as the laws of the United States, and that a less number are still so engaged: it is therefore ordered, that all foreigners claiming any of the privileges of an American citizen, or protection or favor from the Government of the United States, (except protection from personal violence,) shall previously take and subscribe an oath in the form following :

I, ..., do solemnly swear, or affirm, that so long as my Government remains at peace with the United States, I will do no act, or consent that any be done, or conceal any that has been or is about to be done, that shall aid or comfort any of the enemies or opposers of the United States whatever.

(Signed) ....
Subject of ....

At the City Hall, at the Provost Court, at the Provost Marshal's office, and at the several police stations, books will be opened, and a proper officer will be present to administer the proper oaths to any person desiring to take the same, and to witness the subscription of the same by the party taking it. Such officer will furnish to each person so taking and subscribing, a certificate in form following :

DEPARTMENT OF THE GULF, New Orleans, ...1862.
.................., has taken and subscribed the oath required by General Orders No. 41, for a .... of ....
(Signed) ....

By command of

MAJOR-GENERAL BUTLER.

R. S. DAVIS, Capt. and A. A. A. G.

willing to be paroled on his pledge of honor not to do harm to the United States, without the oath of allegiance. The issue of paroles had become more complicated and now needed guidance from higher authority.[30]

After signing sworn oaths in order to be released from the Old Capitol Prison, four Illinois citizens brought criminal action against federal officials for false arrest, deterring public officers from performing their duties. The army's judge advocate had inserted language in the oaths that, in the future, none of those released would "commence or cause any action or suit against officers of any loyal state or of the United States causing any arrest or imprisonment." The U.S. Senate on December 22, 1862, passed a resolution questioning the Judge Advocate's change in the oath, specifically, the promise by released prisoners not to sue Army officials. The day after the Senate inquiry, Secretary of War Edwin M. Stanton assured senators that only one such incident had occurred and that he had already directed that, in the future, under no circumstances, would persons be required to promise not to sue any official for an illegal act. Suspension of the writ of habeas corpus had resulted in a number of private lawsuits in loyal states against state and federal officials for the illegal arrest after the person was released.[31]

The issue of foreign nationals again arose after Rebel raids originated from Canada. The secretary of state, through the War Department's General Order No. 30 of December 24, 1864, declared that any traveler crossing into the United States from Canada had to have a passport issued by a United States consul or minister, unless arriving by ship. After protests again were lodged through diplomatic channels, the State Department withdrew the order after their "friendly neighbor" to the north promised to prevent hostile incursions by enemies of the United States.

Often President Lincoln urged Rebels to renounce the Rebel cause and swear future

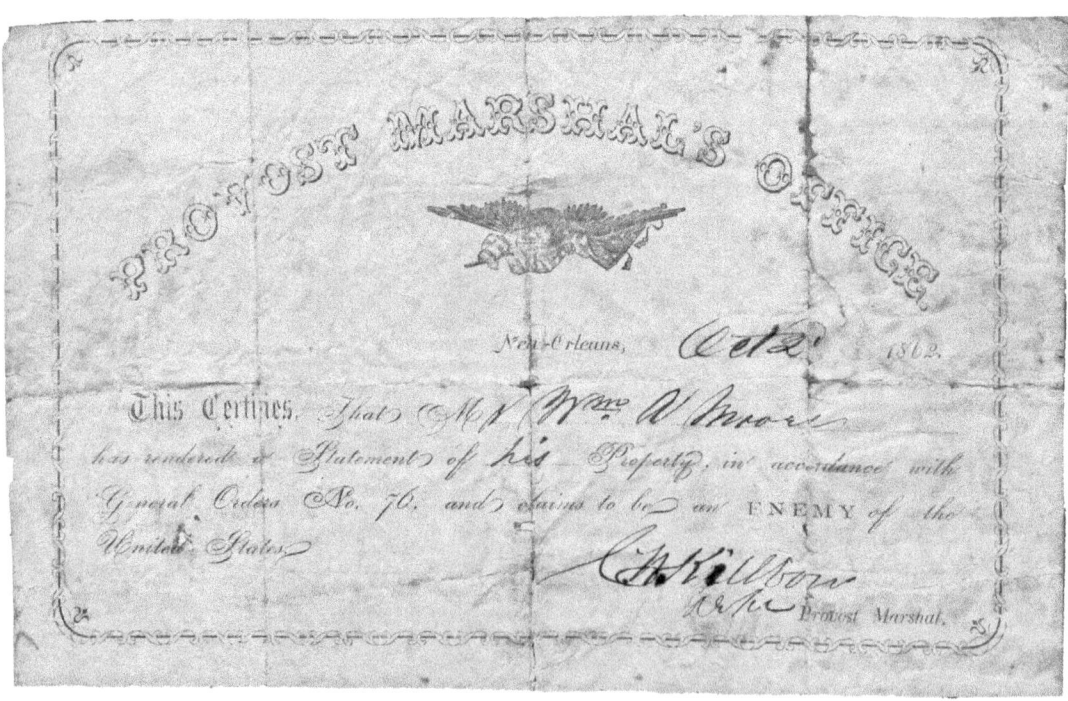

(Fig. 19) Proof that an "Enemy of the State" had rendered property statement to provost marshal. New Orleans. October 2, 1862. 5 × 8 inches. (LA-5.62.02)

Union loyalty. Not surprisingly, Confederate officials abhorred any encouragement for their citizens to become turncoats. After General Butler extracted hundreds of oaths in occupied New Orleans, Confederate lawmakers were incensed. The Confederate senator from that city, on January 13, 1863, introduced a joint resolution to the Congress in Richmond that praised all who risked being declared "enemies of the United States" rather than submitting to Butler's indignity. The joint resolution read:

> *Resolved,* That Congress views with pride the course pursued by the true men and women of the Confederacy, who, falling within the lines of the enemy, have resisted all appeals to their pecuniary interest and refused, in spite of pains and penalties, to foreswear their own government by taking an oath of allegiance to support that of the United States, and regards with peculiar satisfaction the conduct of those citizens of Louisiana, who, by refusing the oath and openly registering themselves enemies of the United States in the immediate presence and in defiance of General Butler's military authorities, have borne most noble testimony by their martyr-like courage to the patriotic spirit and Christian faith of our people.
>
> *Resolved,* That while such conduct has secured them the present respect and sympathy of all good people, it will be esteemed, in the future, a most honorable claim upon the gratitude of their country, and the highest evidence of their devotion to truth and principle.

Within weeks of the resolution, the former Presbyterian bishop of New Orleans, Benjamin M. Palmer, published a monograph discussing the moral and political implications

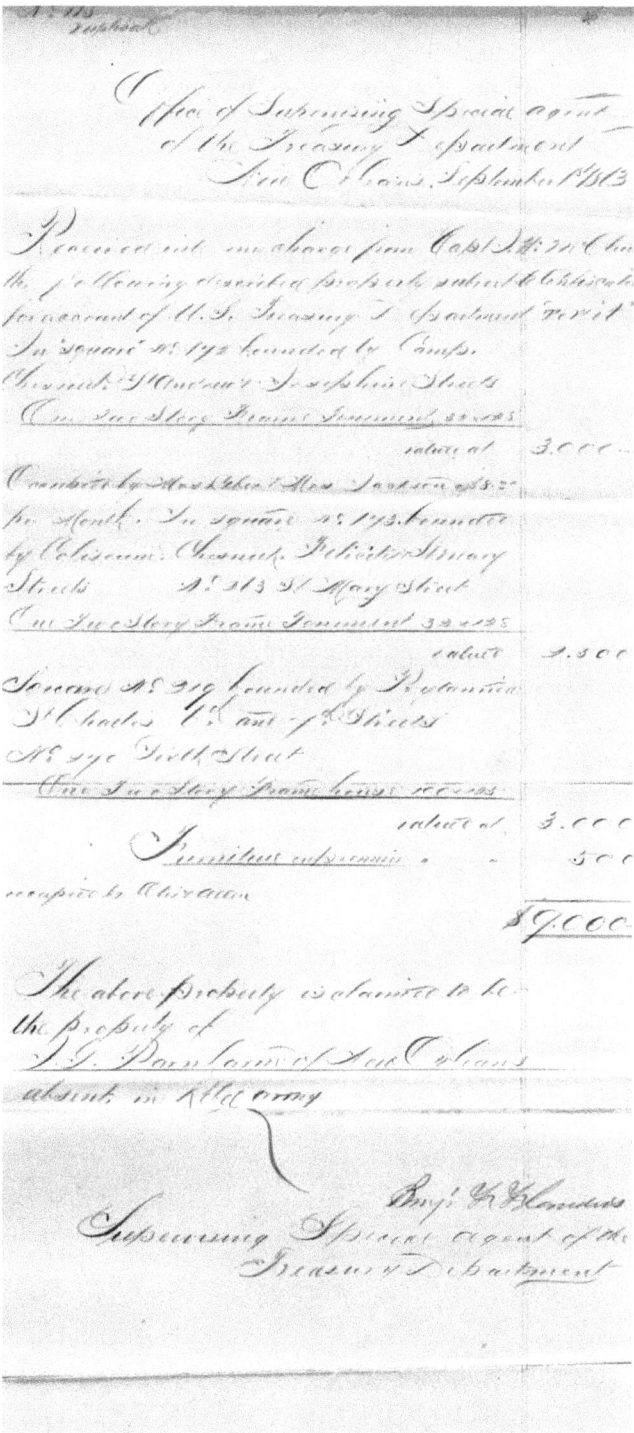

(Fig. 20) Manuscript statement listing three houses seized from "registered enemy," signed by Supervising Special Agent, Treasury Department, Benjamin Flanders. New Orleans. September 1, 1863. (LA-5.63.01)

of southerners giving allegiance to the enemy. He alternated between sympathy and anger for his captured neighbors. In his conclusion he could find no excuse for such acts of shame and warned that dishonor would cleave to them forever.

In a review of the history of oaths, Bishop Palmer reminded southerners that such words were holy pledges witnessed by God. Because the sworn document was solemnly made, any breach was both a crime and a sin. Those who had mental reservations and still took the oath risked "the fearful retribution of eternity." In Palmer's opinion, only two classes of people would give loyalty to the enemy. The most obvious were those who were "simply traitors to the South," who were "destitute of all principle." The more troublesome group were those who claimed to have given oaths because of the "necessities of war," while maintaining in their "secret hearts" loyalty to the Southern cause. They explained their actions as the fortunes of war. If and when the de facto control of the federal government was no more, they promised to return their allegiance to the South. The minister admonished that it was better to be termed an "alien enemy of the United States" than to feign allegiance for the sake of safety and commerce. He reminded captives that early Christians chose martyrdom rather than renounce Christ. The clergyman noted that it was inexcusable for civilians to avoid confiscation and imprisonment while their soldiers suffered wounds and death upon the fields of slaughter. In conclusion, the bishop pleaded that any New Orleans citizen who had subscribed to Butler's infamous oath should recant and "choose the dungeon and the scaffold a thousand times rather than transmit the taint of this leprosy to your offspring."[32]

4

Presidential Pardons

After the first year of the war, political prisons lost public support. Both the press and politicians began to question the necessity of such undemocratic measures, especially within loyal regions of the country. Loved ones of persons arrested for disloyalty began to hire attorneys, against the advice of officials, to file actions for the release of their relatives. After the State Department, without explanation, released Dr. Iver of the New York *Herald* for snooping in the war office telegraph room, the president modified the political prison system. To distance confined political prisons from civilian oversight of the courts and press, the president, on February 14, 1862, directed all future arrests and confiscations to be transferred from the State Department to the War Office.[1]

Most commonly, a disloyal citizen was released from political prison by simply being given a parole of honor after swearing an oath. The form of oaths changed over time and by region. By May of 1862, at Fort Warren in Boston, prisoners were allowed either to give an "oath of allegiance" to the United States, the Constitution, its laws and government; or to sign a parole promising not to render aid or comfort to the enemies of the government of the United States. A prewar United States consul at Cadiz, Spain, Thomas T. Tunstall, a loyal C.S.A. and Alabama citizen, with family and friends in the state, first offered the alternative form of parole in lieu of the normal oath of allegiance. The parole of honor proposed by Mr. Tunstall was considered sufficient to secure his release on May 7, 1862.[2]

In Border States, political arrests increased after the transfer of responsibility to the War Department. Most arrests occurred in Maryland. Unrest increased after slaves were emancipated in the District of Columbia. By July 1862, a group in Baltimore was conducting private inquiries into official corruption and disloyalty, as well as abuse of power. The committee gathered evidence and took the testimony of witnesses. A report was being prepared that allegedly would recommend that charges be filed. However, before the report was completed, the commanding general ordered the evidence seized. Later in the week, members of the investigating committee were arrested and sent to Fort Delaware. After much uproar, the citizens were released without charges being made and with no word of explanation or apology. Loyal citizens in Border States were beginning to grow weary of martial law.[3]

Congress soon adjourned in early summer of 1862. Many lawmakers were preparing to go home to concerned citizens unsure of the continued necessity of martial rule and the suspension of the writ of habeas corpus. Unchecked executive government action without court oversight was uncomfortable and threatening to a growing number of loyal Americans. President

Lincoln, that July, invited representatives and senators of the seven Border States to a meeting at the White House to consider a special appeal prior to their departure home. The president clearly stated a proposal for the gradual emancipation of slaves in Border States along with his recommendation for partial compensation to their owners. A similar proposal had died in Congress in March. He reminded the lawmakers that his friend, General David Hunter, commander of the Department of the South at Port Royal, South Carolina, had tried to free all the slaves within his command without any recompense already that year — but the president had rescinded the order. President Lincoln predicted that as the war continued, slavery eventually would be extinguished as an incident of war, by "friction and abrasion." A gradual plan, as supported by the Maryland Colonization Society, would surely be preferable to the citizens of the Border States. The president went on to suggest cost estimates for compensating slave owners in the Border States. Based on the most recent census of slave populations, and using an average value of $300 per slave, similar to the number used in the District of Columbia, the appropriation in total would be around $359,000,000, spread over decades. To this, the president would even add another $118,000,000 to cover deportation costs, transportation and initial colonization in a distant land. The lawmakers from the Border States all respectfully rejected the proposal for compensated gradual emancipation. All soon left for their home states. Lincoln revisited the subject in his message to Congress on December 1, 1862. Lincoln had dropped the idea after the House again refused to consider the subject. The matter became moot once the president turned to drafting the language of his eventual proclamation of emancipation.[4]

During the summer, more released political prisoners began to claim they were forced to take an oath of allegiance in order to gain their freedom. Questions concerning the validity of the parole system were harming the administration's attempt to release as many of the political prisoners as possible to calm public outcries against the system. The army's adjutant general on August 15, 1862, vowed that no person would be given an oath of allegiance against their will — all oaths were to be entirely voluntary. The order went on to explain that a parole accepted by prisoners to avoid arrest, detention, imprisonment or expulsion beyond the safety of the lines was still considered one that was freely given and voluntary. The adjutants general's Order No. 107 did remind all that a released prisoner, later found in violation of his oath of parole, would be punished to the full extent of military justice.[5]

As more state courts received numerous forms of writs and motions seeking orders to compel the officers of the War Department's military prisons to respond to charges of false imprisonment and like charges, after the writ of habeas corpus was suspended, the secretary of war was forced to provide guidance. The adjutant general was instructed by the secretary to inform the commanding officer of the primary political prison, Fort Warren in Boston, that he would not permit any civil officers or other persons entering the facility to serve a civil process, writ or other document. Further, all army personnel under the command at Fort Warren were not to obey or take notice of any such process or writ, whether served or not. Court interference with the confinement of disloyal citizens was quickly becoming a political problem.[6]

Challenges to the administration's suspension of habeas corpus and declaration of martial law were not solely from within the Border States. Court cases arose in Wisconsin, New Hampshire, Michigan, Pennsylvania, and New York. In New Jersey, a marshal and two deputies were arrested, forced to post bail bonds and indicted by a grand jury in Hunterdon County for false arrest. Similar proceedings occurred in Ohio and Indiana. The largest number of complaints were filed in the two dominant border states of Maryland and Missouri. The issue affected the fall state elections. In November, at the urging of the president's party, Congress decided to relieve the president of some of the blame for martial rule. This occurred after Mr. Lincoln had instructed his secretary of war, on November 22, 1862, to declare that all political prisoners held because of discouraging volunteer enlistments and giving aid to the enemy be released on paroles of honor, if willing to cease hostilities against the government. The order for relief did not apply to any already sentenced by a military tribunal or to captured rebel soldiers. When Congress reconvened, the lawmakers declared suspension of the writ of habeas corpus as a martial act necessitated by emergency. Congress was willing to share the blame.[7]

Wisconsin's governor was particularly upset with martial rule. Governor Edward Salomon on January 13, 1863, complained to the secretary of war that citizens of his state had been convicted by military tribunal for interfering with the recruitment of soldiers. The governor informed the secretary that the Wisconsin Supreme Court, a body of loyal and patriotic judges, had ruled that the president did not have the power to suspend the writ of habeas corpus in the loyal states not threatened by enemy attack. Soon after the letter was received, on March 3, 1863, Congress authorized the President to suspend the writ of habeas corpus wherever, in his judgment, the public safety of the nation required it during the Rebellion. The same day, Congress passed an act that required the army to furnish for the courts "a list of political prisoners." Quickly, the judge advocate ruled that the law did not apply to persons already sentenced by military tribunals. By November, the Judge Advocate added that the law did not apply to persons charged with offenses intended to embarrass the military in an active region threatened by enemy action. Habeas corpus or any other court writ had no effect within a combat zone.[8]

After Rebel troops attacked Morrisville and Laurel, Maryland, burning bridges and stations, and destroying tracks and telegraph lines, all were on edge. Subsequently, during the summer of 1863, provost police arrested almost four hundred civilians suspected of spying, blockade running, sedition and disloyalty. Upon taking the oath of loyalty, three-fourths of the arrested suspects were released. Of those remaining, five were sent to Fort Henry, three to the Old Capitol Prison, 11 banished and 19 were held for examination. Two social clubs, the Germanic Club and Alston Association, were temporarily closed for allowing disloyal meetings. The Maryland Club was permanently closed and seized after complaints that it maintained a place for "those disaffected toward the Government." Major General Robert C. Schenck of the Middle Department tried to force election judges to sign a loyalty oath prior to the fall Maryland elections. On November 2, 1863, the president sent word that the order was revoked and election polling judges could assume their duties without signing an oath of allegiance.[9]

Although Delaware, the second smallest state, remained loyal, its population of 120,000, of which a fifth were "freed colored," included many who had strong financial and political connections with the South. After the election of William Cannon as governor, the general assembly, in spite of his protest, passed a resolution denouncing the "illegal arrests" of disloyal citizens in February 1863. Afterward, General Schenck ordered the provost marshal to closely monitor the fall elections to discourage polling irregularities by Southern sympathizers. In furtherance of Schenck's General Order No. 559, of November 13, 1863, election judges were required to take an oath of allegiance to the United States regardless of any state law or resolution to the contrary. The major general noted that his order was directed to the "many evil disposed persons now at large in the state of Delaware" bent on disrupting the electoral process. Governor Cannon, to the dismay of many citizens, appealed to the people of Delaware to obey all military orders. On election day, as an act of protest, many residents of New Castle abstained from voting.[10]

The growing passions in the North against the war finally erupted into riots. The igniting spark was the passage of the General Conscription Act. Prior to the announced draft lottery for each district to fill state quotas of troops, local police were put on notice for possible disruptions. In New York on Saturday, July 11, 1863, the lottery wheel was scheduled to spin. The Sunday press printed the names of the selected draftees. Residents of working-class neighborhoods were angered by a process that favored the privileged and wealthy who could afford to pay draft substitutes. Riots soon broke out all over New York City. Fires, assaults and mayhem continued for two days. The anarchy resulted in several hundred deaths and over $2 million in damages to property. On July 15, a smaller series of incidents took place in Boston with a dozen deaths. Other outbursts occurred in Portsmouth, New Hampshire; Holmes County, Ohio; and other northern cities. Implementation of further draft notices are delayed for a time. Local police and military authorities were reluctant to charge many of the rioters with a crime fearing that the riots might be rekindled. Finally, many lawmakers in Washington began to understand the practical limits of martial law in loyal zones.[11]

After the riots, the judge advocate of the army was instructed by the solicitor general to clarify the military's response to civil writs issued by the state courts. This was prompted by an opinion by Chief Justice Roger B. Taney of the U.S. Supreme Court in *Alderman v. Booth*. Henceforth, military officers were directed to always reply, in a respectful manner, in writing to any judge issuing a writ to provost marshals or other military officers. The written response should first state that the respondent was a military officer of the United States duly appointed according to the law, followed by a description of his duties. Secondly, the reply should state the reason the soldier, enlisted or conscript, or civilian was being held, and whether on a criminal charge or military offense. Finally, a clear statement that production of the identified person in court, as ordered by the judge, was inconsistent with and in violation of the military officer's duties as ordered by his superiors, and, for that reason, he must decline to produce the said person. In noncombat zones in the future, if requested by court order, the reason for holding a person would be disclosed.[12]

Not until September 30, 1864, did the first of several special commissions publicly report on the circumstances surrounding political prisoners. The report submitted by Commissioners H. L. Bond and John C. King to the secretary of war covered "state prisoners" held at Forts McHenry and Delaware. Prisoners, but not arresting officers, were individually interviewed. The 48 prisoners (16 at Fort Henry and 32 at Fort Delaware) were all suspected of disloyalty and had refused to disavow sympathy for the Rebellion. After the conclusion of the 30-day examination, the commissioners recommended only one prisoner be released. Four prisoners were recommended for trial before military tribunals. Four others were scheduled for a prisoner exchange. One was held as a deserter from the army. Two were to be court-martialed. Eight were to be held in confinement, but for no stated reason. Twenty-eight were now willing to take the oath, and were qualified for release. None were determined by the commissioners to have been held without proper cause, and the arresting officers, in their opinion, had acted with moderation and discretion.[13]

By the end of 1863, public outcries against the Conscription Act assaulted politicians. Many believed the powerful and wealthy were buying their way out of the army while common soldiers were exposed to battlefield carnage and deserters risked capital punishment. Death could be the cost of loyalty while the privileged remained safely at home. Lincoln needed to dispel this mood but still preserve good order and discipline among the public and the ranks.

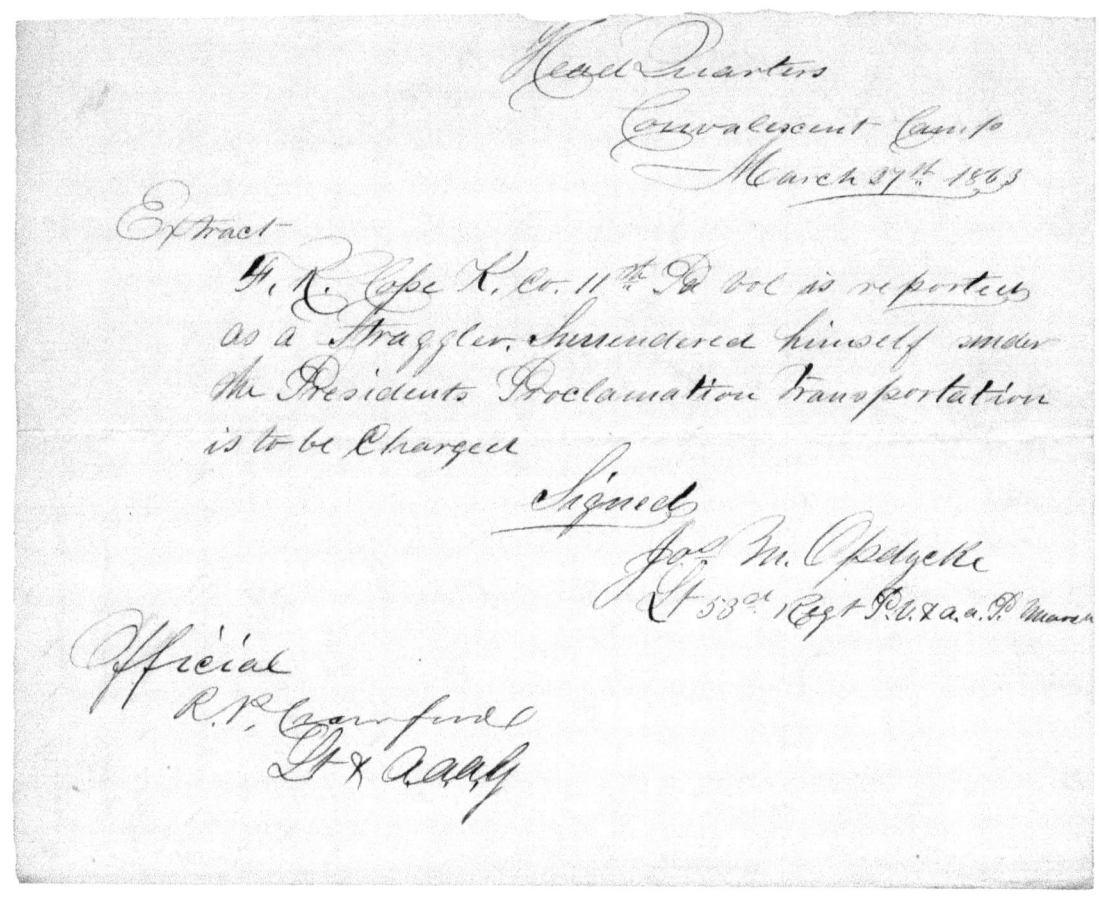

(Fig. 21) Manuscript extract reporting a "straggler" under president's proclamation at Convalescent Camp Headquarters. March 27, 1863. 6½ × 8 inches. (UNK-5.63.01)

He lured Union deserters back with amnesty offers if they returned before April 1, 1863 (Fig. 21). Their only punishment would be loss of pay and allowances. For any who refused his offer, he threatened that they would be "arrested as deserters, and punished as the law provides."

Clemency was well received with positive results both among the troops and general population. On December 8, 1863, the president offered reunion to disloyal citizens. In the preamble to his "Declaration of Pardon," Lincoln listed the sanctions for disloyalty including forfeitures, confiscation and liberation of slaves. He restated that Congress had allowed him "to extend to persons who may have participated in the existing Rebellion, in any State or part thereof, pardon and amnesty, with such exceptions and at such times and on such conditions as he may deem expedient to the public welfare." He declared that civilians could resume their allegiance to the United States and reinaugurate a loyal state government not in rebellion, in return for his amnesty. If pardoned, all property, except slaves and confiscated property, would be restored through court authority. The pardon process required taking an oath, subscribing to a sworn document and registration (Fig. 22).

The president's amnesty offer of December 8, 1863, excluded six groups deemed the most egregious to loyal Americans:

PROCLAMATION OF PARDON.

Whereas, in and by the Constitution of the United States, it is provided that the President "shall have power to grant reprieves and pardons for offences against the United States, except in cases of impeachment;" and

Whereas a rebellion now exists whereby the loyal State governments of several States have for a long time been subverted, and many persons have committed and are now guilty of treason against the United States; and

Whereas, with reference to said rebellion and treason, laws have been enacted by Congress, declaring forfeitures and confiscation of property and liberation of slaves, all upon terms and conditions therein stated, and also declaring that the President was thereby authorized at any time thereafter, by proclamation, to extend to persons who may have participated in the existing rebellion, in any State or part thereof, pardon and amnesty, with such exceptions and at such times and on such conditions as he may deem expedient for the public welfare; and

Whereas the congressional declaration for limited and conditional pardon accords with well-established judicial exposition of the pardoning power; and

Whereas, with reference to said rebellion, the President of the United States has issued several proclamations, with provisions in regard to the liberation of slaves; and

Whereas it is now desired by some persons heretofore engaged in said rebellion to resume their allegiance to the United States, and to reinaugurate loyal State governments within and for their respective States; therefore,

I, ABRAHAM LINCOLN, President of the United States, do proclaim, declare, and make known to all persons who have, directly or by implication, participated in the existing rebellion, except as hereinafter excepted, that a full pardon is hereby granted to them and each of them, with restoration of all rights of property, except as to slaves, and in property cases where rights of third parties shall have intervened, and upon the condition that every such person shall take and subscribe an oath, and thenceforward keep and maintain said oath inviolate; and which oath shall be registered for permanent preservation, and shall be of the tenor and effect following, to wit:

"I, _____, do solemnly swear, in presence of Almighty God, that I will henceforth faithfully support, protect, and defend the Constitution of the United States, and the union of the States thereunder; and that I will, in like manner, abide by and faithfully support all acts of Congress passed during the existing rebellion with reference to slaves, so long and so far as not repealed, modified, or held void by Congress, or by decision of the Supreme Court; and that I will in like manner, abide by and faithfully support all proclamations of the President made during the existing rebellion having reference to slaves, so long and so far as not modified or declared void by decision of the Supreme Court. So help me God."

The persons excepted from the benefits of the foregoing provisions are all who are, or shall have been, civil or diplomatic officers or agents of the so-called confederate government; all who have left judicial stations under the United States to aid the rebellion; all who are, or shall have been, military or naval officers of said so-called confederate government above the rank of colonel in the army or of lieutenant in the navy; all who left seats in the United States Congress to aid the rebellion; all who resigned commissions in the army or navy of the United States and afterwards aided the rebellion; and all who have engaged in any way in treating colored persons, or white persons in charge of such, otherwise than lawfully as prisoners of war, and which persons may have been found in the United States service as soldiers, seamen, or in any other capacity.

And I do further proclaim, declare, and make known, that whenever, in any of the States of Arkansas, Texas, Louisiana, Mississippi, Tennessee, Alabama, Georgia, Florida, South Carolina, and North Carolina, a number of persons, not less than one-tenth in number of the votes cast in such State at the Presidential election of the year of our Lord one thousand eight hundred and sixty, each having taken the oath aforesaid and not having since violated it, and being a qualified voter by the election law of the State existing immediately before the so-called act of secession, and excluding all others, shall re-establish a State government which shall be republican, and in nowise contravening said oath, such shall be recognized as the true government of the State, and the State shall receive thereunder the benefits of the constitutional provision which declares that "The United States shall guaranty to every State in this Union a republican form of government, and shall protect each of them against invasion; and, on application of the legislature, or the executive, (when the legislature cannot be convened,) against domestic violence."

And I do further proclaim, declare, and make known that any provision which may be adopted by such State government in relation to the freed people of such State, which shall recognize and declare their permanent freedom, provide for their education, and which may yet be consistent, as a temporary arrangement, with their present condition as a laboring, landless, and homeless class, will not be objected to by the national Executive. And it is suggested as not improper, that, in constructing a loyal State government in any State, the name of the State, the boundary, the subdivisions, the constitution, and the general code of laws, as before the rebellion, be maintained, subject only to the modifications made necessary by the conditions hereinbefore stated, and such others, if any, not contravening

[General Orders, No. 64.]

WAR DEPARTMENT,
ADJUTANT GENERAL'S OFFICE,
Washington, February 18, 1864.

REFUGEES AND REBEL DESERTERS.

Whenever refugees from within the rebel lines, or deserters from the rebel armies, present themselves at U. S. camps, or military posts, they will be immediately examined by the provost marshal, with a view to determine their character and their motive in giving themselves up. If it appear that they are honest in their intention of forever deserting the rebel cause, care will be taken to explain to them that they will not be forced to serve in the U. S. army against the rebels, nor be kept in confinement. The President's proclamation of December 8, 1863, will be read to them, and, if they so desire, the oath therein prescribed will be administered to them. They will then be questioned as to whether they desire employment from the United States, and if so, such arrangements as may be expedient will be made by the several army commanders for employing them on government works within their commands. Those who come to the army of the Potomac will be forwarded to the military governor of the District of Columbia, at Washington, with reports in their cases, that employment may be given them if desired, or, if not, that they may be sent as far north as Philadelphia.

BY ORDER OF THE SECRETARY OF WAR:

E. D. TOWNSEND,
Assistant Adjutant General.

OFFICIAL:

Assistant Adjutant General.

---

said conditions, and which may be deemed expedient by those framing the new State government.

To avoid misunderstanding, it may be proper to say that this proclamation, so far as it relates to State governments, has no reference to States wherein loyal State governments have all the while been maintained. And for the same reason, it may be proper to further say, that whether members sent to Congress from any State shall be admitted to seats constitutionally, rests exclusively with the respective houses, and not to any extent with the Executive. And still further, that this proclamation is intended to present the people of the States wherein the national authority has been subverted, and loyal State governments have been subverted, a mode in and by which the national authority and loyal State governments may be re-established within said States, or in any of them; and, while the mode presented is the best the Executive can suggest, with his present impressions, it must not be understood that no other possible mode would be acceptable.

Given under my hand at the city of Washington the 8th day of December, A. D. one thousand eight hundred and sixty-three, and of the independence of the United States of America the eighty-eighth.   ABRAHAM LINCOLN.

By the President:

WILLIAM H. SEWARD, *Secretary of State.*

A book whereon to record the taking of the above oath by such persons entitled to take it, as may apply, is in the custody of ————, at ————, who is authorized to administer said oath to such persons of that vicinity, and is required to give to every such person requesting it a certificate in the form below, and which certificate shall be, until some other mode of proof shall be authoritatively provided, sufficient evidence of the facts certified to entitle the rightful holder to the benefits as promised in said proclamation.

"I do hereby certify that on the —— day of ————, 186—, at ————, the oath prescribed by the President of the United States in his proclamation of December 8, 1863, was duly taken, subscribed, and ———— matter of record by ————, of ————."

(Fig. 22) Above and opposite: Proclamation of pardon. Washington. December 8, 1863. Issued with G. O. No. 64, War Department, Refugees and Rebel Deserters. Washington. February 18, 1864. 6½ × 11 inches. (DC-5.63.01)

1. U.S. congressmen who left office to join the Rebellion
2. Federal judges and other justice officials who resigned to join the Rebellion
3. U.S. naval and army officers who resigned their commissions to join the Rebellion
4. High-ranking Confederate military officers
5. Officials and agents of the Confederate government
6. Any person accused of not treating "colored persons" in accordance with the rules of war

The judge advocate general, Joseph Holt, was quick to point out that the president's amnesty proclamation would not serve as "a general jail cleaning." Those persons already sentenced by military tribunals and persons awaiting trial on charges in violation of military law or the Articles of War, would remain confined.[14]

Through 1863, as a matter of policy, a protocol had evolved that application for the release of prisoners held for disloyalty would not be entertained unless the applicant presented good evidence why clemency was in order. For captured enemy, the standards were even tougher. A Rebel soldier's success in receiving a parole, after giving his oath of allegiance, was usually dependent upon his providing evidence that he had been forced to enlist and had tried to desert. A second factor was the willingness of loyal friends or family to vouch for the prisoner's sincerity of loyalty. A prisoner's youthful age was also considered. Prison-camp commissioners examined the facts in doubtful cases. If a prisoner of war were granted parole after taking the oath, he had to register for the federal draft. This policy was highly offensive to the Confederate agents for prisoner exchange.[15]

The second purpose of Lincoln's proclamation of December 8, 1863, was to announce a process whereby a seceded state could rejoin the Union. Whenever "a number of persons, not less than one-tenth of the votes, cast in such State at the Presidential election of [1860], each having taken the oath aforesaid and not having since violated it, and being a qualified voter by the election law of the State before ... secession, excluding all others, shall re-establish a State governance which shall be republican, such shall be recognized as the true government of the State, and the State shall receive there under the benefits of the constitutional provision"

Specifically mentioned were Arkansas, Texas, Louisiana, Mississippi, Tennessee, Alabama, Georgia, Florida, and both Carolinas. State governments in rebellion had to first proclaim the permanent freedom of slaves and promise to provide for education and protection of all citizens from invasion and violence. Some newspapers in occupied Tennessee, Arkansas and Louisiana published the proclamation, but with dismissive editorial comments. Overall, the Rebel press characterized the Lincoln announcement as propaganda from a weakened nation tired of war.

The proclamation also affected those in loyal states. Persons charged with disloyalty were allowed to file a certified copy of their oath and pardon with a local court to clear their names. Even acts of treason could be dismissed. More significantly, pardons removed the risk of confiscation of property. On December 31, 1863, the president extended amnesty to Rebel prisoners of war, if only they too would take the oath of loyalty and remain within loyal territory (Fig. 23). To violate that oath was a sentence of death (Fig. 24).

If any Rebel refused to take the oath, he had to leave the security of the Union lines, but was entitled to a "safeguard" pass of protection. Article 55 of the Rules of War, provided that any Union soldier forcing a safeguard, i.e., harming the pass holder, "shall suffer death" (Fig. 25).

Standard forms were printed implementing these oaths after March 26, 1864. If forms were unavailable, oaths were to be written out on a sheet of "foolscap" stationery, commencing with the words, "We, the undersigned, do solemnly swear...." The oath was to be ruled and dated

(Fig. 23) *Frank Leslie's Illustrated Newspaper.* Administering the oath of allegiance to Confederate prisoners. December 1864. (NY-5.64.01)

with the name and residence of the applicant. After the oath was administered, a provost was to certify, date and sign the document. Afterward, a register detailing all was prepared in duplicate with a copy forwarded to the State Department. The duplicate oath was given to the oath taker.

As procedures for administering oaths became standardized, greater numbers came forward to publicly state their allegiance in order to return to their livelihoods, both in loyal states and occupied Rebel territory. Soon the question arose concerning the citizen wishing to void his loyalty oath after it had been sworn and registered. A political prisoner, Walter H. Powell, within a loyal state, claimed he only took the oath in order to gain his freedom. The army's judge advocate general, Joseph Holt, wrote an opinion to the secretary of war advising that once the pledge was made with an honest intention of becoming a loyal citizen in order to return to civilian pursuits, the statement of conscience could not be voided unless the affiant alleged duress, which he had not. The oath obligations of good citizenship remained. If his subsequent behavior proved otherwise, the affiant would face the legal consequences. The government had no mechanism for declaring an oath inoperative in the abstract.[16]

The politically motivated "10 percent" election rule was not successful in the upcoming national election because voters qualified only if sufficient in number to satisfy the 10 percent rule. Many loyal southerners in Tennessee objected to taking an oath designed for Rebels because their allegiance had always been true. The president insisted all had to take the oath to qualify as voters—primarily as a pragmatic way to eliminate the need for establishing loyalty in each case. Military Governor Johnson designed a special oath incorporating his position that Tennessee never really seceded, but was only "paralyzed" (Fig. 26). The Johnson oath also stated the affiant desired to suppress the Rebellion, hope for success of the Federal armies and wished defeat to those who opposed them. The Tennessee pledge to "aid and assist all loyal people," because it accomplished Lincoln's purpose and satisfied Johnson's policies, was allowed to stand. The modified oath was only good for six months.[17]

Governor Johnson was always quick to distinguish Tennessee from its Rebel neighboring states. This distinction would later save the people of the governor's home state from the full measure of Reconstruction's retribution after the war ended. Johnson always claimed that

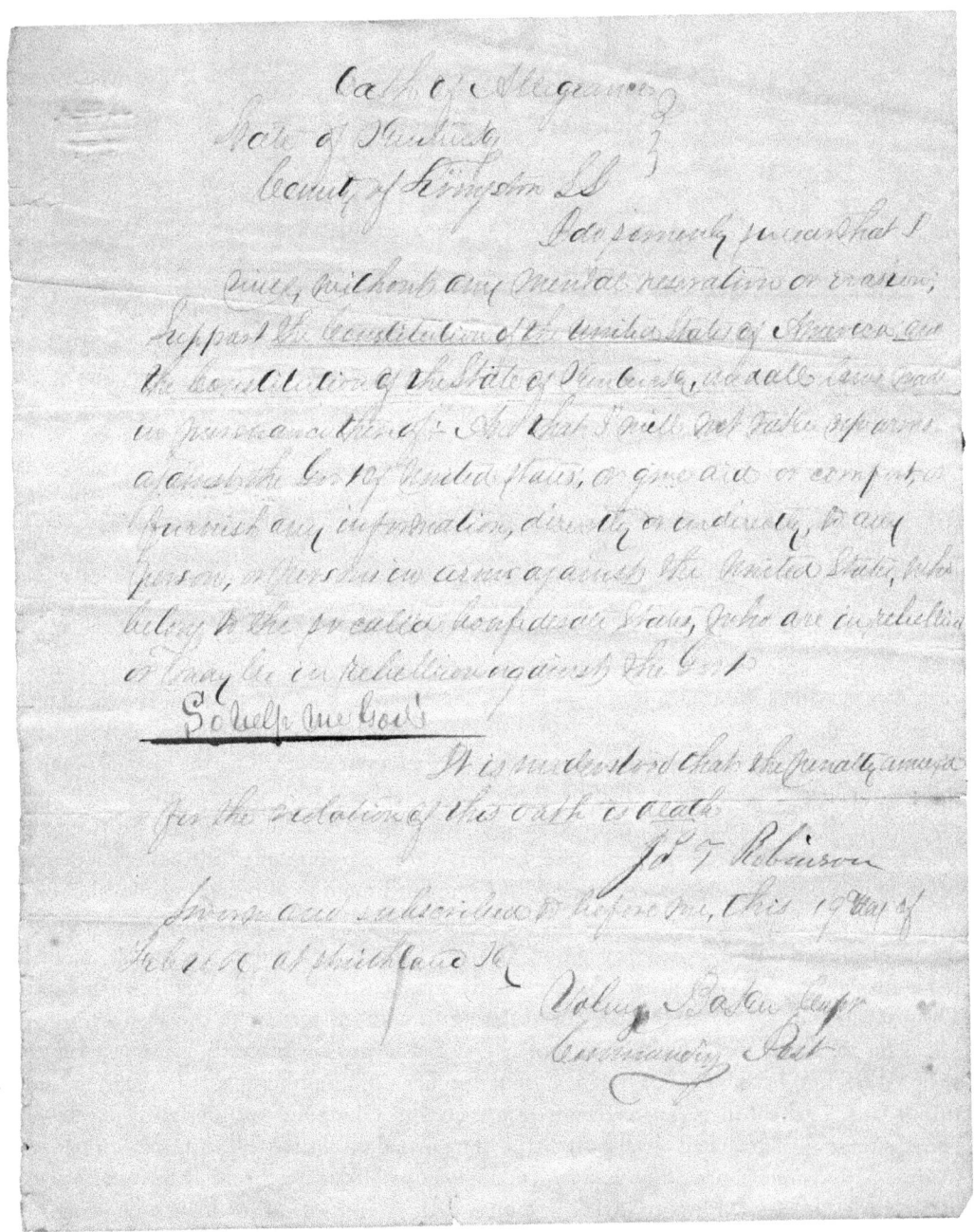

(Fig. 24) Manuscript oath of allegiance. Smithland, Kentucky. February 19, 1864. 10 × 8 inches. (KY-4.64.01)

"Tennessee is not out of the Union, never has been and never will be out." He described his function as military governor as one of an "agent" to aid in the restoration of government. He explained to the people that once elections were again in motion, one by one, state agencies, courts and the legislature would resume. He went on to explain that the president's "10 percent" election process was essential in setting the process in motion and that the voters should not be obstinate—"The metaphysics of politics should not overrule common sense." On January 26, 1864, Johnson set out his plans for a state election. (Earlier a state convention, held in July 1863, had chosen delegates to begin the process of "reorganization.")[18]

(Fig. 25) Union safeguard pass blank, under Article 55, Rules and Articles of War. 1864. (UNK-2.64.02)

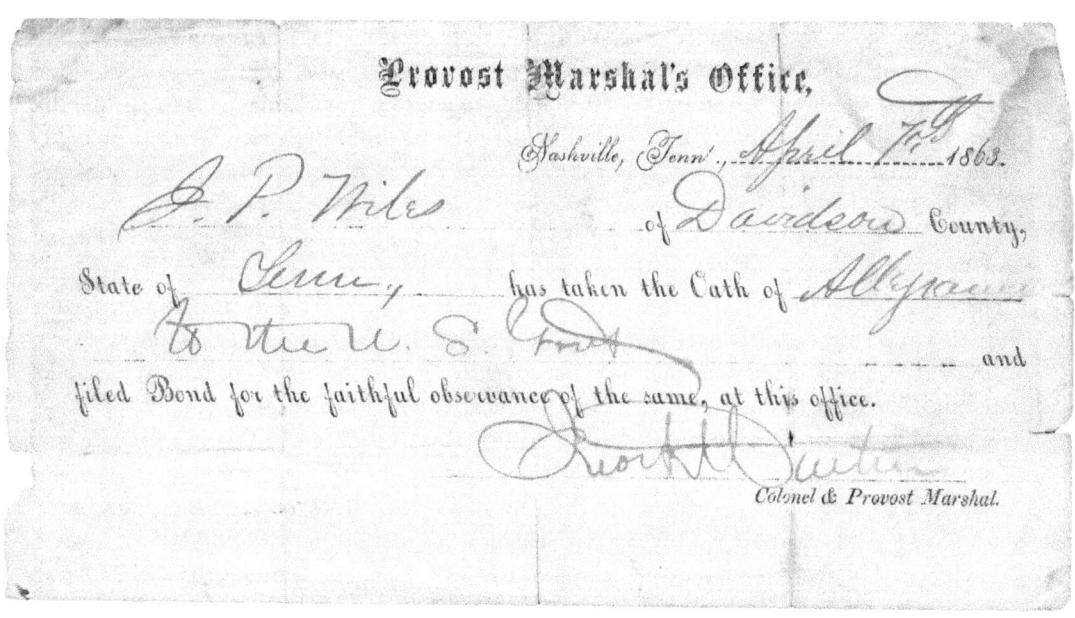

(Fig. 26) Provost marshal's office. Statement of oath of allegiance and bond. Nashville, Tennessee. April 1, 1863. 4¼ × 8 inches. (TN-4.63.01)

The Tennessee election, held in March 1864, resulted in barely enough delegates for the National Union Convention in Baltimore. Although Governor Johnson did not represent his state, he managed to elect Union men. Tennessee eventually supplied 60,000 soldiers to the Union Army, including 20,000 black troops, many of whom served in Kentucky.

On September 7, 1864, Governor Johnson appointed judges and civil tribunals for all districts in Tennessee where the people, by their votes and loyalty, had shown a willingness to restore civil government. This was in preparation for the national election, scheduled for November. Although only loyal, free, white males, who had resided in the state six months, were qualified to vote, all former slaves were offered the rights of "free persons of color." Soon, many loyal residents took issue with the governor's "test oath" required at the polling station prior to voting. After some complained to the president about the governor's use of a more stringent loyalty oath for obtaining their voting rights, his office sent word that it was the governor's decision and that the president would not interfere. The national electoral results of November 8 in Tennessee were not admitted by the congressional electoral college for procedural reasons. Soon after the first of the year, the state constitution added the new amendment affirming the abolition of slavery; and, soon thereafter, elections for governor and the legislature were scheduled.[19]

The *New South* weekly reported on February 20, 1864, that General Order No. 16, Department of the South, Hilton Head, allowed residents of Florida to take advantage of the president's amnesty order and participate in the upcoming national election. This attempt to elect Unionists in Florida under the "10 Percent Majority Rule" failed despite the presence of the president's private secretary, John Hay, on the scene to monitor enrollment. Hay unsuccessfully campaigned in Fernandina and Jacksonville. The South Carolina amnesty program was administered by the post commander of Hilton Head, but there were too few in residence within the enclosure to matter.

After the Battle of Pea Ridge, Union general Samuel R Curtis crossed the White River and occupied Batesville, Arkansas, on May 1, 1862. City officials, including judges and many of the clergy, took the loyalty oath. Next to fold to Federal forces, in Arkansas, was Helena, in the delta of the Mississippi River. Although John S. Phelps was appointed by the president to be the state's military governor, he was not able to relocate from Saint Louis to assume that office. Little Rock was not occupied until September 10, 1863, by Major General Frederick Steele. By that time, the region north of the Arkansas River had been desolated by both sides. Little Rock residents were told to fly the American flag to show their allegiance. Most complied and occupation proceeded smoothly. By the first of 1864, many residents had taken the oath and received amnesty under the president's proclamation of December 8, 1863. Confederate General E. W. Gantt, a prisoner of war, took the oath, received amnesty and became a committed "Union man." Both black and white local residents enlisted in the Federal Army. General Gantt wrote that "old flags that have been hidden in the crevices of rocks, and have been worshiped by our mountain people as holy relics, are flying in the breeze" (Fig. 27).[20]

Only Batesville, Fort Smith, Helena and Little Rock were secure. The Confederate state government relocated to Camden and was supported by the Trans-Mississippi Department of the Confederate general Kirby Smith from his depots in Shreveport, Louisiana, and Marshall, Texas. Arkansas held its "10 Percent" election on March 28, 1864. Only 5,406 voters participated, but the representatives elected to the 38th Congress were not seated. The state constitution was amended abolishing slavery on August 25, 1864. Civil courts did not resume until after the war. Most of the geographic area of the state was subject to Rebel control until the war's last year.[21]

OATH OF ALLEGIANCE.

I, W. S. Satterfield, of _____ County of Pope, State of Arkansas, do solemnly swear that I will bear true allegiance to the United States, and support and sustain the Constitution and Laws thereof; that I will maintain the National Sovereignty paramount to that of all State, County or Confederate powers; that I will discourage, discountenance, and forever oppose secession, rebellion and the disintegration of the Federal Union; that I disclaim and denounce all faith and fellowship with the so-called Confederate Armies, and pledge my honor, my property, and my life, to the sacred performance of this my solemn oath of allegiance to the Government of the United States of America. I do further solemnly swear in the presence of Almighty God, that I will henceforth faithfully support, protect and defend the Constitution of the United States and the Union of States thereunder, and I will in like manner abide by, and faithfully support all acts of Congress passed during the existing rebellion, with reference to slaves so long and so far as not repealed, modified or held void by Congress or by decision of the Supreme Court, and that I will in like manner abide by, and faithfully support, all proclamations of the President made during the existing rebellion, having reference to slaves, so long and so far as not modified or declared void by decisions of the Supreme Court, so help me God.

CERTIFICATE:

Sworn to and subscribed before me, this Fourth day of February A. D. 1864.

Wm. S. Satterfield (SEAL)

At Little Rock, Arkansas,

J. M. Anderson
1st Lieut. and Ass't. Provost Marshal.

WITNESS: O. C. McMahon, Sergt 50th Ind

IN TRIPLICATE.
One copy to be given to the person taking the oath.
One copy to be sent to the Headquarters of the Department.
One copy to the Commanding Officer or Provost Marshal of the camp, garrison, town or county where the oath was taken; and no oath to be administered except by order or with the knowledge of said Commanding Officer or Provost Marshal. And this oath, taken and subscribed by W. S. Satterfield, shall be his safeguard, unless violated in any of its obligations.

DESCRIPTION.

YEARS OF AGE.	EYES.	HAIR.	COMPLEXION.	HEIGHT. FEET.	HEIGHT. INCHES.	OCCUPATION.	RANK.	POST OFFICE ADDRESS.
52	Blue	Grey	Fair	5	8	Cabinet Maker	Citizen	Galley Creek, Ark

(Fig. 27) Oath of allegiance and safeguard. Pope County, Little Rock, Arkansas. February 4, 1864. 11 × 8 inches. (AR-4.64.01)

Although Galveston, Texas, was captured on November 5, 1862, Union occupation was short-lived and by New Year's Day, the Rebels had retaken the island. President Lincoln, in anticipation of full occupation, appointed Alexander J. Hamilton military governor for Texas, but he was unable to assume that office until after the war ended. The Union army was more successful in Brownsville, Texas. Draft-aged males remaining within the Federal lines of Fort Brown after occupation were required to take the loyalty oath and register for the draft. Although the president declared the port of Brownsville open, it was soon closed. Few loyalty oaths were taken in Texas during the war.[22]

Rebel action in Kentucky was minimal during the early months of 1863. The Kentucky General Assembly resolved to differ with the President regarding slave emancipation after the proclamation of January 1, 1863. To remain in office, city and county officials were required to take loyalty oaths. The highest state civil court, the court of appeals, embarrassed federal officials by holding in *Norris v. Dompleon* that the national confiscation act was an unconstitutional denial of due process because no indictment, arrest, or summons against the slave owner was issued. The court was of the opinion that a Civil War was not "war" with a foreign nation and such reprisals as Letters of Marque and confiscation of the property of enemies did not apply to domestic insurrections. Kentucky remained a divided border state.[23]

In Kentucky, Colonel John Hunt Morgan's Tennessee partisans terrorized rural communities. Late in June 1864, while still in Georgia, General William T. Sherman instructed commanding officers in Kentucky that a state of anarchy existed. He reminded them that guerrillas were not soldiers, and their actions constituted murder and arson, and if captured they should be treated as common criminals. On July 5, 1864, President Lincoln suspended the writ of habeas corpus and reinstituted martial law for Kentucky. That order was not lifted until October 29, 1865. As areas were retaken, new loyalty oaths were required. As a sign of the uncertain times, many citizens filed pledges of loyalty to both sides — sometimes on more than one occasion.

West Virginia's constitutional convention in February 1863 requested a federal appropriation to compensate slave owners for losses that would result from emancipation. None was granted. On March 26, the constitution of the state was amended and slaves were freed, after which President Lincoln declared that the people had met all necessary conditions for statehood. A full slate of Union candidates was elected to office in May, followed by the inauguration of Governor Arthur I. Boreman at Wheeling on June 20. Departing governor Francis H. Pierpont urged all to never forsake the national flag. At the ceremony, Governor Boreman vowed to extirpate all visages of slavery. He stated that no man in West Virginia should ever be allowed to vote or hold office unless he had given his full allegiance to the United States and the U.S. Constitution.[24]

Although geographically extending east to Alexandria, the West Virginia government had little influence over most of the state. West Virginia residents took the same loyalty oath as persons in Rebel-held areas. Passes were required for travel beyond the protected Union lines, which extended to Harper's Ferry. In that vital stronghold, residents took an oath in 1864, "on the Holy Evangely [sic] of Almighty God," that they disclaimed the Rebellion and Confederate government (Fig. 28).

Citizens in occupied towns often were reluctant to take a loyalty oath, since the protection offered by Union forces could be both temporary and ineffectual. In Norfolk, the commander of the Eastern District of Virginia, on September 22, 1864, warned all males and females over 16 years of age that failure to take the presidential oath of allegiance by October 15 meant expulsion. To that end, all adults had to appear at a place designated and either take the oath or register as an "enemy." Further, none would be threatened or promised benefits to induce

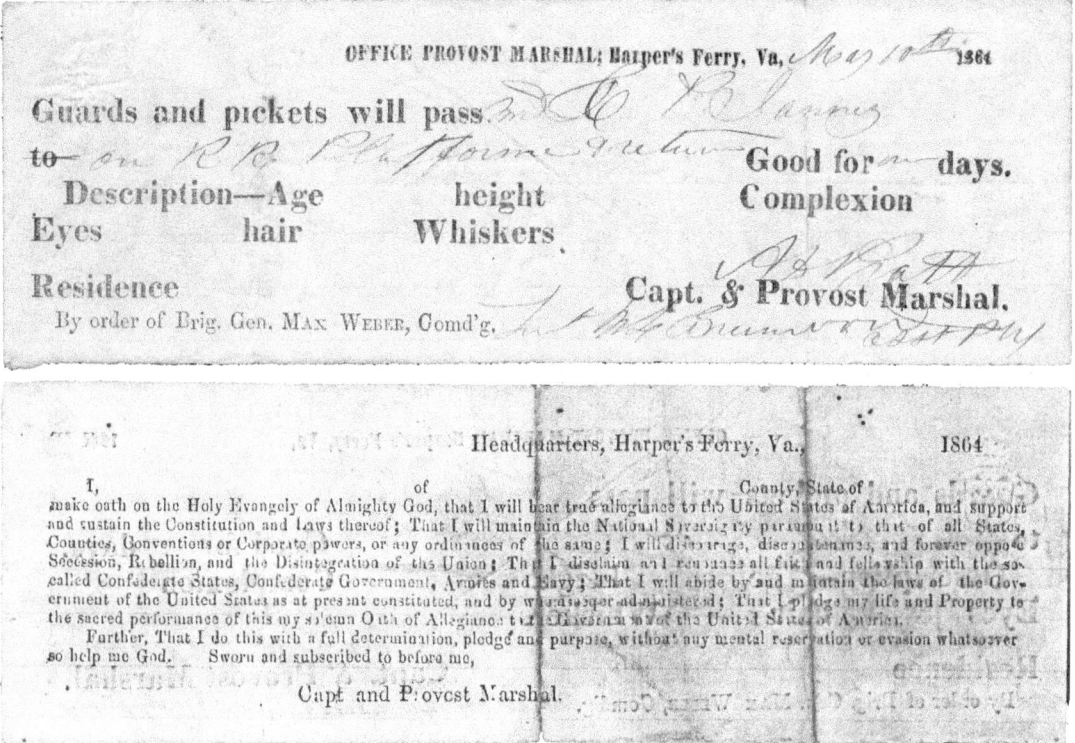

(Fig. 28) Pass and oath of allegiance. Harper's Ferry, Virginia. May 10, 1864. 2¾ × 8 inches. (VA-2.64.03)

them to take the oath, since the oaths were deemed "voluntary." Oaths were given at Portsmouth, Cherrystone, Yorktown and at City Hall, Norfolk (Fig. 29).

Guerrilla action, rather than organized raids, threatened Missouri after 1862. The Emancipation Proclamation on New Year's Day created an uproar in state politics. By May 1863, a considerable number of disloyal citizens had been banished. Property, in excess of the $1,000 per family exemption or $200 per individual, was seized to offset the cost of providing medical care for sick and wounded soldiers. After the state convention, state Republicans pushed through a resolution that was sent to the party offices in Illinois and Kentucky in hopes of voicing an appeal to the president that he replace General J. M. Schofield as commander of the Department of Missouri. He was considered too tolerant of the growing influence of the Democrats in state politics. He had declined to prohibit those openly opposed to emancipation from participating in the elections. General Schofield warned all to follow the law and restrained his officers from interfering in the process by threatening dismissal if any soldiers were permitted to get involved. Violators of his warning would be brought before a military court or commission.[25]

Major General Rosecrans replaced Schofield. Subsequently, on October 12, 1864, he issued Department of Missouri General Order No. 195, prescribing a rigid loyalty oath for voters to participate in the national election. Although the legislature passed the required state constitutional ordinance abolishing slavery, the delegates of the state convention still pleaded that loyal slave owners should be compensated for their losses. Gradual or compensated emancipation were no longer options. However, the movement to compensate loyal slave owners

NOTICE!

HEAD QUARTERS,
District of Eastern Virginia,
NORFOLK, VA., Sept. 22d, 1864.

GENERAL ORDERS NO. 31.

In pursuance of orders from Head Quarters Department, all persons within the District of Eastern Virginia, over 16 years of age, who have not taken the Oath of Allegiance, will be sent outside of the lines.

This order will be carried into effect on and after Oct. 15th, 1864.

Col. H. T. SANDERS, 19th Wisconsin Vols., Provost Marshal, will make immediate arrangements to administer the oath, and will afford every facility for this purpose.

Col. SANDERS is charged with the execution of this order.

By order of Brig. Gen. GEORGE F. SHEPLEY.

WICKHAM HOFFMAN, Asst. Adjt. Gen.

Head Quarters Provost Marshal's Office,
NORFOLK, VA., Sept. 24th, 1864.

To carry the foregoing order into effect at the time limited, all persons, (male and female,) over the age of 16 years, residing within the limits of the District Eastern Virginia, who have NOT taken the Oath of Allegiance, will, before the expiration of the time above stated, appear at one of the places herein designated, and either take the Oath of Allegiance or register their names in the list of persons DECLINING to take the Oath.

Officers charged with administering the Oath and making the Registry, will be especially careful that no one takes the Oath under threats, intimidation, or promises of any kind; but, on the contrary, the nature of the oath, its obligations and penalties in case of violation, will be fully and particularly explained.

Major H. G. O. WEYMOUTH, Provost Marshal of Portsmouth, will be charged with the execution of this order in Portsmouth and vicinity.

Major WHITE, Provost Marshal at Cherrystone, will be charged with the execution of this order on the Eastern Shore.

Capt. J. E. FLEMMING, Provost Marshal at Yorktown, is charged with the execution of this order in Yorktown, Williamsburg, and vicinity.

All persons residing in the City and County of Norfolk, will report at the CITY HALL, in Norfolk.

H. T. SANDERS,
Col. and Provost Marshal.

(Fig. 29) Broadside notice of General Order No. 31, District of Eastern Virginia, directing all over 16 years of age to take oath or leave district. Norfolk, Virginia. September 22, 1864. 10½ × 7½ inches. (VA-5.64.01)

did receive recognition from a most unlikely authority. Slaves that voluntarily enlisted in a regiment of "Colored Troops," organized from both the border and occupied Rebel states, received federal pay and bonus money. A later series of laws, both federal and in Missouri and Maryland, offered up to $100 compensation for those black enlistees to be paid to loyal former owners. Claims had to be filed after the war.[26]

The Missouri Constitutional Convention, convened in Saint Louis on January 6, 1865, was controlled by the radical wing of the Republican Party. The assembly abolished slavery, approved adoption of the 13th Amendment and drafted a new state constitution with little debate. The so-called "Section 3, Article II Oath" was adopted, which required both future and past loyalty (Fig. 30). Former Rebels were effectively excluded from holding public office, serving as trustees, teachers, ministers, or members of the state militia. Jury trials were purged of disloyal citizens through the requirement of "juror oaths." The Convention hinted at the future of "Jim Crow" laws by adding literacy to future voting requirements.

More than any other Border State, Missouri experimented with different forms of loyalty oaths. Various modifications were produced for voters, poll watchers, and members of the state militia. Major General John Pope withdrew his troops as monitors as soon as regions of the state showed a willingness to observe the laws and allow the courts to protect the laws of old. By August 1865, only a dozen military posts remained in Missouri for the protection of government property. After the legislature approved emancipation of slaves, it funded a board of immigration to encourage newcomers to resettle in Missouri. State literature promoted the accessibility of good agricultural lands, as well as valuable timber, minerals and transport resources, open to those willing to take advantage of the opportunities now that the war was over. Willing workers were welcomed to fill the vacancy created by the emancipation of black farm workers.[27]

Like its neighboring Border States, Maryland politics in 1864 were consumed by passage of an amendment to the state constitution abolishing slavery. Maryland convention delegates were almost all loyal citizens as a result of "test oaths" and military oversight of the polling places. Voters, poll watchers and delegates were all first required to file loyalty oaths. The emancipation amendment, although much debated, passed. The second challenge for the army in Maryland was assuring protection of the newly freed slaves on the eastern and western shores. Guidance for that protection came through Major General Lew Wallace's General Order No. 112, Middle Department, at Baltimore, on November 9, 1864. A Freedmen's Bureau with agents was established to carry out the pronouncement. The previously confiscated Maryland Club became the Freedmen's Rest, a place of safety, lodging and meals. To cover the cost of maintaining the home for former slaves, the provost marshal used provost police to collect fines and request contributions. Shortfalls were made up by assessments against "avowed rebel sympathizers" residing in Baltimore. Major Williams was in charge of the department's Freedmen's Bureau. His charge was to investigate and confiscate property or arrest persons interfering with the rights of freedmen.[28]

A common practice in Tennessee, Missouri, Maryland and Kentucky was to assess disloyal citizens during the war to compensate loyal citizens for losses sustained as a result of raids by Rebel guerrillas. Although extrajudicial, the practice was sustained by the judge advocate general as necessary under the urgencies of war. Neither the executive department nor several military governors had an issue with the practice while martial rule was in effect. After peace and the reopening of civil courts, the necessity ended. Only then did the courts begin to question extrajudicial and punitive sanctions against uncharged citizens in occupied cities.

Before the fall election, Major General John M. Palmer in the Department of Kentucky

SECTION 3, ARTICLE II,
OF THE
CONSTITUTION OF THE STATE OF MISSOURI.

At any election held by the people under this Constitution, or in pursuance of any law of this State or under any ordinance or by-law of any municipal corporation, no person shall be deemed a qualified voter, who has ever been in armed hostility to the United States, or to the lawful authorities thereof, or to the Government of this State; or has ever given aid, comfort, countenance, or support to persons engaged in any such hostility; or has ever, in any manner, adhered to the enemies, foreign or domestic, of the United States, either by contributing to them or by unlawfully sending within their lines, money, goods, letters, or information; or has ever disloyally held communication with such enemies; or has ever advised or aided any person to enter the service of such enemies; or has ever, by act or word, manifested his adherence to the cause of such enemies, or his desire for their triumph over the arms of the United States, or his sympathy with those engaged in or exciting or carrying on rebellion against the United States; or has ever, except under overpowering compulsion, submitted to the authority, or been in the service, of the so-called "Confederate States of America;" or has ever left this State, and gone within the lines of the armies of the so-called "Confederate States of America," with the purpose of adhering to said States or armies; or has ever been a member of, or connected with, any order, society or organization, inimical to the Government of the United States, or to the Government of this State; or has ever been engaged in guerrilla warfare against loyal inhabitants of the United States, or in that description of marauding commonly known as "bushwhacking;" or has ever knowingly and willingly harbored, aided or countenanced any person so engaged; or has ever come into or left this State, for the purpose of avoiding enrollment for or draft into the military service of the United States, or has ever with a view to avoid enrollment in the militia of this State, or to escape the performance of duty therein, or for any other purpose, enrolled himself, or authorized himself to be enrolled, by or before any officer, as disloyal, or as a Southern sympathizer, or in any other terms indicating his disaffection to the Government of the United States in its contest with rebellion, or his sympathy with those engaged in such rebellion; or, having ever voted at any election by the people in this State, or in any other of the United States, or in any of their Territories, or held office in this State, or in any other of the United States, or in any of their Territories, or under the United States, shall thereafter have sought or received, under claim of alienage, the protection of any foreign government, through any consul or other officer thereof, in order to secure exemption from military duty in the militia of this State, or in the army of the United States; nor shall any such person be capable of holding in this State any office of honor, trust or profit under its authority; or of being an officer, councilman, director, trustee or other manager of any corporation, public or private, now existing or hereafter established by its authority; or of acting as a professor or teacher in any educational institution, or in any common or other school; or of holding any real estate or other property in trust for the use of any church, religious society or congregation. But the foregoing provisions in relation to acts done against the United States shall not apply to any person not a citizen thereof, who shall have committed such acts while in the service of some foreign country at war with the United States, and who has, since such acts, been naturalized, or may hereafter be naturalized, under the laws of the United States; and the oath of loyalty hereinafter prescribed, when taken by any such person, shall be considered as taken in such sense.

Sec. 6. The oath to be taken as aforesaid shall be known as the Oath of Loyalty, and shall be in the following terms:

OATH OF LOYALTY.

STATE OF MISSOURI, } ss
Ray COUNTY.

I, _John A. Cash_, do solemnly swear, that I am well acquainted with the terms of the third section of the second Article of the Constitution of the State of Missouri, adopted in the year eighteen hundred and sixty-five, and have carefully considered the same; that I have never, directly or indirectly, done any of the acts in said section specified; that I have always been truly and loyally on the side of the United States against all enemies thereof foreign and domestic; that I will bear true faith and allegiance to the United States, and will support the Constitution and laws thereof, as the supreme law of the land, any law or any ordinance of any State to the contrary, notwithstanding; that I will, to the best of my ability, protect and defend the Union of the United States, and not allow the same to be broken up and dissolved, or the Government thereof to be destroyed or overthrown, under any circumstances, if in my power to prevent it; that I will support the Constitution of the State of Missouri; and that I make this oath without any mental reservation or evasion, and hold it to be binding on me.

John A. Cash

Subscribed and sworn to before me this......24th......day of ......April...... 186_6_

(Fig. 30) Opposite: Missouri oath, Article II, Section 3, of Constitution. April 24, 1866. 10¼ × 7¼ inches. (MO-4.66.01)

used martial law to protect voters. Anyone suspected of trying to exclude any person in Kentucky from voting was subject to arrest under an act passed by the legislature on March 3, 1865. Test oaths and a two-year residency were required before voters were allowed to participate in the election. General Palmer announced on December 7, 1865, that since three-quarters of the state population had ratified the amendment to the Constitution prohibiting slavery, as far as he was concerned, for all intents and purposes it was "now part of the Law of the Land." On October 12, 1865, President Johnson finally abolished martial law for Kentucky and civil authority was restored.[29]

After the twin defeats in Gettysburg, Pennsylvania, and Vicksburg, Mississippi, during the summer of 1863, the reality of the Emancipation Proclamation took hold. Secret organizations sympathetic to the Southern cause formed in the loyal states, especially in the Midwest and along the border. Groups, similar to the postwar Ku Klux Klan, gained popularity with their fraternal-like trappings of rituals, codes and oaths of secrecy. After recruitments were noted in Indianapolis, a number of suspects were arrested by the provost marshal. Three of those arrested were tried in the federal district court for treason and convicted. Afterward, Major General Alvin P. Hovey, commanding the District of Indiana at Indianapolis, on September 3, 1864, instructed the provost marshal to maintain a registry of all incoming refugees recording their place of origin, reason for moving, and to arrest and examine those suspected of disloyalty. Most were released after taking a loyalty oath and those that refused were held and brought before a military commission. After the war, the three convicted by the Indianapolis district court were pardoned by the president, thereby dismissing the case pending before the U.S. Supreme Court.[30]

The administration exhibited its confidence in the progress of the war and began to prepare for the upcoming national elections, set for November 1864. Accordingly, the secretary of war instructed the commissary general of prisoners to reduce the number of political prisoners. On September 3, 1864, the commissary of prisoners issued a circular ordering that prisoners of war, held in close confinement or in irons, be released from their bonds and placed in the general population. Most held as "state prisoners" were encouraged to take the oath to qualify for early release. Clemency did not apply to common criminals or those awaiting trial.[31]

The army's judge advocate later submitted a report covering the origin, purpose and organization of secret associations of traitors conspiring against the United States. Included were such groups as the Knights of the Golden Circle, Sons of Liberty, Southern League, and other so-called temples in Missouri, Ohio, Illinois, Indiana and Kentucky. All members of these organizations swore to protect from disclosure membership lists, rituals, and passwords. All swore to support the Confederacy, with sword and life. Their members resisted the draft, circulated publications, gathered vital intelligence, cooperated with guerrillas, and destroyed government property. The ultimate goal of these organizations was the establishment of a northwestern branch of the Confederate government. The first public exposure of the groups was by a military commission trial of Harrison H. Dodd in Indianapolis. His charges included conspiracy, citing insurrection, aiding the Rebels and other disloyal acts. The eleven-day trial in October 1864 was interrupted after the accused escaped to Canada. He was later convicted in absentia and sentenced to be hanged.[32]

Not until after the national election was held, and as General W. T. Sherman turned his army north from Charleston to close the gap on Rebel forces between his troops and General Grant's in Virginia, with victory finally in view. Only then did the secretary of war permit the judge advocate to begin to provide the Senate a list of names of all political prisoners remaining confined in military prisons. Earlier the Senate had asked that the list be given to circuit and district judges of the United States. For months, appointed commissioners toured most military prisons, including those in Saint Louis, Chicago, New York and the District of Columbia. For more than a year, numerous judges, both state and federal, questioned the circumstances surrounding the continued necessity of resisting the writ of habeas corpus as a means of testing loyalty; and of the arrests and imprisonment of civilians without any criminal charges being filed. By the beginning of 1865, few "state prisoners" remained.[33]

An actual count of confined political prisoners was not publicly reported until 1867. The commissary general of prisoners compiled a listing by month, from July 1862 through March 1866, of prisoners confined in Union military prisons. This list identified the number of political prisoners as distinct from military prisoners. The census was incomplete because names of prisoners in custody at provost jails, civilian jails and hospitals were not always available. Most political prisoners were soon released after their arrest on suspicion of some form of disloyalty after signing an oath of loyalty. Very few remained incarcerated during the course of the war. During the Rebellion, the public was seldom informed of the number of political prisoners and persons who were arrested, examined, jailed and released after being paroled. The last civilians released were in 1866—one in January, two in February and the final one in March. The commissary general's prison count was published as part of the adjutant general's report to the secretary of war on May 16, 1867. Remarkably, the Confederate governors, cabinet members and other high-ranking officials imprisoned at Fort Pulaski, Georgia, were not included in the report.[34]

Civilian Political Prisoners
Confined in U.S. Military Prisons

Prison	1862	1863	1864	1865
Alton IL		190	206	
Camp Chase OH	605	57	156	
Camp Morton IN		13	33	
Elmira NY			47	
Ft. Delaware DE		77	73	
Ft. Lafayette NY		70	59	4
Ft. McHenry MD		29	151	2
Ft. Pickens FL		18	11	17
Ft. Warren MA		70	78	5
Johnson's Island OH	26	39	32	2
Little Rock AR			61	3
Louisville KY		156	46	
McLean OH			16	
Memphis TN			12	
Nashville TN			136	105
Old Capitol DC		349	180	39
Point Lookout MD			185	
Rock Island IL			24	
Saint Louis MO		168		
Wheeling WV		130	17	

Note: No prison census available for 1861.

After Atlanta was burned in 1864, General Sherman turned his army south toward the port of Savannah. On Christmas Day, General Sherman made a gift of the city of Savannah to President Lincoln. After New Year's Day, Savannah residents formed a line at Charles Green's mansion, where Sherman had his headquarters, to take their loyalty oaths (Fig. 31). The

(Fig. 31) *Frank Leslie's Illustrated Newspaper.* "General Geary Issuing Passes to Citizens of Savannah, Georgia." January 1865. (NY-5.64.02)

process was pictured by northern journalists in *Harper's Weekly* and *Frank Leslie's Journal.* No disruptions or incidents were reported. Sherman warned rural residents if any soldier or loyal farmer was murdered, commanders would retaliate in kind, at the rate of five to one. If perpetrators were not known, lots would be drawn for punishment. If any loyal family was run out of town, a Rebel family would be selected for exile. Other than in Savannah, few Georgians took the loyalty oath during the war.

After crossing the Savannah River, General Sherman turned his army north toward Virginia through South Carolina. Charleston soon surrendered and martial law declared. As in Savannah, men and women were invited to take the oath of loyalty. Tradesmen and men of commerce led the way, in order to reopen their businesses. As published in a Charleston newspaper, the loyalty oath directive read:

> All loyal citizens of the United States residing in [city] or its vicinity, are invited to call at the office of the Post Provost Marshal and register their names, take the Oath of Allegiance to the Government, and receive Certificates of having done so.
>
> Post of Brigade Commanders will grant no passes or favors to persons (owing allegiance to the United States) who have not, by taking the oath, shown their loyalty to the government.
>
> No guards will be placed over the houses of citizens for the protection of private property. Any person fearing molestation will best secure their property by placing in some conspicuous position on the premises the Flag of the United States. Persons detected depredating on houses so protected, will be punished with additional severity (Fig. 32).

Unlike Georgia, South Carolina had a United States Direct Tax Office that had been operational since 1863. Three U.S. tax commissioners, residing in Beaufort, South Carolina, already had assessed, posted, foreclosed and sold property for unpaid taxes when Sherman's

(Fig. 32) **Charleston, South Carolina, citizens taking the oath of allegiance after General Hardee's evacuation, 1864.** *Frank Leslie's Illustrated History of the Civil War, 1893.* 9½ × 11 inches. (NY-5.93.01)

army arrived. Citizens of Charleston were afraid of these tax foreclosures, already used in neighboring Beaufort as well as in Florida and Louisiana. Once ownership passed to a third party, valid title would be vested in the buyer and the foreclosed owner was shut out. Beyond a short statutory redemption period, tax-delinquent owners had little legal redress. Some Charleston property owners managed to pay their federal tax liens to the U.S. direct tax collector soon after the occupation. Halfway through the year, a suggestion was made to the state convention that South Carolina should assume all federal taxes for the benefit of destitute citizens. However, the federal Direct Tax Act was suspended before South Carolina took action.

Citizens in occupied Richmond, Virginia, also soon saw the consequences of disloyalty, especially if they were property owners. Notices went out soon after Union troops took control of the city. Tenants ceased paying rents on leased dwellings in towns and farmlands after condemnation proceedings began against delinquent direct-tax owners. Proceedings of foreclosure later were suspended while cases worked their way through the courts. At the same time, district attorneys in Norfolk and Richmond awaited a pending decision from the Supreme Court. Confiscation cases filed against disloyal owners before the war ended that were in progress were also held in abeyance. Ultimately, the courts ruled that pardoned disloyal citizens could file claims for the return of seized property, if not already conveyed to an innocent third party by the tax commissioner or other federal official. Political clemency of formerly disloyal Americans had significant consequences for property rights.[35]

5

Prisoner Oaths

When Fort Sumter surrendered in April of 1861, no Union prisoners were taken. All in the garrison were allowed to return home unmolested. Most troops of the Union Department of Texas, after surrendering to the Texas militia, also in April, were allowed to leave after officers gave their paroles of honor. Federal outposts were abandoned. Some Union soldiers were held in the Bexar County jail for a year. Prisoner exchanges were difficult because of the politics of civil war. To negotiate a prisoner exchange was considered recognition of the confederate government as legitimate, something Washington was reluctant to concede. However, sheer numbers of captives eventually outweighed politics. More than 400,000 prisoners were captured over the course of the war, divided roughly equally, but formal exchanges did not begin until the summer of 1862.

Soldier-artist of the Texas frontier, Captain Arthur T. Lee, Eighth Infantry, Company C, was stationed at Fort Stockton, Texas, before the Civil War. Fearing upcoming events, he moved his family to San Antonio the first of April 1861. His post was ordered abandoned a week later. In route to the coast, Lee's company was taken prisoner by the Texas volunteer militia on April 21. Confederate major S. Macklin, formerly of the U.S. Army, released Lee upon the condition that he would "not for the present do army duty for the United States." Lee's parole of honor and safe passage are housed in the library of the Rochester Museum and Science Center, New York. Under his parole, Lee promised he would not take up arms against the Confederate States or correspond with the United States until regularly exchanged (Fig. 33). More than a year passed before an exchange cartel included Lee's name. In the interim, Lee served in West Point, New York, as a member of a court-martial board and a drill instructor (Fig. 34).

On May 10, 1861, the Missouri militia was captured by Union forces. The certificate of release issued at Camp Jackson by commanding officer Captain N. Lyon, U.S.A., simply read, "You do solemnly swear that you will not serve in any capacity against the Government of the United States during the civil war now existing." For officers of the captured Missouri brigade, the pledge was longer:

> We, the undersigned, do pledge our words as gentlemen that we will not take arms or serve in any military capacity against the United States during the present civil war. The parole to be retained upon our surrendering ourselves at any time as prisoners of war. While we sign this parole with a full intention of observing it, we nevertheless protest against the justice of its exactions.

Head Quarters Confederate
States Army in Texas
San Antonio April 26/61

To all guards, patroles, Citizens and all Concerned, within the limits of the Confederate States. The bearer Captain A. T. Lee 8th Infantry U.S.A. a prisoner of war on his parole of honor, is hereby permitted to pass through each and any of the Confederate States, without let or hinderance or molestation of any kind whatever

S. Maclin
Major Infy C S Army
Commanding

(Fig. 33) Capt. A. T. Lee, parole of honor. San Antonio, Texas. April 24, 1861. (TX-3.61.01)

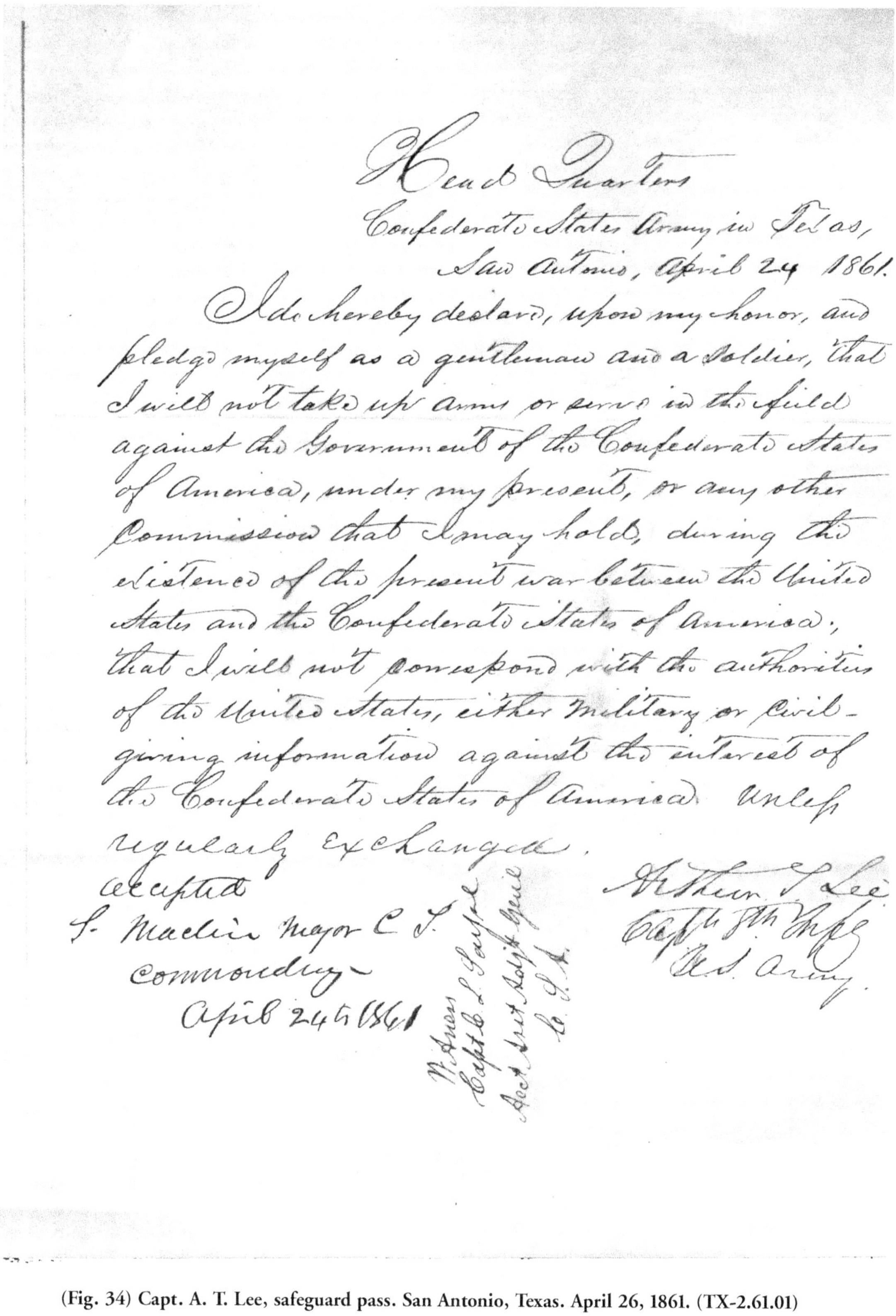

5. Prisoner Oaths

Head Quarters
Confederate States Army in Texas,
San Antonio, April 24 1861.

I do hereby declare, upon my honor, and pledge myself as a gentleman and a soldier, that I will not take up arms, or serve in the field against the Government of the Confederate States of America, under my present, or any other Commission that I may hold, during the existence of the present war between the United States and the Confederate States of America; that I will not correspond with the authorities of the United States, either Military or Civil, giving information against the interest of the Confederate States of America. Unless regularly exchanged.

Accepted
S. Maclin Major C. S.
Commanding
April 24th 1861

Witness
Capt C. L. Sayre
Act Asst Adjt Genl
C. S. A.

Arthur T. Lee
Capt 8th Infy
U.S. Army.

(Fig. 34) Capt. A. T. Lee, safeguard pass. San Antonio, Texas. April 26, 1861. (TX-2.61.01)

Generally, the rule was one prisoner per parole. Group paroles were the exception. Technically, officers' releases were termed paroles of honor, while enlisted men were released on certificates of parole.

The Battle of Bull Run, Virginia, resulted in more than one thousand Union enlisted men and fifty officers being taken as prisoners. Some who were seriously wounded were returned under a flag of truce for "reciprocal humanity." After letters to the press reached Congress, the lawmakers pressed for prisoner exchanges. The general of the army, through Special Order No. 170, dated October 12, 1861, activated prisoner exchanges with a required "oath of obligation not to bear arms" against the United States. The first formal exchange took place at Fort Monroe in Virginia where Union prisoners had been transferred from Richmond and from as far away as Montgomery, Alabama (Fig. 35). Most were confined in the Henrico County jail pending their release.

Prisoner exchanges initially relied on the personalities of commanders in the field and battlefield exigencies rather than formal cartels. Such exchanges were referred to as battlefield paroles or indirect exchanges. Registration of prisoners' names was often lax, but as numbers of captives grew, paper work increased and delays became common. Soon, the press and public opinion brought pressure for negotiation of a protocol agreement. Both Congresses agreed. Confederate paroles mirrored their federal counterparts, including the penalty of death if parolees' promises were broken (Fig. 36).

Prisoner exchanges were easier to negotiate within the interior theaters, beyond the critical eyes of Congress. General of the army, Winfield Scott, instructed Major General McClellan, in western Virginia, to release prisoners on July 14, 1861, if they would agree not to "take up arms against the United States or serve in any military capacity" until discharged according to the usages of war. By October, prisoner exchanges had

(**Fig. 35**) Confederate safeguard and parole for Union prisoner to travel to Richmond for exchange. Montgomery, Alabama. February 21, 1862. 9½ × 7½ inches. (AL-1.62.01)

become common in the Missouri theater. After the Battle of Lexington, Kentucky, Major General John C. Frémont, U.S.A., and Major General Sterling Price, C.S.A., negotiated an informal exchange agreement on October 26, 1861, that released five hundred Rebel prisoners at Columbus, Kentucky. There were no official guidelines from Washington or Richmond — personalities and conditions in the field still set the terms (Figs. 37 and 38).[1]

The guidance issued to Major General George McClellan for parole of captured Rebel soldiers held in Beverly, Virginia, was brief. As normal, commissioned officers had to pledge not to take up arms against the United States or serve in any military capacity whatsoever. Further, until discharged according to the usages of war from that obligation, they swore to keep that promise on their "words of honor as officers and gentlemen." The paroles were given and signed as a group rather than individually. Excluded from the authorization for granting paroles were any other prisoners who had previously been members of the U.S. Army or Navy and had left that service with the intention to bear arms against the United States. These former United States commissioned officers were to be sent, under guard, to the political prison at Fort McHenry.[2]

Prisoner exchanges negotiated by field commanders slowly evolved. An October 1861 agreement involved the swap of 57 Federal prisoners held in Richmond jails with an equal number of Confederate soldiers confined in Washington and New York. The Rebel prisoners were given the choice of taking an "oath of allegiance" to support and protect the Constitution and government of the United States; or simply swearing not to bear arms until regularly discharged under the usages of war from that obligation. Soon the adjutant general of the army issued guidance to the armies in the field incorporating such guidelines. Unchanged was the exclusion of exchanges or paroles of former commissioned members of the United States military service. All were considered traitors and were to be held as prisoners to await trial.[3]

(Fig. 36) Confederate parole oath for Union prisoners of war. Headquarters, Army of Mississippi. September 23, 1862. 9½ × 7 inches. (MS-4.62.01)

> **HEAD QUARTERS, ARMY OF KENTUCKY,**
> LEXINGTON, OCTOBER 9, 1862.
>
> I, L. C. Bell, Col. _____ a prisoner of War, captured by the Confederate Forces under Maj. Gen. E. KIRBY SMITH, having been this day paroled, do solemnly swear that I will not take up arms against the Confederate States of America until duly exchanged, and that I will not communicate any military information to the enemies of the Confederate States, which I may obtain whilst in their lines. The penalty for the violation of this parole is death.
>
> OFFICIAL:
>
> H. Elcan Troy
> Provost Marshal
>
> L. C. Bell

(Fig. 37) Confederate Parole for Union prisoner of war. Lexington, Kentucky. October 9, 1862. 4 × 9 inches. (KY-1.62.01)

> **Headquarters Post Commandant,**
> Lebanon, Ky., Nov 1st 1862.
>
> I, W. H. Organ Co. B 4th Battalion 4th Regiment of Tennessee Cavalry, being a prisoner of war, do solemnly pledge my word of honor that I will not take up arms against the United States, nor give any information or aid to the prejudice of the United States, during the present war, unless sooner exchanged.
>
> Sworn to and signed before me
> this 1st day of November 1862.
>
> W. H. Organ
>
> Lt. Col. C. S. Poorman
> Lt. Col. 98th O. V. I., Commanding Post

(Fig. 38) Union Parole for Confederate prisoner of war. Lebanon, Kentucky. November 1, 1862. 4 × 9 inches. (KY-4.62.01)

By the end of the year, another variation of prisoner exchanges became common. A number of captives were taken by the U.S. Navy's blockading fleet all along the Eastern Seaboard. Flag Officer Louis M. Goldsborough, commander of the North Atlantic Blockading Squadron, from his flagship USS *Minnesota*, held these Confederate prisoners. He wrote Confederate major general Benjamin Huger at Hampton Roads, Virginia, on December 21, 1861, with an offer of parole. The terms required the Confederate captives to promise to voluntarily return as prisoners at the expiration of 50 days, if an equal number of acceptable captured United States soldiers were delivered to the fleet. The release and subsequent exchange was completed in February 1862. Major General John E. Wool, U.S. Army, at Fort Monroe, Virginia, made a similar offer of exchange that only granted six days to complete the transaction with his Confederate counterpart.[4]

The Union army's leading authority on international law, General Henry Halleck, argued that prisoner exchanges did not recognize the Rebel government, but were merely a "military convention" under the normal rules of *commercia belli*, with precedents dating back to the Revolution. The sole consideration, in his opinion, should be humanitarianism, not politics. Soon after receiving Halleck's opinion, the Adjutant general created a standard "Military Oath" dated October 12, 1861, as a guide for future prisoner exchanges. The order required each prisoner to sign under oath the following: "I do solemnly swear (or affirm) that I will not take up arms against the United States or serve in any military capacity whatsoever against them until regularly discharged according to the usages of war from the obligation."[5]

In Missouri, General Samuel R. Curtis, U.S. Army, on December 28, 1861, received word he could accept Rebel deserters into his lines conditional upon their stated allegiance to the United States. Afterward, most were required to post a bond to assure performance. Security bonds for officers could be as high as a thousand dollars, but were usually was waived for enlisted men. Bond amounts were at the discretion of the officer in charge of administering paroles. The use of security bonds became standard in the Border States.[6]

On April 15, 1861, President Lincoln called on loyal states to provide 75,000 volunteers to supplement the standing army to "repossess the forts and places seized from the Union" along the newly designated border of the Confederate States. Two days later, Jefferson Davis offered Letters of Marque and Reprisal to captains, crews and vessels willing to post a $5,000 bond entitling them to become privateers. The threat of prize-seeking Rebel vessels attacking United States shipping caused the U.S. Navy to begin a crash program to charter and build war vessels. To justify the international legality of the offered Letters of Marque, the Confederate Congress on May 6, 1861, declared a state of war between its government and the United States. In response, both the politicians and courts of the United States insisted that the seceding states were in a state of insurrection, and any ships flying flags on the presumed protection of the Confederate Letters of Marque and Reprisal would be charged with piracy and treason. One of the first vessels to fly a privateer's flag for the Confederacy was the former pilot boat N0.7 from Charleston, seized by South Carolina. The vessel, renamed C.S. privateer *Savannah*, was promptly captured on June 3, 1861, by the U.S. brig *Perry*. The Confederate captain, Harrison Baker, and 14 of his crew were first imprisoned at Fort Lafayette in New York (Fig. 39).[7]

The Rebel privateers were charged with piracy and stood before federal judge Samuel Nelson in New York. Eight of the defendants were foreign nationals. After the presentation of evidence, the jury was instructed that under the "law of nations," the affirmative defense of acting under Letters of Marque was not available to the rebel sailors. Instead, the crew were deemed pirates under the law because they roved the sea in an armed vessel without any valid authority from a sovereign nation for the sole purpose of seizing, by force, any vessel available. The Letters of Marque could not be presented in evidence since the Confederate government was not recognized by the United States. The jury became deadlocked and were unable to return a verdict. A new trial was ordered. In retaliation for not recognizing the validity of the Letters of Marque, Jefferson Davis advised President Lincoln that a like number of Federal

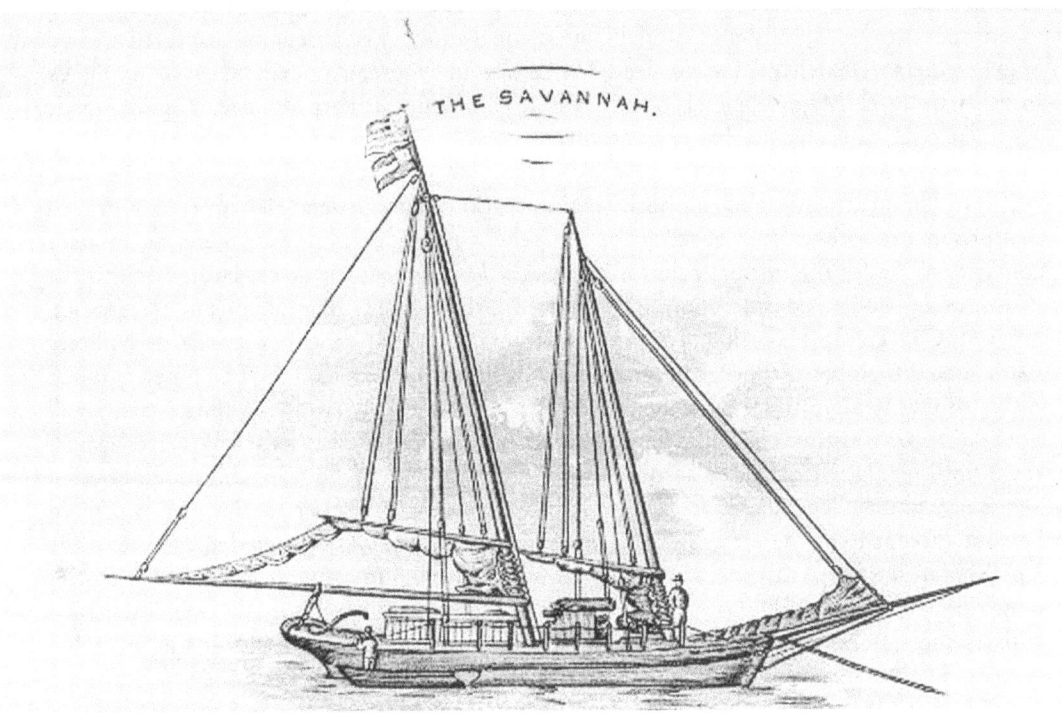

(Fig. 39) C.S. privateer *Savannah*. Library of Congress, reproduction no. LC-Z62-136802, 1861.

prisoners, drawn by lot, would be executed should the Rebel privateers be convicted and hanged. Eventually both sides backed down, and the prisoners were exchanged.[8]

Rebel privateers, upon capture, presented a difficult problem for both sides. Federal law considered them pirates beyond the protection of the Articles of War. Confederate lawmakers viewed them as citizen combatants entitled to the same treatment as soldiers. The Confederate government was reluctant to enter formal prisoner negotiations until captured privateers, held in New York, were considered prisoners of war, rather than common criminals. General U. S. Grant after the Battle of Belmont, Missouri, in November 1861, was unable to reach an agreement with Confederate general Leonidas Polk for the exchange of prisoners because of this concern. President Lincoln instructed Secretary of War Stanton to appoint two exchange commissioners to try and resolve the problem. Consequently, Edward R. Ames, bishop of the Methodist Episcopal Church, and Hamilton Fish, former governor of New York and U.S. senator, traveled to Norfolk, Virginia, to meet with their Confederate counterparts. After negotiation, each side agreed to an exchange protocol, but execution of the agreement was held in abeyance until the status of the New York privateers was resolved. This occurred in May 1862.

Before the cartel, separate negotiations by individual area commanders were the standard, but this practice lacked both uniformity and predictability. Almost three thousand prisoners from each side benefited from another understanding reached by Union admiral Louis M. Goldsborough and Confederate major general Benjamin Huger. The Roanoke Island Agreement of February 1862, benefited 2,488 Rebels, including two colonels, one naval lieutenant, nine musicians, 12 surgeons and 29 servants. The language of the exchange parole read:

> Having been taken a prisoner of war ... I ... do solemnly pledge my sacred word and honor that if released I will give no information I may have derived or mention anything I have seen or heard since my capture that might injure the government of the United States of America, and that I will not take up arms ... until ... regularly exchanged.... The information to me of said exchange to be beyond the possibility of a doubt.[9]

Admiral Goldsborough once informed General Huger that he took it for granted that the terms of any parole he granted a soldier or sailor would be "religiously observed and that no countenance whatever will be given to them from any quarter to do otherwise." The naval officer's parole, given to the released prisoners, clearly stated, "This paper is intended to release me on parole," and all had given their pledge of sacred honor to not take up arms or divulge any information until released under the rules of war. The smaller vessels of the Atlantic Blockading Squadron were forced to parole and release as many prisoners as possible, on their words of honor. Space limitations of their ships and requirements they remain unrelieved on station for long periods of time made holding captives impractical.[10]

Informal accommodations to battlefield conditions created variations from the standard prisoner-exchange process. Conditional exchanges were one example of such practical modifications. General W. S. Rosecrans, Department of Western Virginia, at Wheeling, on January 27, 1862, released Confederate colonel Milton J. Ferguson in hopes of exchanging him for Lieutenant Colonel George W. Neff, of the Second Kentucky Volunteers, captured after the Battle of Scary Creek in far western Virginia. The exchange offer provided that Ferguson had 60 days to effectuate the release and return of Neff. If that was not possible, Ferguson swore on his honor to surrender himself to the Ohio County jail, at Wheeling, where he would remain until discharged. The effort was unsuccessful. On April 10, 1862, another Confederate captive, Lieutenant Colonel Frank P. Anderson, requested that the Confederate secretary of war, in Richmond, trade him for Lieutenant Colonel Neff who was then confined in Richmond's Libby Prison. Lieutenant Colonel Neff was exchanged soon after.[11]

Not until June 28, 1862, did the adjutant general publish guidelines to direct the organization of former prisoners paroled back to the Union lines. The adjutant general's Order No. 72 provided that paroled soldiers from regiments in the Middle Atlantic and New England states would be sent for organization to a camp of instruction in Annapolis, Maryland. Released Union prisoners from the western theater were to go to Jefferson Barracks, Missouri, and all others to Camp Chase in Columbus, Ohio. No furloughs would be granted paroled Union soldiers in the future. All parolees were to be organized by states and assigned duties compatible with the conditions of their individual paroles. Qualified duties included guard, police and fatigue duty. Permanently disabled men would be eligible for a medical discharge if confirmed by a medical board. No paroled soldier could be assigned duties such as military police, prison guards or depot watchers since such would be inconsistent with their parole. Any paroled soldier or officer failing to comply with the guidelines would be charged with desertion.[12]

Medical officers and chaplains were treated differently than other prisoners. Chaplains, as unarmed soldiers, were usually given greater freedom when captured and often released early. For instance, after the Battle of Manassas, Virginia, on August 2, 1862, Confederate General P. G. T. Beauregard granted seven Union surgeons paroles to attend to the needs of their wounded men. The seven doctors first gave their "unqualified parole of honor" not to take up arms against the Confederate States until released from their parole or when duly exchanged. After treating the injured men in the field, the group of physicians was allowed to return to their homes under the conditions of their parole. The general explained that these men were noncombatants who easily might have escaped had they imitated others and ran from the battlefield. They had remained under fire only because of the duty of their profession.[13]

The long delayed cartel was executed on July 22, 1862, between General John A. Dix, U.S.A., and General D. H. Hill, C.S.A. The methodology of the Hill-Dix Cartel system was rank equivalencies whereby captives were weighted by rank. A general or admiral would be 60 times more valuable on the exchange scale than a private or seaman. Civilians, sutlers and agents of the military were treated as privates. Releases were to be completed in ten days, but seldom was that accomplished. Surplus prisoners held by one side were paroled, but the formal exchange awaited more captives from the deficient side (Fig. 40). Exchange points were Aiken Landing at Dutch Gap, Virginia, and Vicksburg, Mississippi.

The Hill-Dix Cartel clarified the rights of prisoners. A captive could promise not to attempt an escape in exchange for less severe confinement. They also could do extra work for better rations. According to the War Department's General Order No. 207 of July 3, 1863, any prisoner exchange accomplished outside the guidelines of the Hill-Dix agreement was null and void. The War Office referred to cartels as military paroles to distinguish them from

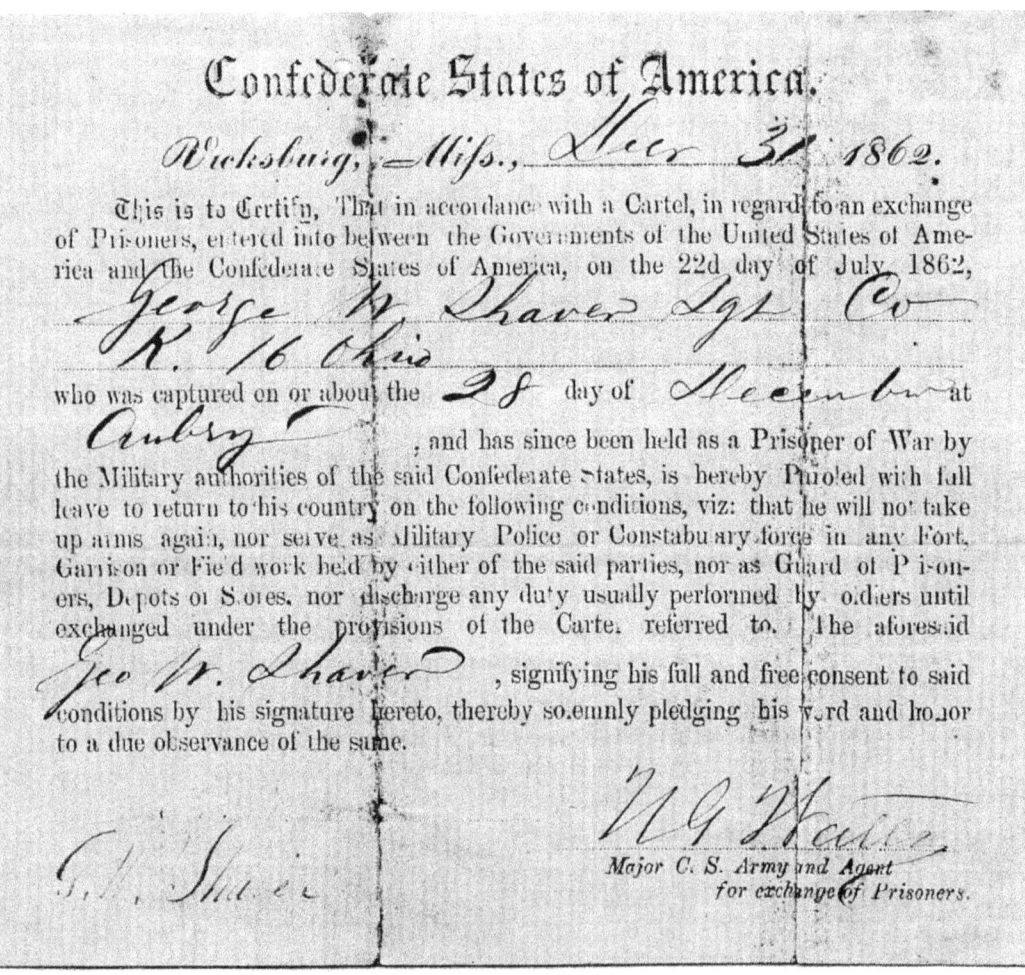

(Fig. 40) Confederate parole of Union prisoner of war exchanged under cartel of July 22, 1862. Vicksburg, Mississippi. December 31, 1862. 8 × 9¼ inches. (MS-1.62.02)

the customary paroles of honor. The fine distinction between the two was not always observed in the field, especially in the western theatre.

After the Hill-Dix Cartel, exchanges increased. The Confederates exacted statements from Union soldiers similar to the federal form. Standard Rebel language read, "I will not take up arms against the Confederate States of America until duly exchanged." A promise not to reveal military intelligence was sometimes added. The standard penalty for any parole violation was death. Paroles were often handwritten and usually contained personal identification of the released prisoner.

In the early war years, paroled Union prisoners were sent home on furlough to await word of their names appearing on the list of exchanged prisoners. Once exchanged, the paroled prisoner was relieved of his obligation not to take any duty involving actual combat. Paroled prisoners, for a time, were better off than active duty personnel or the medically discharged. On September 17, 1862, a plan was launched to change that anomaly. Major General Lew Wallace was instructed to organize a regiment of paroled prisoners in Columbus, Ohio, in preparation for service against northern Indian tribes who had been disruptive after the army withdrew from the area. Within two weeks of training, General Wallace reported to Washington that almost all parolees had protested the assigned Indian-fighting duty. Wallace would have preferred dishonorably discharging the lot of mutineers but knew they would only encourage more disruptions. Instead, he asked that no more paroled prisoners be sent to him. He recommended that future recruits be transported directly to Minnesota, armed and equipped there, and put to work. The only bright spot in Wallace's report was a favorable impression of the regimental commander, the recently paroled Lieutenant Colonel George W. Neff, previously held captive in Richmond. Although military service against hostile Indians did not violate the conditions of parole, the idea seemed much better in Washington than out West.[14]

The Indian War training facility at Columbus, known as Camp Wallace, was closed by the end of the war. All the recently constructed buildings, hospitals and warehouses were abandoned. Cords of firewood stored for the winter were also left for the locals. (To transport the 1,200 cords of wood across to Camp Chase was considered too costly — although only eight miles away.)[15]

General Henry Halleck encouraged Tennessee military governor Andrew Johnston to release Rebel deserters held in the Union prison at Corinth if they would take a loyalty oath. Many took advantage of this offer in Tennessee and Kentucky. Later, the commissary general of prisoners, through his General Order No. 49, transferred deserters to Camp Chase, Ohio, to remove any temptation to join guerrilla bands active in those states.[16]

The battle at Stone's River, Murfreesboro, Tennessee, in January 1863, resulted in heavy losses for both sides. True to the intent of the Hill-Dix Cartel, prisoners of war were exchanged within ten days. Rebel prisoners subscribed to "Almighty God, the Sovereign Judge" that they would not bear arms against the United States Government until regularly exchanged (Fig. 41).

It was not long before some soldiers realized the benefits of being a former prisoner of war, released back to friendly lines without the risk of future enemy fire. First noticed loitering around Washington, D.C., were allegedly released Union prisoners with questionable parole documents. The commissary general of prisoners on January 10, 1863, alerted all commanders to be on the lookout for forged parole certificates carried by unassigned soldiers. A number of these men were spotted in Alexandria and Fredericksburg. The growing number of stragglers threatened morale as battle casualties increased. Being caught malingering with a fake parole certificate was not as risky as actual desertion, which always contained the possibility of capital

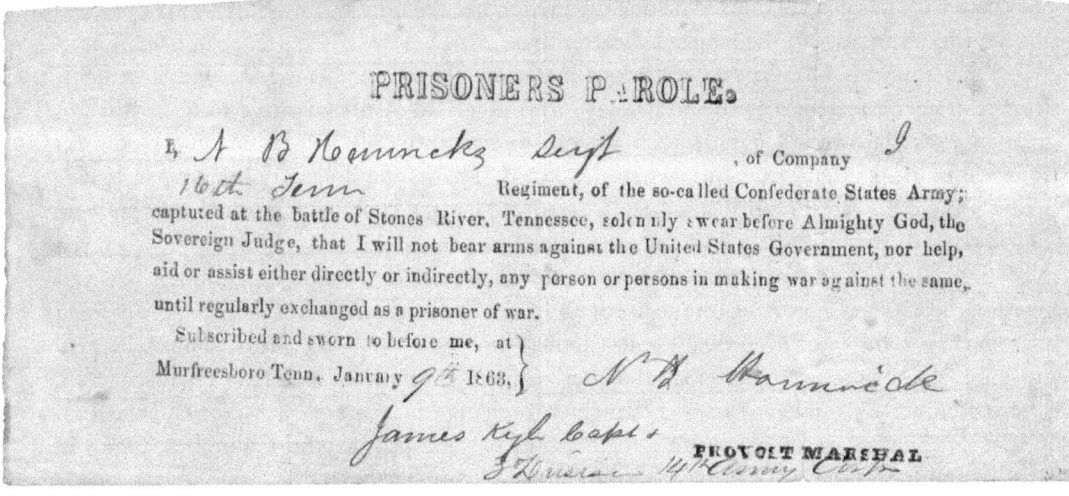

(Fig. 41) Union parole for Confederate prisoner of war. Murfreesboro, Tennessee. January 9, 1863. 3½ × 7¾ inches. (TN-1.63.02)

punishment. Paroled Union soldiers, before being admitted to one of three camps of instruction, were thoroughly questioned. Those in possession of doubtful documents were arrested as deserters until the certificate of parole could be validated. Valid names were listed on the cartel papers compiled prior to prisoner exchange or were on authentic parole documents given prior to the release.[17]

The adjutant general of the U.S. Army on February 28, 1863, through his General Order No. 49, outlined the rules for issuing paroles under the "common law and usages of war." Each was to be written, in duplicate, complete with full name and rank. Only the senior officers could grant paroles for the lower grades. Battlefield paroles, group paroles and general dismissals of prisoners were not allowed and, if given, that officer would be deemed a deserter. No one could be forced to accept a parole. For a while, Rebel parolees taking up residence in a loyal state were subject to conscription like any other loyal citizen — a requirement modified a year later. Excluded from parole were Rebel officers and members of irregular units.

Additional guidance for prisoner exchange and the use of paroles was included in General Order No. 100 from the War Department, issued April 24, 1863. It established rules of governance of the U.S. forces in the field. Section VII of the order provided that the release of prisoners of war was to be accomplished by agreed upon exchanges, and paroles were considered exceptions to that general rule. Every parole was to be prepared in duplicate, one given and one retained. Only commissioned officers could sign paroles for their men. Once paroled, released soldiers could be assigned duties such as recruiting, drilling recruits, quelling civil commotions, as well as diplomatic duties and general fatigue duties. The breaking of a parole was considered a breach of an individual's good faith and word of honor, and, if the parole was registered, punishable by death. Paroled soldiers could be used for combat against belligerents only if the enemy was in no way connected with the paroling forces. This directive supplemented General Order No. 49 of the War Department.[18]

The Confederate Congress was annoyed with the Union army's use of black regiments formed with former slaves. President Davis stated that captured black soldiers would not be treated as prisoners of war and their white officers would be charged with inciting slave revolts. In response, General David Hunter, U.S. Army, from Hilton Head in April 1863, proclaimed that "the United States flag must protect all its defenders, white, black or yellow." Hunter promised to execute the highest ranking Rebel held should any black soldiers be murdered. On July 30, President Lincoln announced he would protect all its citizens, especially those in uniform. He echoed General Hunter's threat of retaliation, should black prisoners be mistreated. Insincere oaths and the presence of captured black soldiers thwarted the expansion of prisoner exchanges.

Execution of prisoners of war was the exception rather than the general rule and was usually reserved for spies, bridge burners and parole breakers. Two Rebel recruiters in the North, who had entered the country from Canada, were held at Johnson's Island, Lake Erie. After being convicted by a military commission, the two, T. P. Graw and William Corbin, were executed on May 15, 1863. Outraged Confederate politicians and officials retaliated. Two Union captives, held in Richmond, were selected by lot for a similar fate. Union exchange agent, Colonel William H. Ludlow, informed his Confederate counterpart, Colonel Robert Ould, that unless the two Union captains, H. W. Sawyer and John Flynn, were spared, a similar execution awaited two Confederate officers. Two officers were selected to emphasize the resolve of the Union negotiator. The confederates, General W. H. Lee and Captain Winder, were placed in close confinement to await the fate of the two Federal officers. Colonel Ludlow assured the Confederates that his government would "retaliate for every similar barbarous violation of the laws of civilized war." Six months passed and tempers subsided. The four were duly exchanged.[19]

As battlefield victories began to favor the North, an imbalance of confined prisoners grew in favor of the Union side. Political disagreements between cartel negotiators regarding the issue of retaliation for the use of Federal black troops contributed to a stalemate. Paroles in possession of prisoners dated after May 22, 1863, were not considered valid. An exception was made for one group of Rebel prisoners after that date. This group was permitted to take the oath and move to Philadelphia by order of the commissary general of prisoners, W. Hoffman. The commissary general explained that the POWs had already expressed their desire to give the oath and stay within the Federal lines when the cutoff date was announced. He felt to leave them in the general population, among other Rebel prisoners, subjected those individuals to bodily injury and perhaps death. After the Battle of Gettysburg, the secretary of war informed Major General Robert C. Schenck that no Confederate prisoners of war were to be released on taking the oath of allegiance. By August 5, 1863, the general in chief, Henry W. Halleck relaxed this policy. Accordingly, General Burnside was allowed to receive the oath of Rebel prisoners if the individuals seemed sincere, were willing to post a bond and wished to be paroled. The parole policy was, again, confused and applied inconsistently.[20]

Large numbers of captives after the Battles of Gettysburg and Vicksburg created logistical problems. At first, General Grant, from Vicksburg, declined exchange, recognizing the loss of men affected the enemy more than him. As prisoner populations grew, Grant relented (Fig. 42). In August 1863, paroles resumed at Fort Pillow, Tennessee. Rebels were released with a promise to "bear true allegiance to the United States of America" and defend the nation "especially against the Rebellious League known as the Confederate States of America" (Fig. 43). On December 8, the president issued a comprehensive Proclamation of Pardon covering both civilians and soldiers. Grant followed with his own General Order No. 10, Military Division of Mississippi, dated December 12, 1863, that encouraged Rebel desertions in return for a full pardon.

Six prisoner cartels under Hill-Dix occurred between August 1862 and the fall of 1863. The first cartel, in August, covered captives from Virginia, North Carolina and Tennessee. A month later, prisoners taken in Georgia, Arkansas, Texas and New Mexico were added. By November, confinees from Kentucky, western Virginia and Pennsylvania went home. The following year saw prisoners from Mississippi, Missouri, Kansas, Arizona, Alabama and Louisiana exchanged. The fifth agreement, in April, released men from Virginia and North Carolina. The final Hill-Dix exchange took place at City Point, Virginia, where prisoners held in Georgia were freed. The six releases by the War Department as approved by the adjutant general were as follows:

General Order Nos.	Date	Capture Date
118	August 27, 1862	To August 1, 1862
147	September 30, 1862	To September 1, 1862
191	November 19, 1862	To November 1, 1862
10	January 10, 1863	To January 1, 1863
17	May 9, 1863	To April 1, 1863
167	June 8, 1863	To May 30, 1863

The commissary general of prisoners filed a report on the number of captured and exchanged prisoners of war to date. The secretary of war later included the information in his annual report to the Congress. As of the end of 1863, the United States had accepted 110,866 Federal prisoners in exchange for the release of 121,937 Confederates. The rank-weighted protocol accounted for the disparity in number. Still held were 29,229 Confederate

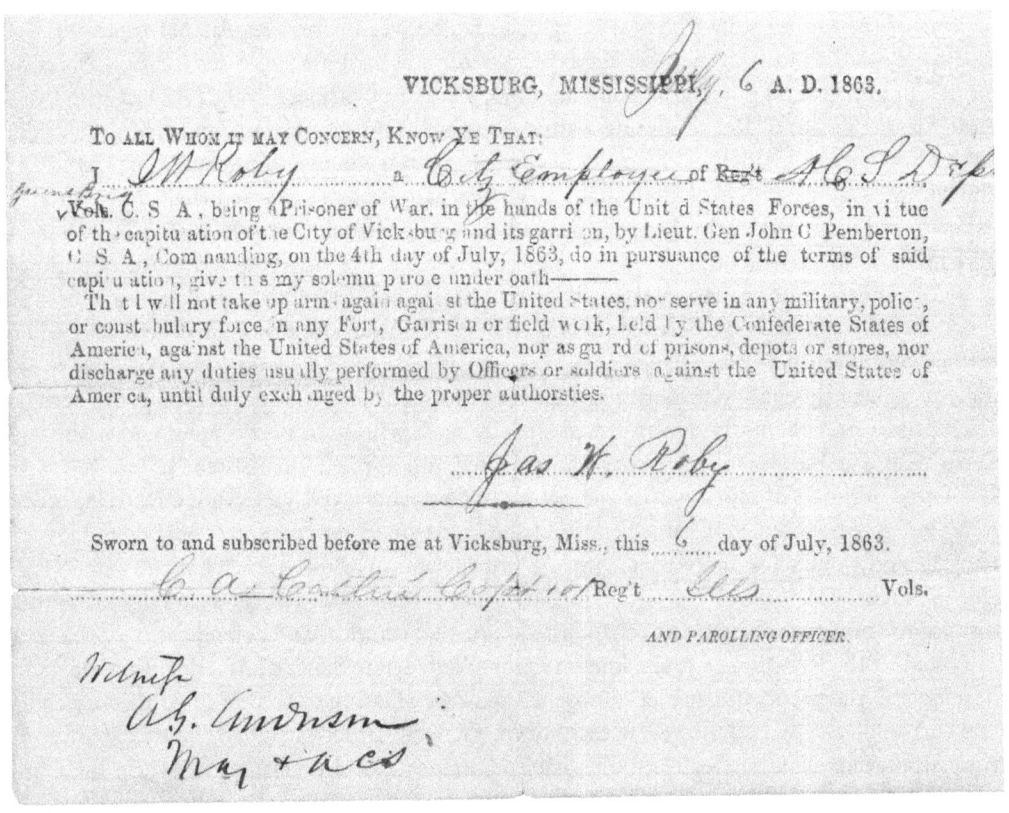

(Fig. 42) Union parole of Confederate prisoner of war at Vicksburg on July 6, 1863. Vicksburg, Mississippi. 6 × 7½ inches. (MS-1.63.03)

Provost Marshal's Office,

6th Division, 16th Army Corps,

Fort Pillow, Tenn., Aug. 22 1863.

I do Solemnly Swear, In the presence of Almighty God, that I will bear true allegiance to the United States of America, and will obey and maintain the Constitution and Laws of the same, and will defend and support the said United States of America against all enemies, foreign and domestic, and especially against the *Rebellious League* known as the Confederate States of America. *So help me God.*

CERTIFICATE:

Sworn and subscribed to before me, this 22 day of Aug. 1863.

Ross Griffin
Capt. Co. G, 52d Ind. Inf. Vols. and Prov. Mar'l.

Residence _____

Age, ___ years; Height, ___ feet ___ inches; Hair, black; Eyes, ___

(Fig. 43) Union oath of Confederate prisoner of war. Fort Pillow, Tennessee. August 22, 1863. 8 × 5⅛ inches. (TN-4.63.02)

prisoners of war, including one major general and seven brigadiers. The reported number of Confederate captured, by rank, was as follows:

Lieutenant General	1
Major General	5
Colonel	186
Lieutenant Colonel	146
Major	244
Captain	2,497
Lieutenant	5,811
Noncommissioned Officer	16,563
Private	121,156
Civilian	5,800[21]

On February 18, 1864, the War Office's General Order No. 64 encouraged more Rebel desertions. Deserters had to assure officials they were sincere in their renouncement of the Confederacy. They no longer would be subject to the Union draft. If their loyalty was accepted, employment at government shops, docks and warehouses was available. Further inducements included transportation within the Federal lines and temporary rations.

After several formerly paroled Rebel prisoners were recaptured and incarcerated in the military prison at Louisville, the army's judge advocate general wasted no time deciding their fate. The judge advocate general, Joseph Holt, instructed Brigadier General Stephen G. Burbridge to "proceed with the utmost promptitude and vigor in bringing these perjured traitors to punishment." Most of these men still had in their possession the actual oaths signed upon their original release. All faced judgment before a military commission. The judge Advocate had firmly stated in his letter that those recaptured should receive the "heaviest chastisement known to the law." Sentence of execution was swift and without hesitation in May 1864.[22]

A number of former Rebels volunteered for military duty on the western frontier, even after being relieved of exposure to the Union draft. About six thousand "turncoats" became "galvanized Yankees," "tranfugees" or "whitewashed Rebs," as labeled in the press. Desertions continued to take a toll on Rebel troop strength and morale. In response the Confederate Bureau of Conscription increased efforts to capture and punish deserters (Fig. 44).

Lieutenant General Grant realized that pardoned Rebels, if recaptured, would probably be executed. That possibility had a chilling effect on the number of Rebel deserters willing to accept amnesty. Accordingly, on August 24, 1864, Grant issued Special Order No. 82, in the field in Virginia, declaring that no "forced military duty or service endangering them to capture by the Confederate Forces" would be imposed on surrendered Rebels. Northern families with draft-aged sons were not pleased with Grant's concern for captured enemy. Many suspected the Rebels were not sincere, and their oaths were only given in exchange for government housing, food and protection.

Guidelines provided by the U.S. War Department in General Order No. 242, of August 8, 1864, clarified rules for those entitled to the benefits of the President's Amnesty Proclamation. The notice was prompted by increasing evidence that some had "fraudulently and treacherously" applied for clemency with no intent to restore peace or respect national authority. Afterward, if any person received amnesty for any purpose other than "restoring peace and establishing the national authority, the benefits would be denied." Amnesty was not intended to protect Rebels from punishment unless they were sincere and forever loyal.

As the year came to a close, Rebel commissary stores became scarce. Many soldiers and civilians surrendered because of hunger and need for medical treatment. At City Point, Virginia, General Grant had to endure the drain on his army's rations. On September 12, 1864,

War Department,
BUREAU OF CONSCRIPTION,
Richmond, _____ 1864.

To Lieut. General T. H HOLMES,

 In charge of Conscription in North Carolina:

  General: The name of Private _____ *Co.* ___, _____ *N. C. Regiment, has been reported to this Bureau as a Deserter, with the information that he will be found in* _____ *county*

You will forthwith proceed to investigate this case, and if absent without proper authority, have him arrested and forwarded to the nearest Provost Marshal, Commandant of Military Post, or Camp of Instruction, to be forwarded to his command.

In this matter you will act promptly and report to this Bureau the result of your action or inquiries.

  By command of the Secretary of War.

    JOHN S. PRESTON,
    Brigadier General and Superintendent.

OFFICIAL:

  A. A. A. General.

NOTE.—The report, if *brief*, may be endorsed on the back of this order. If written on a detached sheet, it should be disconnected from any other subject matter, and in all cases this order must be returned with the report.

(Fig. 44) Confederate Bureau of Conscription notice for deserters in North Carolina. Richmond, Virginia. December 23, 1864. 11 × 8½ inches. (NC-5.64.02)

To all whom it may concern:

Know Ye that I, _____ a _____ of Co. _____ Regiment _____, U.S.A. being a **PRISONER OF WAR** in the hands of the Confederate States Forces, in virtue of the surrender of _____ at _____ on the _____ day of _____ 186__, Do give this **MY SOLEMN PAROLE**, under oath:

That I will not take up arms again against the Confederate States of America, nor serve in any Military, Police, or Constabulary Force, in any Fort, Garrison, or Field Work, held by the United States of America against the Confederate States of America; nor as guard of any prisoners, depots, or stores; nor discharge any duties usually performed by officers or soldiers, against the Confederate States of America, until duly exchanged by proper authorities.

Sworn to & subscribed before me _____ this _____ day of _____, 186__

(Signed in Duplicate.) _____ Co. _____ Reg't _____ C.S.A., **PAROLING OFFICER.**

(Fig. 45) Confederate parole of Union prisoner of war. Hempstead, Texas. December 5, 1864. 9¾ × 6 inches. (TX-1.64.01)

he issued General Order No. 35, Army of the Potomac, stating any citizen within the Federal lines who refused to take the oath of allegiance would be denied government rations and expelled from the protection of the Union enclave. As the war's conclusion became obvious, officials began to appreciate the enormous burden ahead once the enemy was subdued.

Despite suspension of the Dix-Hill Cartel, prisoner exchanges by regional commanders continued. For instance, General Benjamin Butler, at Fort Monroe, successfully accomplished an exchange of three thousand men. Unofficial exchanges also took place in the Trans-Mississippi Department at Camp Ford, in Tyler, and Camp Gore in Hempstead, Texas (Fig. 45). Larger numbers also were exchanged at Charleston and Savannah in early 1864.

Despite the official position, informal exchanges by regional commanders continued. Battlefield exchanges reported included the following:

Date	Officers	Location
July 1, 1863	Franklin-Taylor Cartel	New Iberia, TN
January 21, 1863	Thomas-Johnston Cartel	Chattanooga, TN
August 3, 1863	Blunt-Hindman Cartel	St. Louis, MO
January 4, 1864	Banks-Taylor Cartel	Red River, LA
July 28, 1864	Canby-Smith Cartel	Red River, LA

(Fig. 46) Confederate Special Order for furloughs of Confederate paroled prisoners to report to Richmond or Macon. Richmond, Virginia. January 23, 1865. 6½ × 8¼ inches. (VA-1.65.07)

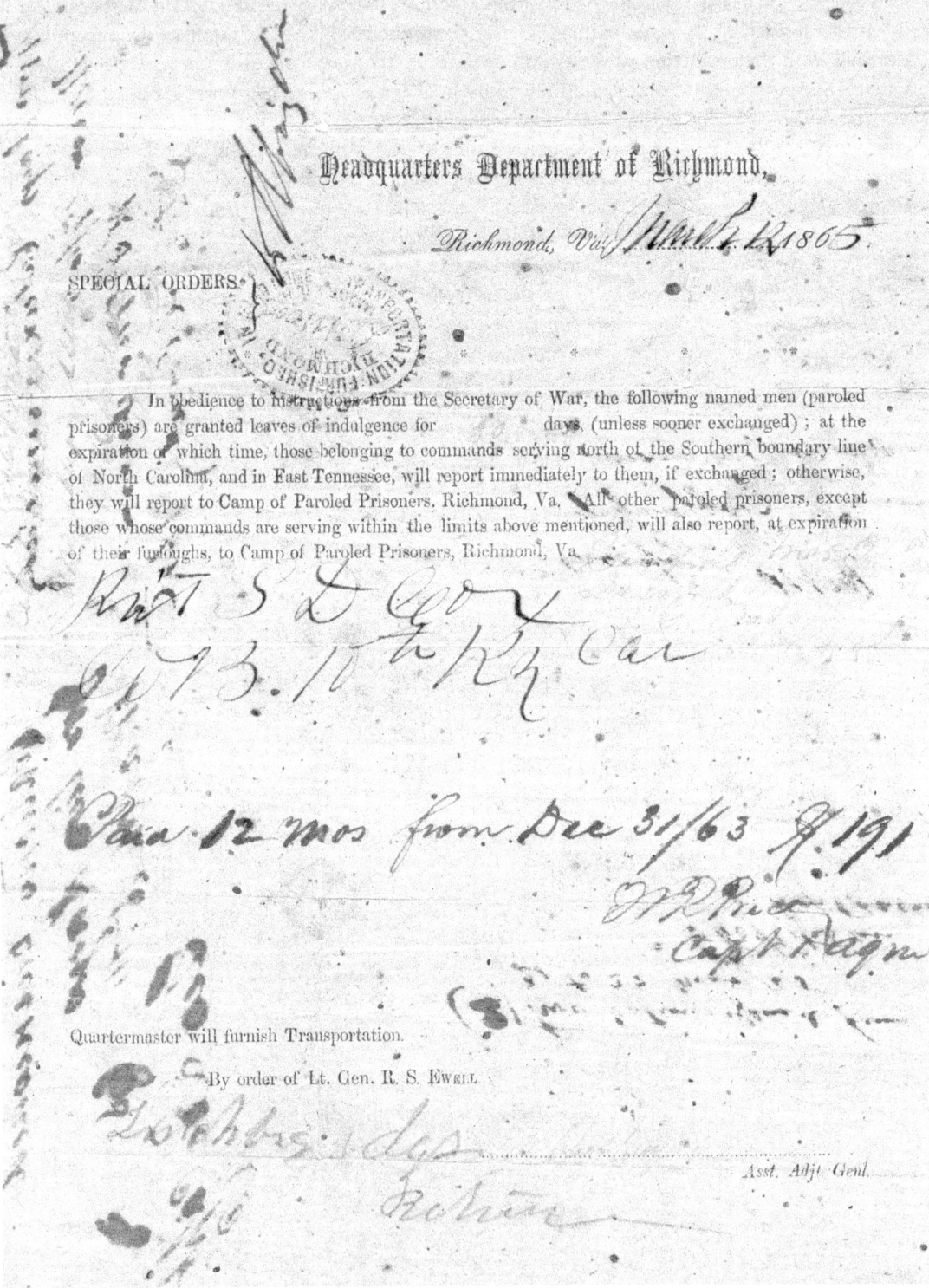

(Fig. 47) Confederate special order granting "leaves of indulgence" for 30 days unless exchanged. Richmond, Virginia. March 12, 1865. 10½ × 8 inches. (VA-1.65.06)

Not until 1865 did Secretary of War Stanton reinstitute formal prisoner exchanges. War Office General Order No. 109, dated January 6, 1865, announced resumption for both enlisted and lower-rank commissioned officers. Grades lower than major in the army and lieutenant in the navy qualified. Employment, subsistence and transportation continued for Rebels willing to desert. According to reports, almost sixty thousand more Confederate prisoners took the oath. Thousands of Union prisoners still remained confined at Andersonville Prison, Georgia. The Confederate Camp of Rebel Paroled Prisoners awaiting exchange in Richmond became so crowded that many were granted furloughs or leaves of indulgence and sent home (Figs. 46 and 47).

Not all prisoners of war were willing to trade oaths for amnesty or even make promises to cease hostilities in return for parole until duly exchanged. Not surprisingly, some of the more resistant were residents of the Border States where emotions ran higher because of the differences of loyalties within neighborhoods and among families. No captive was forced to be exchanged unless the prisoner clearly volunteered. The army's chief, Major General Henry Halleck, wrote the secretary of war on February 17, 1865, "that it was much cheaper to feed an enemy in prison than fight him in the field." Afterward, Halleck recommended that all who did not wish to participate in the prisoner release-exchange program be sent to the military prison in New York.[23]

Less formal exchanges were not preapproved by the adjutant general. Some were never reported. Exchanges that were reported and approved include the following:

Agreements*

Approval	Officers	Location
December 30, 1863	Hurlbut-Forrest	Memphis, TN
May 31, 1864	Dwight-Levy	Red River, LA
July 18, 1864	Dwight-Szymunski	Red River, LA
August 10, 1864	Mulford-Ould	Richmond, VA
August 22, 1864	Dwight-Watts	Mobile, AL
September 10, 1864	Mulford-Ould	City Point, VA
December 1, 1864	Carter-Vaughn	Knoxville, TN
January 6, 1865	Forrest-Washburn	Nashville, TN
February 14, 1865	Mulford-Ould	Varina, VA
February 16, 1865	Forrest-Thomas	Nashville, TN
February 21, 1865	Smith-Watts-Henderson	Huntsville, AL
February 28, 1865	Ord-Longstreet	Army of the James, VA
March 16, 1865	Smith-Watts-Henderson	Vicksburg, MS
April 10, 1865	Grant-Ould	Appomattox, VA

*Compiled from *War of the Rebellion* (ORR), Series II, Volumes 3–8.

6

Paroles on Surrender

The war was coming to an end in late 1864 and more Union converts came forward. By the act of March 2, 1865, Rebel deserters were required first to surrender before being qualified as prisoners of war entitled to amnesty. When the war concluded, almost 32,000 Confederate prisoners had taken the loyalty oath. Tennessee, North Carolina and Arkansas had the greatest number of converts during the war. In areas of relative peace, released prisoners were allowed to live among the loyal citizens after swearing they would, "in the presence of Almighty God," support, protect and defend the Constitution, Congress and proclamations of the president regarding slaves. Personal identification noted on the amnesty document included complexion, hair, eye color, height and age, as well as name, unit and rank (Fig. 48).

The mechanics for administering presidential amnesties became more complex as peace approached. As published in Field Order No. 2, Army of West Mississippi, on March 8, 1865, only commanders of divisions, brigades, districts or posts and their superiors could administer oaths. Applicants had to disclose, under oath, detailed service or aid rendered to the Rebel cause. If any acts were omitted, amnesty was voided. Further, the applicant had to convince authorities that his intent was sincere and that he would loyally support the government of the United States. If the provost marshal was satisfied, the ledger noted the acts disclosed in the petition. All documents were prepared in duplicate, registered and the records were forwarded to Washington.

Final surrender of the Rebel armies in the East occurred over a two-month period beginning in April. Some surrender ceremonies were formal and dignified, others ad hoc. Some Rebel units merely disbanded and went home. A few Rebel commanders discharged their soldiers before sending them home, lessening the trauma of a formal surrender (Fig. 49). Union commanders were advised, in no uncertain terms, by the secretary of war that terms of surrender could not be negotiated—"unconditional surrender" was the only option. The first army to surrender was at Wilmer McLean's residence, across from the Appomattox Court House in Virginia. The armies of Generals U. S. Grant and Robert E. Lee awaited results of a conference on April 9, 1865. General Lee announced in General Order No. 9, dated April 10, 1865, Army of Northern Virginia, Appomattox Courthouse, that after "four years of arduous service" he was "compelled to yield to overwhelming numbers and resources" (Fig. 50).

The previous day Lee and his six staff officers had given their "solemn parole of honor" they would no longer serve in the Rebel army or in any military capacity for the Confederate

Head Quarters U. S. Forces,

1st. Division, Department of Kentucky,

OFFICE PROVOST MARSHAL,

Louisa, Ky., April 13th 1865.

UNITED STATES OF AMERICA, ss.
STATE OF KENTUCKY.

I, _Jos W H Owens_, do solemnly swear, in the presence of Almighty God, that I will henceforth faithfully support, protect and defend the Constitution of the United States, and the Union of the States thereunder; and that I will, in like manner, abide by and faithfully support all acts of Congress passed during the existing rebellion with reference to slaves, so long and so far as not repealed, modified, or held void by Congress, or by decisions of the Supreme Court; and that I will in like manner abide by and faithfully support all proclamations of the President made during the existing rebellion having reference to slaves, so long and so far as not modified or declared void by decision of the Supreme Court: So help me God.

Jos W H Owens

Subscribed and sworn to before me, this _13_ day of _April_, A. D. 1865.

J. W. Ellison
LIEUT. AND PROVOST MARSHAL.

The above named has _Fair_ complexion, _Light_ hair, _Blue_ eyes, and is _5_ feet, _1_ inches high, _24_ years of age.

Last Military Organization: _22 Va Cavalry_

(Fig. 48) Loyalty oath of paroled Confederate. Louisa, Kentucky. April 13, 1865. (KY-4.65.01)

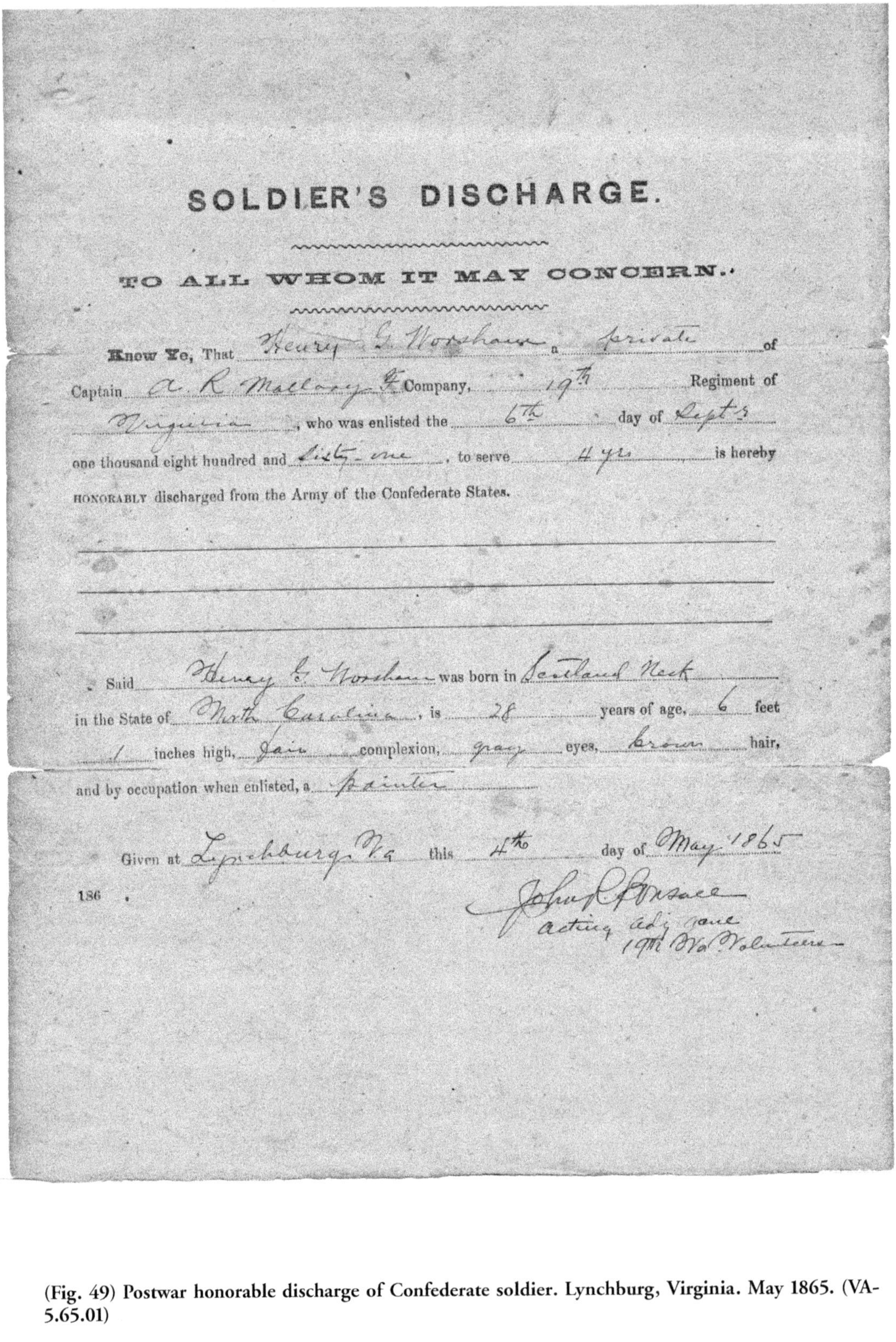

SOLDIER'S DISCHARGE.

TO ALL WHOM IT MAY CONCERN.

Know Ye, That Henry G. Worsham a private of Captain A. R. Mallory's Company, 19th Regiment of Virginia, who was enlisted the 6th day of Sept's one thousand eight hundred and sixty one, to serve 4 yrs is hereby HONORABLY discharged from the Army of the Confederate States.

Said Henry G. Worsham was born in Scotland Neck in the State of North Carolina, is 28 years of age, 6 feet 1 inches high, fair complexion, gray eyes, brown hair, and by occupation when enlisted, a painter.

Given at Lynchburg, Va this 4th day of May 1865.

John R. Forsale
acting adj. vance
19th Va. Volunteers

186

(Fig. 49) Postwar honorable discharge of Confederate soldier. Lynchburg, Virginia. May 1865. (VA-5.65.01)

(Fig. 50) Lee Surrenders to Grant, McLean House, Appomattox C.H. Virginia. April 9, 1865

(Fig. 51) *Harper's Weekly.* "Surrender of Gen. Lee's Army, April 9, 1865." November 4, 1865.

States "until properly exchanged" by respective authorities. All were assured they would "not be disturbed by the United States authorities so long as they observe their parole and the law in force where they may reside," as noted by George H. Sharpe, assistant provost-marshal-general, U.S. Army. Word of the surrender ignited the North. Later, the November 4, 1865 issue of the popular *Harper's Weekly* published illustrations of "Lee's Army" at Appomattox

Court House, April 9, 1865 (Fig. 51). The artist, Colonel Battersby of the First New York Calvary, described the events and formalities in the accompanying text.[1]

Each surrendered soldier received a parole certificate and safeguard pass, dated April 10, 1865, Appomattox Court House, on one of two preprinted forms (Fig. 52). Confederate officers signed paroles for their men. Almost thirty thousand paroles and safeguards printed on field presses were executed (Fig. 53). After presses broke down, remaining forms were completed in manuscript (Fig. 54). The protocol of the surrender negotiated at the initial meeting called for rosters in duplicate and recorded in a register. Officers promised not to take up arms against the government of the United States until properly exchanged, before signing their parole of honor. Next, Confederate arms and artillery were turned over to the Federals. Side arms of officers, private horses and baggage were retained by prisoners. Prior to their departure, the captives received food, passes and necessary medical care.

The next in order to surrender were artillery and cavalry units camped outside Appomattox, where colors and arms were relinquished in solemn ceremonies. For weeks, surrenders followed in Lynchburg, Winchester and Farmville with similar terms. Officers signed paroles of honor at Lynchburg on special forms (Fig. 55).

Federal prisoners held in Rebel prisoner-of-war camps presented a special problem. Safety,

(Fig. 52) Two styles of preprinted parole and safeguard forms. Appomattox Court House, VA. April 10, 1865. (VA-2.65.02)

(Fig. 53) Signed parole and safeguard. Appomattox Court House, VA. April 10, 1865. (VA-2.65.02)

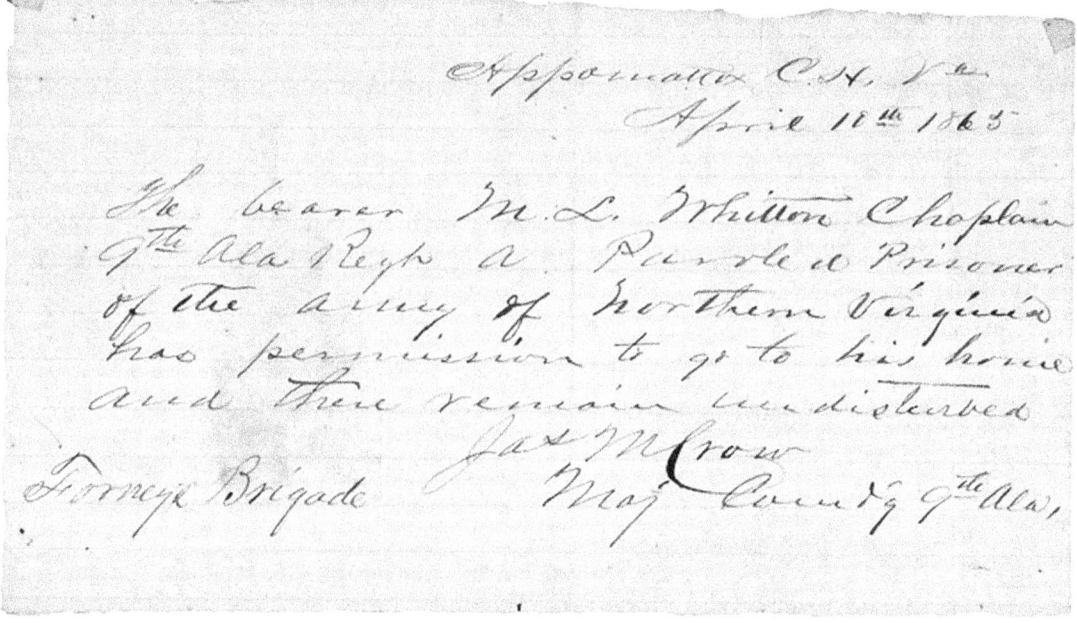

(Fig. 54) Manuscript parole and safeguard. Appomattox Court House, VA. April 10, 1865. (VA-2.65.04)

welfare and security were the primary concerns of Union commanders. Under the convention, Union prisoners were transferred to Camp Parole at Annapolis as provided in General Order No. 42, 24th Army Corps, Appomattox Court House, April 11, 1865. Belongings were forwarded from Rebel prisons to Camp Parole. For months after the peace, items from all across the South were shipped to Annapolis (Fig. 56).

As the two armies wound down at Appomattox, Secretary of War Stanton made it clear no general had "authority to tread on the subject of peace." Lee's surrender affected only his army; all others remained at war. Protocols were soon signed in North Carolina, Alabama, Georgia and Texas after Rebel commands laid down their arms. Paroles and safe passage became standard to the surrender process. In the interim, President Lincoln was assassinated

> We, the undersigned Prisoners of War, belonging to the Army of the Confederate States, having been this day surrendered by General Robert E. Lee, C. S. A., Commanding said Army, to Lieut. Gen. U. S. Grant, Commanding Armies of United States, do hereby give our solemn parole of honor that we will not hereafter serve in the armies of the Confederate States, or in any military capacity whatever, against the United States of America, or render aid to the enemies of the latter, until properly exchanged, in such manner as shall be mutually approved by the respective authorities.
>
> Done at Lynchburg, Va.,
> this   day of April,
> 1865.

(Fig. 55) Parole of honor, POW officer belonging to the army of General R. E. Lee surrendered. Lynchburg, Virginia. April 8, 1865. 3½ × 8 inches. (VA-1.65.09)

at Ford's Theater. For months afterward the nation was in mourning, while uncertainty prevailed.

The second surrender of a Confederate army took place near Durham's Station, North Carolina. At that time, Confederate general Joseph E. Johnston tried to discuss surrender terms with the Union commander, Major General W. T. Sherman. After Sherman began to consider issues other than unconditional surrender he was reprimanded by Secretary Stanton. General Johnston finally agreed, on April 26, to an unconditional surrender (Fig. 57). The provisions were:

1. All acts of war on the part of the troops under General Johnston's command to cease.
2. All arms and public property to be deposited at Greensborough, with an ordnance officer of the United States Army.
3. Rolls of all the officers and men to be made in duplicate, and each will give his individual obligation in writing not to take up arms against the government of the United States until properly released.
4. The side-arms of officers and private horses and baggage to be retained by them.
5. All were permitted to return to home, not to be disturbed by the United States authorities so long as they observe their obligation and the laws in force where they may reside.

The terms of the military convention were approved by Lieutenant General U. S. Grant at Greensboro, the same day.

The Greensboro parole process took a week, and the terms were extended to scattered units across the state. Paroling stations were established at Morganton and Statesville for Rebel cavalry units. Georgia cavalry received paroles from Savannah in May. Likewise, South Carolina Cadets from the Citadel in Charleston were paroled at Augusta in May (Fig. 58). All were allowed to return home peacefully, as long as they observed the terms of their parole and local laws.

Confederate forces in northern Georgia, commanded by General W. T. Wofford, C.S.A, surrendered at Kingston, Georgia, on May 2. His men agreed "not to take up arms against the Government of the United States, until duly exchanged." Afterward, all had permission

> **Head-Quarters, Camp Parole, near Annapolis, Md.,**
> _June 1_, 1865.
>
> *Lieut D C Lewis*
> *14 Regmt N.Y. Vols*
>
> SIR:
>
> Information has been received at this Camp, from BREVET BRIG. GEN. J. E. MULFORD, U. S. Agent for Exchange, that, on the occupation of Richmond, Va., by the Federal forces, a number of packages and boxes were found addressed to Union prisoners of war, confined in Rebel prisons in the South; among which was _One (1) Box_ bearing your address. Be pleased to advise GEN. MULFORD, by mail, (at Richmond, Va.,) as to the disposition you wish to be made of _it_.
>
> _H. H. Fox_
> _Capt and Post Adjutant._

(Fig. 56) Transmittal letter for packages and boxes forwarded to Union POWs, Camp Parole, Annapolis, Maryland. June 1, 1865. 9 × 8¼ inches. (MD-5.65.02)

to go home and not be disturbed as long as the conditions for the parole were observed and laws in effect on January 1, 1861 were not violated (Fig. 59). Similar ceremonies took place in Griffin, Augusta and Macon soon thereafter.

The next army to surrender was Confederate general Richard Taylor's Department of Alabama, Mississippi and East Louisiana. On May 4 at Citronelle, Alabama, Major General E. R. S. Canby, U.S. Army, dictated terms to General Taylor. Officers signed paroles of honor (Fig. 60). The conditions, finalized on May 8 were more detailed than earlier conventions:

> GREENSBORO', NORTH CAROLINA,
> May 5, 1865.
>
> In accordance with the terms of the Military Convention, entered into on the twenty sixth day of April, 1865, between General Joseph E. Johnston, Commanding the Confederate Army, and Major-General W. T. Sherman, Commanding the United States Army in North-Carolina, *Pvt S J Johnson Co K's Art attached 22 Va Batt* has given his solemn obligation not to take up arms against the Government of the United States until properly released from this obligation; and is permitted to return to his home, not to be disturbed by the United States authorities so long as he observe this obligation and obey the laws in force where he may reside.
>
> Fris C Dow
> Maj + A.D.C. U.S.A.,
> Special Commissioner.
>
> .... C.S.A.,
> Commanding.

(Fig. 57) Parole and safeguard under military convention of April 26, 1865, between General J. E. Johnston, C.S.A. and Maj. Gen. W. T. Sherman, U.S.A. Greensboro, North Carolina. May 5, 1865. (NC-2.65.01)

> **Office Provost Marshal,**
> DISTRICT OF SAVANNAH,
> May 9, 1865.
>
> In accordance with the terms of a Military Convention held on the 26th day of April, 1865, in the State of North Carolina, between Maj. Gen. W. T. Sherman, commanding U. S. Forces, and Gen. Joseph E. Johnson, commanding Confederate Forces, I hereby obligate myself not to take up arms against the Government of the United States, until properly released from this obligation, having been a *Captain* in the *Fifth* Regiment of *Ga. Cav.* Vols., in Gen. Johnson's command.
>
> Given the *Ninth* day of *May* 1865.
>
> H. A. Strobhar
>
> By command of Brevet Maj. Gen. GROVER.
>
> Lt. Col. 75th N. Y. V. Vols.,
> **Provost Marshal, District of Savannah.**

(Fig. 58) Parole under military convention of April 26, 1865. District of Savannah, Georgia. May 9, 1865. 5½ × 9 inches. (GA-4.65.01)

1. The officers and men were to be paroled until duly exchanged or otherwise released from the obligations of their parole by the authority of the Government of the United States. Duplicate rolls of all officers and men surrendered were to be made, one copy of which will be delivered to the officer appointed by Major-General Canby and the other retained by the officer appointed by Lieutenant-General Taylor; officers giving their individual paroles and commanders of regiments for the men.
2. Artillery, small-arms, ammunition, and such other property of the Confederate Government were to be turned over to Government of the United States. Duplicate inventories of the property surrendered were to be prepared, one copy to be retained by the officer delivering and the other by the officer receiving.
3. The officers and men paroled under this agreement were allowed to return home, with the assurance that they will not be disturbed by the authorities of the United States so long as they continue to observe the conditions of their paroles and the laws in force where they reside, except those persons residing in Northern States.
4. The surrender of property will not include the side arms, private horses or baggage of officers.
5. All horses which are, in good faith, the private property of enlisted men will not be taken.
6. The time and place of surrender will be fixed by respective commanders, and will be carried out by the commissioners appointed.
7. The terms and conditions of the surrender of the armies lately commanded by Generals Lee and Johnston, will apply.
8. Transportation and subsistence will be furnished at public cost.

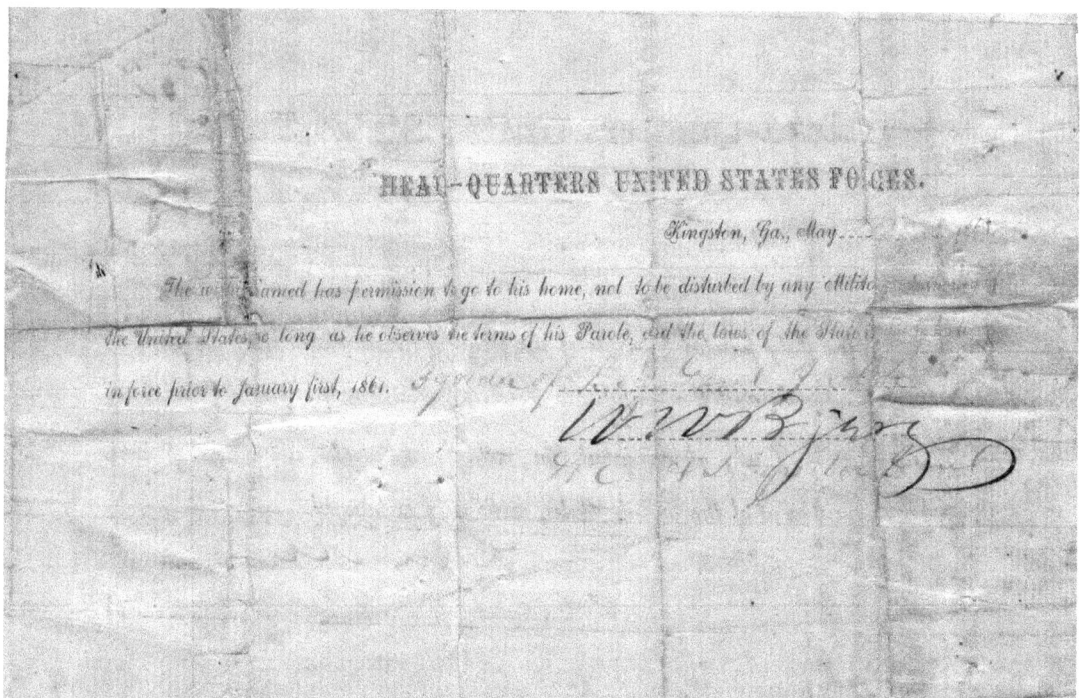

(Fig. 59) Parole under terms of surrender of Confederate forces of northern Georgia on May 2, 1865. Kingston, Georgia. May 2, 1865. (GA-1.65.01)

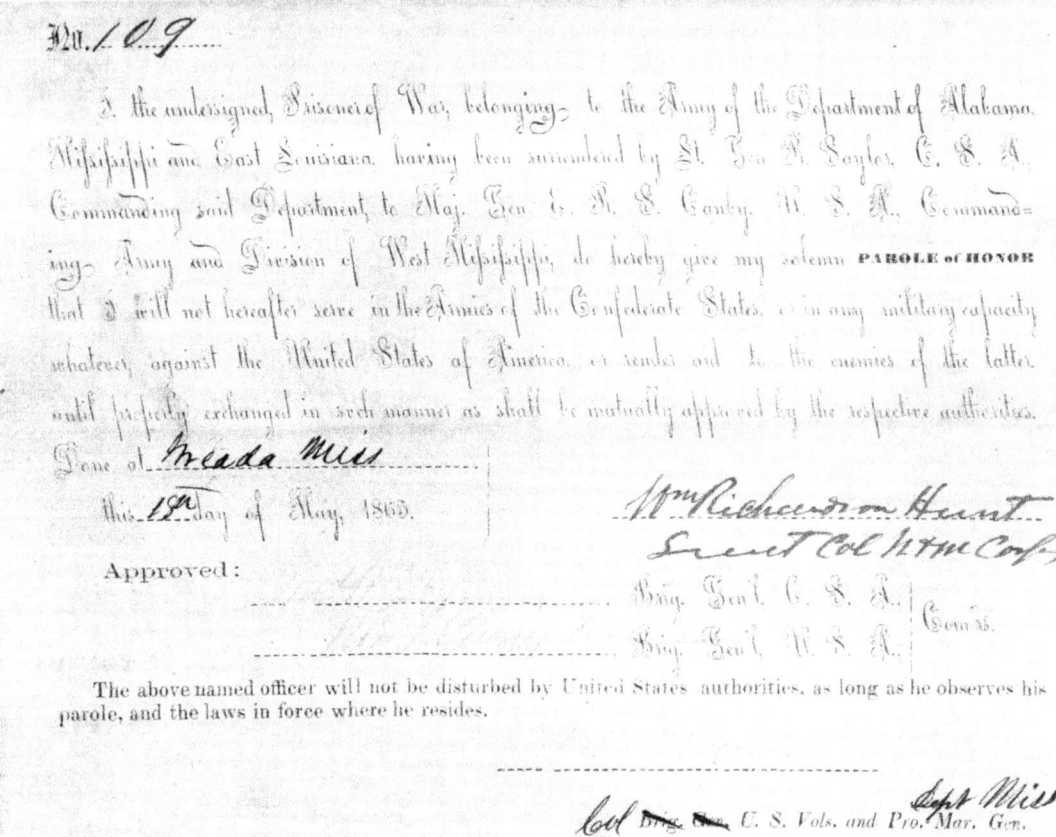

(Fig. 60) Parole of honor and safeguard for surrender of Department of Alabama, Mississippi and East Louisiana of May 4, 1865. Columbus, Mississippi. May 16, 1865. 9½ × 7¼ inches. (MS-1.65.02)

More than 42,000 men of General Taylor's army were paroled at nine locations: Citronelle, Mobile, Gainesville, Demopolis, Selma and Montgomery, Alabama; and in Mississippi at Meridian, Columbus, Jackson and Grenada. Duplicates of the Citronelle surrender agreement, identified by the heading "Memorandum," were dispatched to the nine field commands as evidence of the terms. The officers received "paroles of honor" while "certificates of parole" were given to enlisted men. All received safeguard passes and transportation in kind (Fig. 61).

Lieutenant General Nathan B. Forrest, C.S.A., never formally surrendered. He disbanded his cavalry near Selma, Alabama, on May 9. The next day, near Tallahassee, Florida, Major General Samuel Jones surrendered the Department of South Georgia and Florida to Brigadier General Edward M. McCook under terms similar to the Virginia and North Carolina conventions. On May 11, General Jeff Thompson delivered almost eight thousand men of the Northern Subdistrict of Arkansas who had raided from the Arkansas River to Iowa (Fig. 62). Paroles were issued to these irregular troops by order of Major General J. J. Reynolds, Headquarters, Department of Arkansas at Little Rock. Other small commands were processed in Tennessee, Kentucky and Missouri.

After the Rebel surrenders in the eastern theatre were completed, the tenor changed. General Grant announced in War Department General Order No. 90, on May 11, that Rebels would no longer be considered covered by the Articles of War. After June 1, any "found in arms against the United States, or who may commit hostility against it east of the Mississippi River, will be regarded as guerrillas, and punished with death."

After weeks of negotiations by western commissioners, General E. Kirby Smith, C.S.A., surrendered his Army of the Trans-Mississippi to Major General E. R. S. Canby, U.S. Army, on May 26 at New Orleans. The convention had nine points, the most detailed of all the cartels. The surrender, covering both soldiers and sailors, provided:

1. All acts of war and resistance against the United States shall cease from this date.
2. The officers and men are paroled until duly exchanged, or otherwise released from the obligation of their parole by the authority of the Government of the United States. Duplicate rolls of all paroled will be retained by both parties.
3. Artillery, small arms, ammunition and other property of the Confederate States, including gunboats and transports, will be turned over to the Government of the United States and duplicates will be maintained by both parties.
4. The officers and men will be allowed to return home, with the assurance that they will not be disturbed by the authorities of the United States as long as they continue to observe the conditions of their parole and the laws in force where they reside; except that persons resident in the Northern States; and not excepted in the amnesty proclamation of the PRESIDENT, may return to their homes on taking the oath of allegiance to the United States.
5. The surrender of property will not include the side-arms, or private horses, or baggage of officers.
6. All horses, which are, in good faith, the private property of enlisted men, will not be taken.

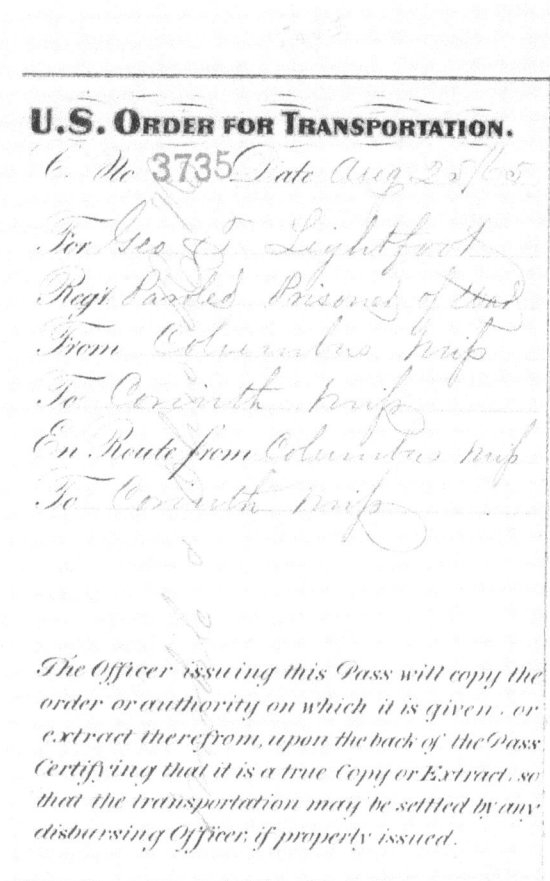

(Fig. 61) U.S. order for transportation of paroled prisoner of war to Corinth from Columbus, Mississippi. August 25, 1865. 5½ × 3½ inches. (MS-5.65.05)

Headquarters Dept. of Arkansas,

Little Rock, Ark June 8th 1865.

I Certify, That Jenks Brown Pvt of Pulaski county, State of Ark is this day paroled on oath "not to take up arms against the Government of the United States until properly exchanged." He is permitted to return to his home, there to remain; not to be disturbed by United States authorities, so long as he observes his parole, the laws of the Government, and those in force where he may reside.

Done by order of MAJ. GEN. REYNOLDS.

L. S. Nash

Capt. & Asst. Provost Marshal General Department of Arkansas.

(Fig. 62) Parole and safeguard of confederate prisoner of war of Northern District of Arkansas surrendered on May 11, 1865. Little Rock, Arkansas. June 8, 1865. 7 × 5½ inches. (AR-1.65.02)

No. 133

I, the undersigned, Prisoner of War, belonging to the Army of the Trans-Mississippi Department, having been surrendered by Gen. E. Kirby Smith, C. S. A., Commanding said Department, to Maj. General E. R. S. Canby, U. S. A., Commanding Army and Division of West Mississippi, do hereby give my solemn Parole of Honor, that I will not hereafter serve in the Armies of the Confederate States, or in any military capacity whatever, against the United States of America, or render aid to the enemies of the latter, until duly exchanged, or otherwise released from the obligations of this parole by the authority of the Government of the United States.

J. R. Brophy,
B Co. 16" T V I

Done at Brenham, Texas, this 31 day of July 1865.

No. 88

Brenham, Texas, July 31 1865.

J R Brophy a Musi of B Company 16th Regiment Tex Inf C.S.A., residing in Washington Co Tex having been, with the approval of the proper authorities, Paroled, is permitted to return to his home, not to be disturbed by the United States authorities, so long as he observes his parole and the laws in force where he may reside.

By order
Maj. Gen'l Granger, U. S. A.
J S Post
Captain & Provost Marshal

(Fig. 63) Parole of honor and safeguard of prisoner of war of the Army of the Trans-Mississippi surrendered May 26, 1865. Brenham, Texas. July 31, 1865. 11 × 7½ inches. (TX-1.65.03)

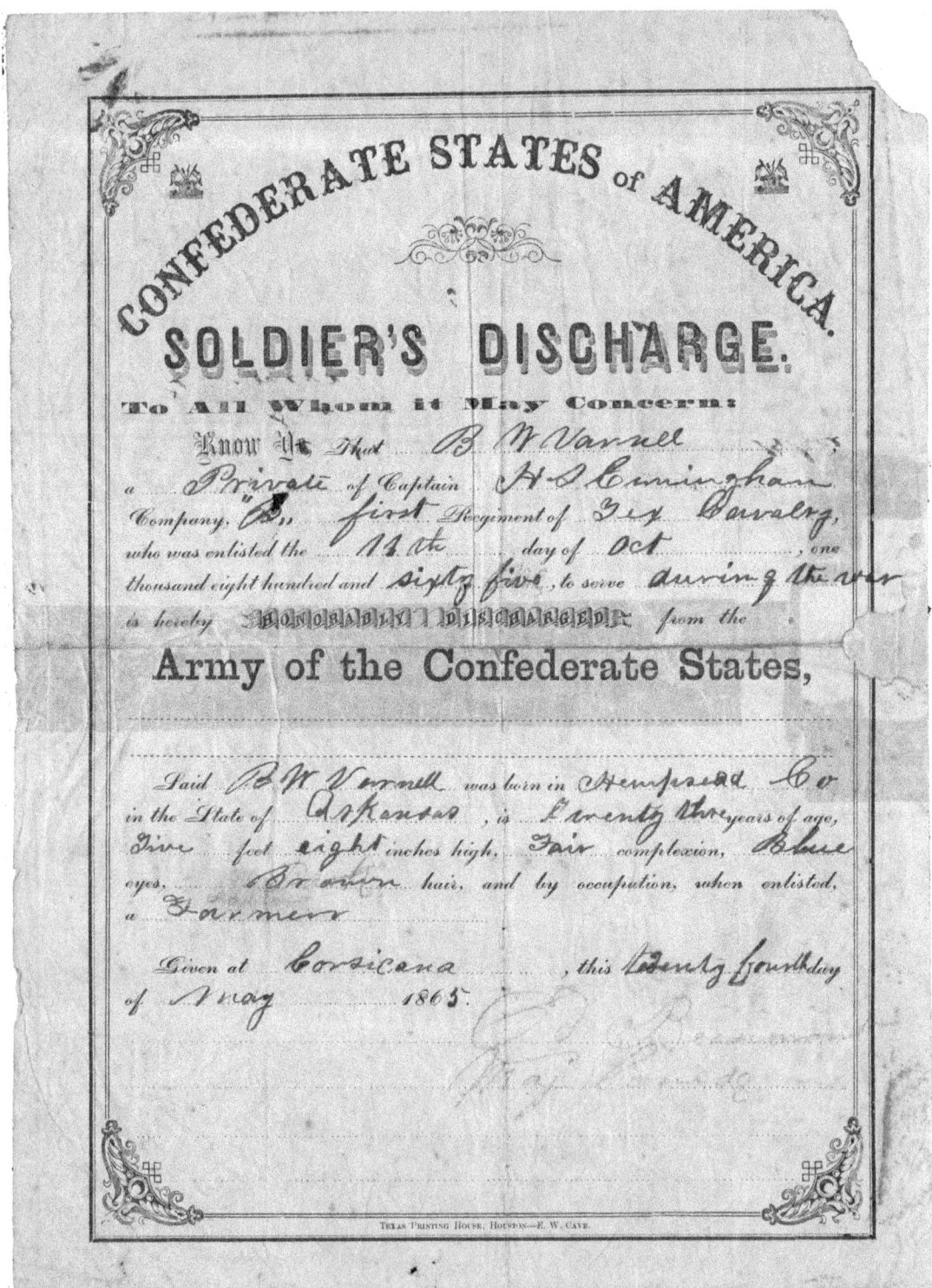

(Fig. 64) Confederate soldier's discharge from Texas Cavalry. Corsicana, Texas. May 24, 1865. 10½ × 8 inches. (TX-5.65.01)

7. The time, mode, and place of paroling and surrender of property will be fixed by the respective commanders, and will be carried out by commissioners appointed by them.
8. The terms and conditions of this convention will extend to all officers and men of the army and navy of the Confederate States, belonging to the Trans-Mississippi Department.
9. Transportation and subsistence will be furnished at public cost to the nearest practicable point near their homes.

From Houston, Confederate general Kirby Smith sent word to New Orleans, on May 30, that his Department was ready for occupation by United States forces. The final ceremony took place aboard the USS *Fort Jackson* in Galveston Bay on June 2, but General Smith was absent. He, along with the governors of Texas and Missouri, had already departed for Mexico ahead of the Federal occupying army. Only at Houston and Brownsville were formal surrenders conducted. The surrenders continued through July (Fig. 63). Most Confederate troops merely disbanded or were discharged by their regimental commanders prior to surrender and occupation (Fig. 64). Smaller informal ceremonies continued through June in Louisiana at Shreveport, Monroe, Washington, Franklin, New Iberia, Natchitoches, Alexandria and New Orleans,

(Fig. 65) Safeguard for member of Louisiana Cavalry, surrendered and paroled at Natchitoches, Louisiana. June 12, 1865. 5¾ × 9 inches. (LA-1.65.02)

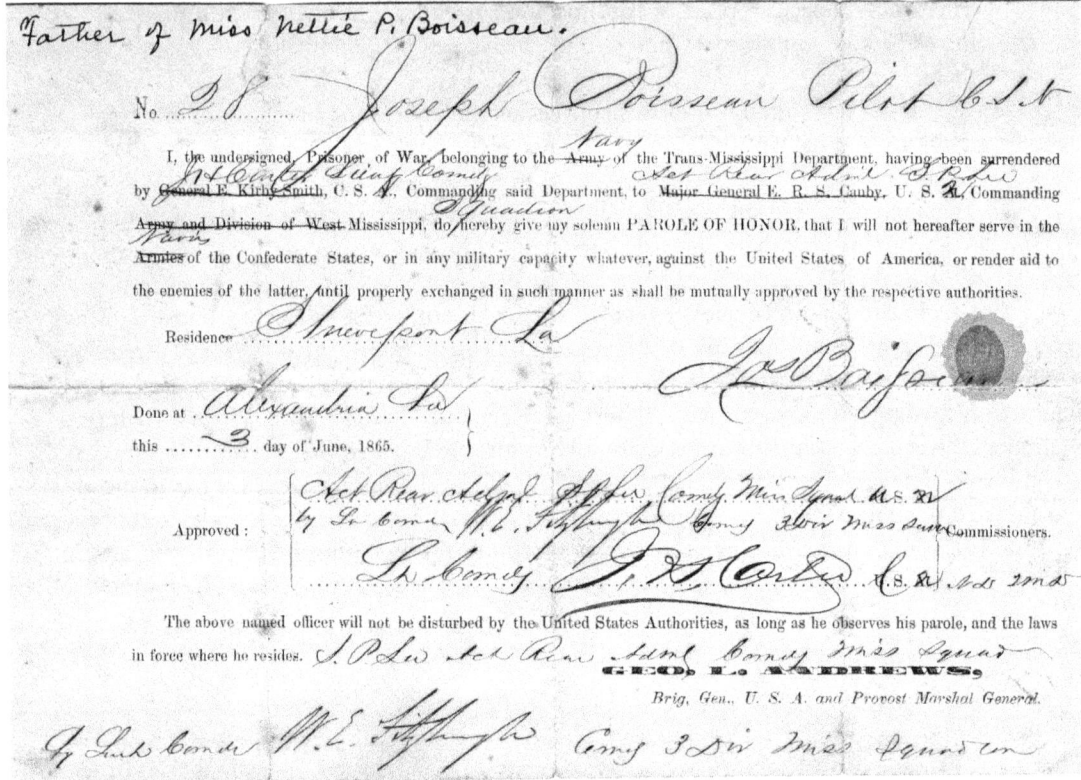

(Fig. 66) Parole of honor of Confederate Navy pilot and Safeguard. Alexandria, Louisiana. June 3, 1865. 5¾ × 9 inches. (LA-1.65.01)

under federal oversight (Fig. 65). Confederate naval personnel operating on the Mississippi River were also surrendered one ship at a time (Fig. 66).

Word of the surrenders finally reached the Indian Territory. Leaders of the tribal nations supporting the Confederates requested a peace commission with federal officials. Technically, their members were neither citizens of the United States nor of the Confederate States, and were on a different standing than the Rebels. On June 23, the governor of the Chickasaws and principal chief of the Choctaws met with the commanding general of the Territory Division of the Trans-Mississippi Army, General Stand Waite, C.S.A., a Native American, who agreed to surrender his division to Lieutenant Colonel A. C. Matthews, U.S. Army, at Doakville in the Indian Territory.

Not until April 28, 1866, was "permanent peace and friendship" between the United States and the Choctaw and Chickasaw Nations diplomatically restored. Treaties followed for the Creeks and Cherokees on June 14 and July 19, respectively. These were the only peace treaties associated with the Civil War. President Andrew Johnson afterward proclaimed a "universal amnesty" for all tribal members for offenses committed against the United States in return for their agreement to forever abolish and outlaw slavery. This was a sharper conclusion of the Rebellion than experienced by the balance of the Confederacy, which was never covered by any peace treaty.

A report produced by the United States commissary general of prisoners, dated November 22, 1865, recapitulated the number of surrenders filed with the U.S. parole commissioner,

Provost Marshal General George L. Andrews. Although almost 175,000 individual surrenders were reported, many Rebels were omitted because they had elected to avoid capture and escaped. Included below are both formal and informal surrenders through the date of the report; not included are individual paroles granted after that date:

Army of Alabama Surrender	42,293
Army of North Carolina Surrender	31,243
Army of Northern Virginia Surrender	27,805
Army of Trans-Mississippi Surrender	17,686
Army of Missouri Surrender	7,978
Nashville and Chattanooga Surrender	5,029
Paroled in Virginia	9,072
Paroled in Cumberland, Maryland	9,377
Paroled in Alabama and Florida	6,428
Paroled in Department of Washington	3,390
Paroled in Virginia, Tennessee, Georgia, Alabama, Louisiana and Texas	13,992
Total Surrendered and Paroled	**174,223**

7

Postwar Amnesty

For four arduous years, President Lincoln invested all to save the Union. Pardons and amnesty seemed to herald his hope of national reconciliation. After his assassination, efforts halted after emotions flared. Policy was at a standstill. The War Department, by General Order No. 69 on April 17, 1865, closed for the funeral of the late President. All flags flew at half-staff, while 21-gun salutes were fired from all forts, posts and ships of the fleet (Fig. 67). The government resumed when the military commission opened to hear the case of the accused assassins. The nation remained in mourning for a year.

When news of President Lincoln's assassination reached California, a gathering of mourners took to the streets of San Francisco. Crowds gathered outside the offices of newspapers considered disloyal. Before police could arrive, a crowd of about 50 destroyed the *Democratic Press*. Another group of rowdies trashed the press of Englishman Frederick Marriott's *New Letter*. Officers managed to save the disloyal *Catholic Monitor* and the *Echo du Pacifique*. Finally, the district commander spoke to the citizens admitting he should have suppressed some of the disunion newspapers, but urged a return to order for now. Two other papers were later stoned by the unruly mob. Both the *Occidental* and the *La Voz de Mejico* were lost. The latter was not disloyal, but being a foreign press, sadly it was mistakenly believed to be so. No arrests were made after the army restored order. The state legislature was chiefly Republican and ratified the amendment to the Constitution abolishing slavery on December 18, 1865.[1]

The secretary of war, on May 8, announced in General Order No. 85 that Rebels held at Richmond, after taking the oath, could go home without a formal exchange. Prison-camp commanders administered oaths of allegiance. The early release was not available to ranking Rebel officers, since their degree of culpability was assumed to be equal to their rank.

War Department Special Order No. 211, of May 6, 1865, appointed Major General David Hunter as president of the nine-member military commission considering the evidence against the accused presidential assassins. The tribunal commenced on May 13 and concluded seven weeks later. Guilty findings were approved on July 5 by President Johnson, and the four executions were carried out two days later. None, however, were charged with or convicted of treason. Jefferson Davis was captured on May 10 in Georgia and transported in chains to Fort Monroe, Virginia, where he was held in solitary confinement. Confederate vice president Alexander H. Stephens was imprisoned at Fort Warren in Boston Harbor. A few Rebel officials escaped to Cuba, Brazil, England and Mexico; some not to return for a decade.

Cases heard by military commissions increased during the first half of 1865. After the

GENERAL ORDERS, }   WAR DEPARTMENT,
　　　　　　　　　　　ADJUTANT GENERAL'S OFFICE,
No. 69.   }   Washington, April 17, 1865.

By direction of the President of the United States, the War Department will be closed on Wednesday next, the day of the funeral of the late President of the United States.

Labor on that day will be suspended at all military posts, and on all public works under the direction of the War Department. The flags at all military posts, stations, forts, and buildings, will be kept at half-staff during the day, and at 12 o'clock, meridian, twenty-one minute guns will be fired from all forts, and at all military posts, and at the Military Academy.

BY ORDER OF THE SECRETARY OF WAR:

　　　　　　　　　　　　　W. A. NICHOLS,
　　　　　　　　　　　　　Assistant Adjutant General.

OFFICIAL:

　　　　　　　　　Assistant Adjutant General.

(Fig. 67) War Department General Order No. 69 closing all offices for funeral of president. Order outlined in black. Washington. April 17, 1865. 7 × 5 inches. (DC-5.65.02)

Lincoln assassination trial, the trial of the former commandant of the Confederate prison at Andersonville, Georgia, Captain Henry Wirz, was the most noteworthy. Before these two high-profile cases, attorney general James Speed had advised President Johnson on the subject of jurisdiction of military tribunals. The Attorney General began his opinion by stating that in times of civil war, "secret enemies" were almost as active as open combatants and the laws of civilized nations allowed the taking of human life without legal process during such times. For example, "Jayhawkers" and "highway bandits" were also punishable "public enemies," as were "secret enemies," such as traitors and members of subversive organizations. These enemies were all engaged in activities contrary to the laws of war and nature. Persons breaking laws of war, as practiced by civilized nations, the attorney general advised, should be tried before military rather than civil tribunals. He further stated that it would be "palpably wrong for the military to hand [public enemies] over to the civil courts as it would be wrong in a civil court to convict a man of murder, who had in time of war, killed another in battle." Later in the year, the U.S. Supreme Court declined to hear an appeal of the conviction, by a military commission, of several Indiana conspirators accused of treason. President Johnson eventually pardoned those prisoners.[2]

The same day Jefferson Davis was captured, President Johnson declared that "the armed resistance to the authority of the Government in the said insurrection States may be regarded as virtually at an end." Soon, southern ports, post offices and customshouses reopened under the American flag. Courts and state legislatures remained closed while Congress debated the course of Reconstruction. Radicals argued for stringent military rule of the defeated states. Senator Benjamin Wade of Ohio and Representative Henry Winter Davis of Maryland proposed military governorships during Reconstruction. Other proposals included "ironclad" oaths, denial of the right to vote to former Rebels, and repudiation of all Confederate debt. Failing to gain sufficient votes for passage, the Wade-Davis proposal remained at the forefront of the Radical policy agenda.

As the war approached its end, President Johnson, asked his Attorney general, James Speed, on April 21, 1865, to determine if Lincoln's amnesty proclamation was sufficient for postwar use. The president, on May 9, declared the war in the eastern theater at an end. The attorney general advised President Johnson that another pronouncement was in order. President Lincoln's first amnesty, issued December 8, 1863, had only excepted Confederate politicians and military leaders from clemency. Somewhat less than one thousand Confederates were excluded from the benefits of the first amnesty, and even those could request presidential pardons. As before, outside of the clemency of the amnesty offer were persons awaiting trial by civil and military authorities. On March 26, 1864, President Lincoln had extended clemency to Rebel prisoners of war. All those that requested Lincoln's amnesty had to swear to "the purpose of restoring peace and establishing the national authority."

President Lincoln's approach for Reconstruction had required only faithful loyalty for restoration to full citizenship. President Johnson wanted assurance of both past and future loyalty before allowing those deemed "treasonable" back into the Union. Both presidents supported the "10 percent" majority rule to elect congressmen for occupied Louisiana, Arkansas and Tennessee. The "10 percent" rule was a political ploy rather than a constitutionally based Reconstruction doctrine.

President Johnson announced a more gradual approach in the General Amnesty Proclamation of May 29, 1865. He forgave all but 14 excluded classes, if sincere. Oaths could be administered by any federal official, including military officers, tax collectors and postmasters. Within months, sixty thousand Rebel prisoners were repatriated. The oath, although carefully worded, was simple — a solemn promise to support and defend the Constitution, laws and proclamations concerning the emancipation of slaves. All oaths closed with "So help me God." Confederate veterans reluctantly took the oath — referring to it as having "to swallow the dog" (Fig. 68).

President Johnson's 14 exclusions from amnesty included high-ranking Rebel officials, those who had resigned from federal office to support the Rebellion, and wealthy southerners. Wealth was defined as more than $20,000 as measured in 1860. This definition excluded planters and businessmen even though they were now bankrupt. In contrast, Lincoln had only six exclusionary classes in his amnesty of March 2, 1864. Rebels unqualified for amnesty still could apply for a presidential pardon, but that procedure took time, money and was discretionary. Presidential pardons over time became simpler, but sincerity was always the overriding concern.

Rebel deserters could not receive amnesty because of a law passed on March 2, 1865, that provided that they surrender before taking the oath. Prison camps holding Rebel military populations were: Point Lookout, Maryland; Newport News, Virginia; Hart's Island, New York; Elmira, New York; Camp Chase, Ohio; Camp Morton, Indiana; Camp Douglas,

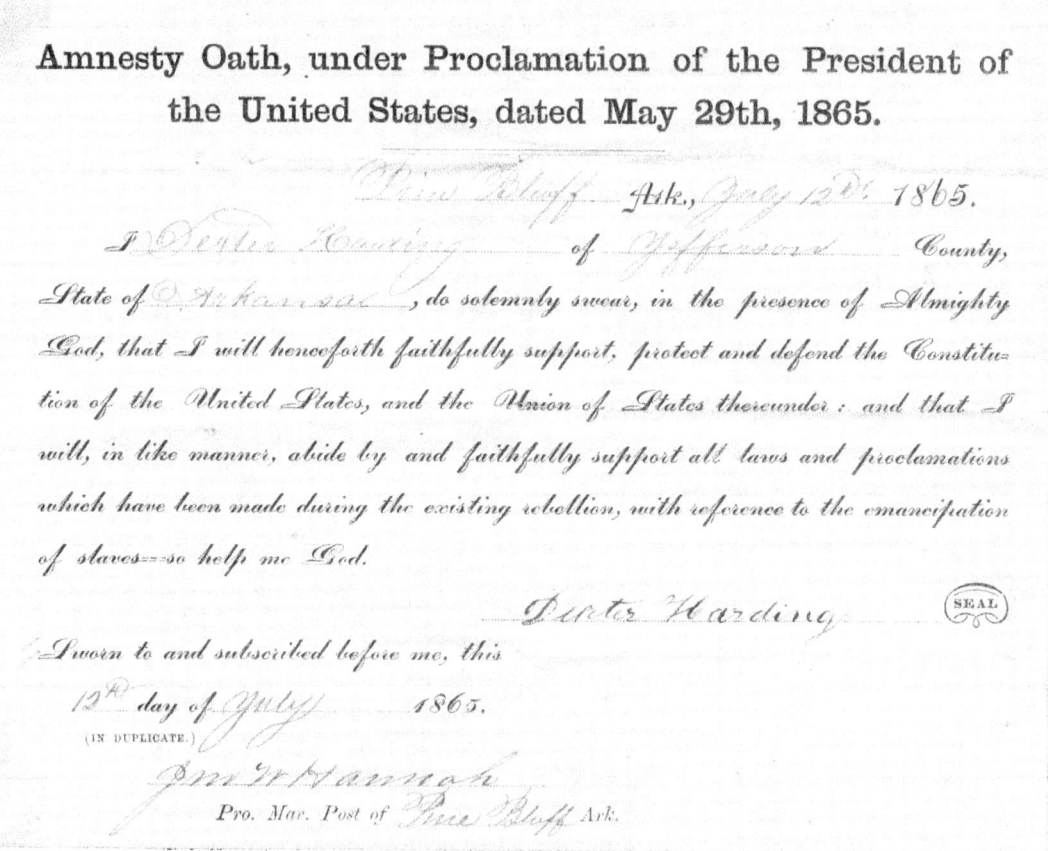

(Fig. 68) Amnesty Oath under proclamation of the president, dated May 29, 1865. Pine Bluff, Arkansas. July 12, 1865. 7 × 8 inches. (AR-4.65.03)

Chicago; Rock Island, Illinois; Alton, Illinois; Fort Delaware; and Old Capitol Prison, District of Columbia. Political prisoners were segregated at Fort Pulaski, Fort Monroe, Fort Warren and Fort Lafayette. On May 28, President Johnson announced, through War Department General Order No. 98, that "all cases of sentences by Military Tribunals of imprisonment during the war" were remitted and the prisoners released. However, those charged with treason or serious felonies were beyond the provisions of that order of remission.

Confined in the political prison at Fort Pulaski, Georgia, located at the mouth of the Savannah River, were most of the high-ranking Rebel officials, all of whom were outside the Amnesty Proclamation:

> George A. Trenholm —(South Carolina) Secretary of Treasury
> (Confined June 5, 1865)
> R. M. T. Hunter —(Virginia) Secretary of State
> (Confined June 5, 1865)
> J. A. Campbell —(Alabama) Assistant Secretary of War
> (Confined June 5, 1865)
> James A. Seddon —(Alabama) Secretary of War
> (Confined June 5, 1865)
> A. G. Magrath — Governor of South Carolina
> (Confined June 11, 1865)
> A. B. Moore — Governor of Alabama
> (Confined June 15, 1865)
> A. R. Allison — Governor of Florida
> (Confined June 19, 1865)
> Charles Clark — Governor of Florida
> (Confined June 25, 1865)

The War Department reported 98,802 Rebel soldiers under control of the commissary general of prisoners, of which 33,127 were exchanged. Detainees released after becoming "galvanized Yankees" numbered only 1,955. The largest number, 63,442, were simply released after surrender and parole. Most "prisoners of war" were confined at Point Lookout, Maryland, and eventually received amnesty (Fig. 69).

The commissary general of prisoners devised a prisoner-release plan to commence after May 31, 1865. His goal was the release of 50 prisoners a day per prison. All prisoners would take the oath of allegiance prior to being issued a parole and safeguard pass. The prisoners would be released in alphabetical order, saving the rank of general until last. All those awaiting charges would be held back. Initially, there were 17 military prisons still housing more than fifty thousand men and the plan was to empty these facilities in about two months. The five thousand Confederate officers who were prisoners were to be paroled on a case-by-case basis. Approximately one thousand civilian political prisoners also remained. By June 15, 1865, a total of 53,679 more men had been released since the start of the process on April 15. Brigadier General W. Hoffman, on June 16, suggested that, unless awaiting trial, all civilians still held in military prisons be released. On July 20, President Johnson directed that all prisoners of war, except those captured with Jefferson Davis, or others held for special reasons, be discharged after they took the oath of allegiance to the United States and proved good behavior.[3]

President Johnson next turned to the civilian population of the former Rebel states. On July 24, the president informed the former Georgia governor, Joseph E. Brown, that he would permit, as soon as possible, persons to be appointed in that state to administer amnesty oaths

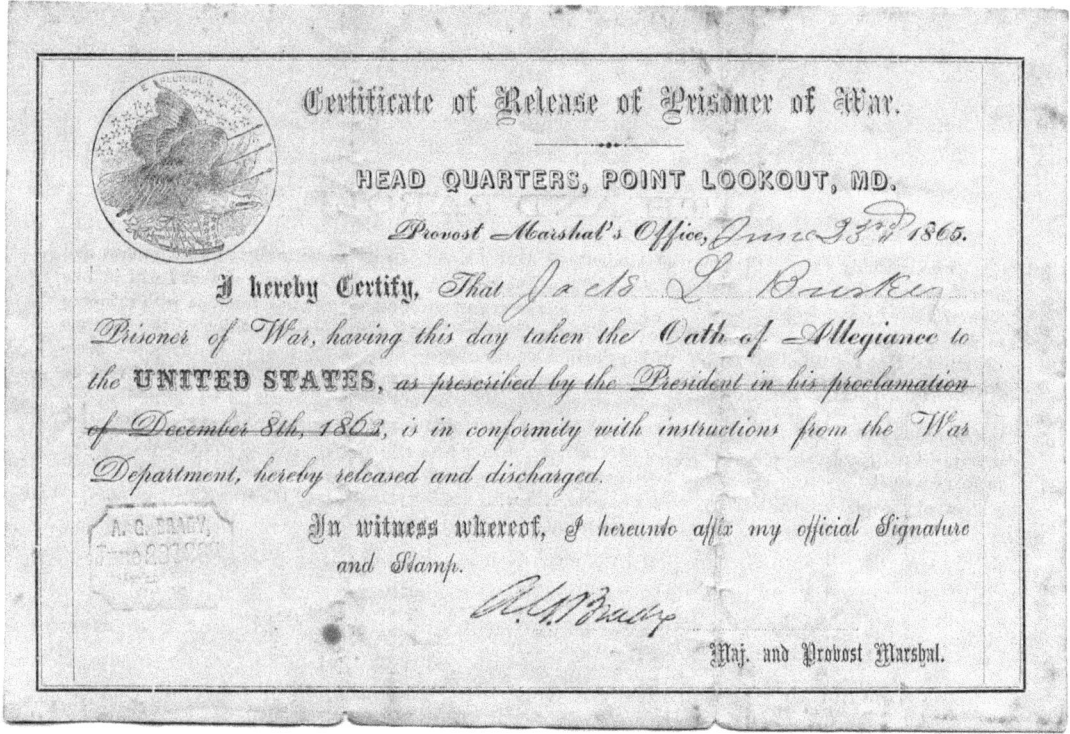

(Fig. 69) Certificate of Release of POW. Point Lookout, Maryland. June 23, 1865. Note: Presidential Proclamation date of December 8. 1863, crossed out. (MD-1.65.01)

to all adults. Any civil or military official loyal to the United States government would qualify to receive the oath. The president expressed his appreciation to the people of Georgia for their prompt restoration of civil authority. He further stated to Governor Brown that he hoped for complete success for his state's return to the Union. The last political prisoners were finally released from military prison in March of 1866. Jefferson Davis remained confined until May 13, 1867. On that day, President Johnson instructed the warden at Fort Monroe to comply with a writ for Davis's release issued by Judge John Underwood of the Richmond circuit court.[4]

Former Confederate states slowly began to assume self-rule. Tennessee and North Carolina, President Johnson's home and birth states, respectively, were the first to seek representation in Congress and a return to state government. However, giving amnesty to individual Rebel soldiers proved simpler than granting the right to vote to all civilians.

By the end of 1865, all the states, with the exception of Texas, were declared sufficiently "reconstructed" to qualify for representation. Congress was not as convinced as President Johnson, however. Mississippi and South Carolina were reluctant to repudiate their Confederate debts. Even more irritating to Congress was Mississippi's refusal to ratify the Thirteenth Amendment, abolishing slavery. Congress was convinced punitive measures were necessary.

Reopening southern state legislatures and district courts was not easy. Courts in Missouri had never closed. In Texas, two former federal judges were appointed. Within occupied Virginia, Kentucky, Tennessee, Florida, Arkansas and Louisiana, courts had only limited jurisdiction. Although a judge was appointed in Alabama, the court remained closed. No one could take the "ironclad" oath in the Carolinas, Mississippi and Georgia. Registration was a prerequisite for being appointed to the bench. To register, a southerner had to produce a loyalty oath, amnesty certificate and be qualified under state election laws (Fig. 70). The strongest evidence to begin the franchise process in a southern state was a Union army discharge (Fig. 71).

The "ironclad" oath in effect January 24, 1865, excluded attorneys from practicing in federal courts if they could not swear past loyalty. Even oaths, amnesty and presidential pardons were not enough to satisfy Congress. The Supreme Court finally settled the question. It ruled a pardoned Arkansas attorney, Augustus H. Garland, who had served in the Confederate Congress, had been unconstitutionally denied his right to practice law. Subsequently, most southern attorneys returned to their law practices.[5]

Surprisingly, oaths of loyalty were just as essential in Border States, despite the general support of the Union. All in West Virginia had to swear fealty to the State "as restored by the convention which assembled at Wheeling on 11th of June, 1861" (Fig. 72). The Missouri "Oath of Loyalty" forced subscribers to defend the government against enemies both domestic and foreign, and swear they had "always been truly and loyally on the side of the United States" (Fig. 73). Only after subscribing to such a pledge could Missouri citizens assume elected or public office or practice as an attorney, minister or educator.

The economic benefits gained by swearing a loyalty oath in a Border State proved just as advantageous as the political consequences, even during the war, after civil order was assured. In reply to the question of why he was at district headquarters, one Missouri diehard about to swear the oath remarked, as he stood before the provost, that he had come to "vomit" it up. The distinction in the minds of these former Rebels was that while the words may sound of loyalty, in their consciences they were no more voluntary than "a dog spitting up rotten food." The oath-taking ceremony was a required prerequisite before persons of doubtful allegiance could be permitted to open their stores, practice their chosen professions or conduct any government business.[6]

Citizens suffering property losses as a result of government action were entitled to submit claims for compensation. Their right to seek damages was assured by the constitutional provision that asserts that the government will not take "private property" for "public use" without just compensation. On July 4, 1864, Congress delegated to the quartermaster general of the army responsibility for settling claims submitted by loyal citizens of states not in rebellion. For instance, when an army forage party took livestock or firewood, regulations provided that the owner be given a signed receipt detailing the property seized for the benefit of the government, which documented the owner's right to file a claim. If in Rebel territory, or if the property were Rebel contraband, no receipts were given. Later, claims officers would review the submitted claims. Particular facts and circumstances of each case, as well as the authenticity of the evidence presented, determined the claims officers' recommendations. Loyalty of the owner was an essential fact that had to be established by both documents and creditable witnesses.[7]

The Congressional Claims Payment Act of July 4, 1864, was limited to states not in rebellion. To clarify the act's extent, President Lincoln proclaimed that the Border States of Maryland, West Virginia, Kentucky, Tennessee and Missouri were "not in rebellion" on the date the act was passed. Even the most loyal of citizens suffering legitimate losses in the Rebel states were only able to file claims with the Washington, D.C., Court of Claims. This was slower, more cumbersome and costly. Normally, claimants were forced to retain a member of the Washington bar specializing in claims work. The standard contingent fee was 50 percent of the claim amount plus expenses up front. Many claims were for damages for which the owner was unable to prove original responsibility. Thieves, guerrillas and marauders from

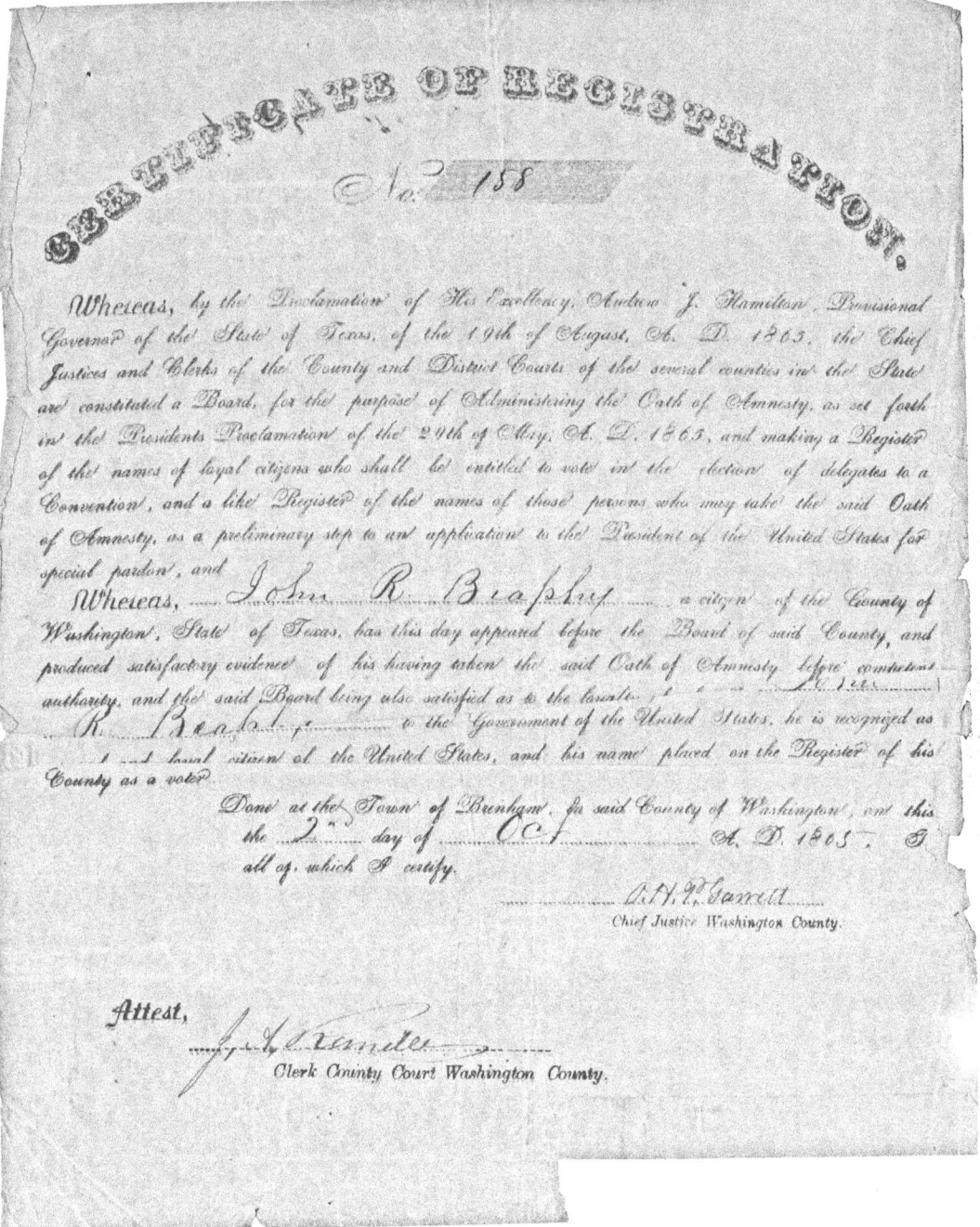

(Fig. 70) Certificate of registration to vote of loyal citizens under Provisional Governor Andrew J. Hamilton's Proclamation of August 19, 1865. Washington County, Texas. October 2, 1865. 10 × 8 inches. (TX-4.65.09)

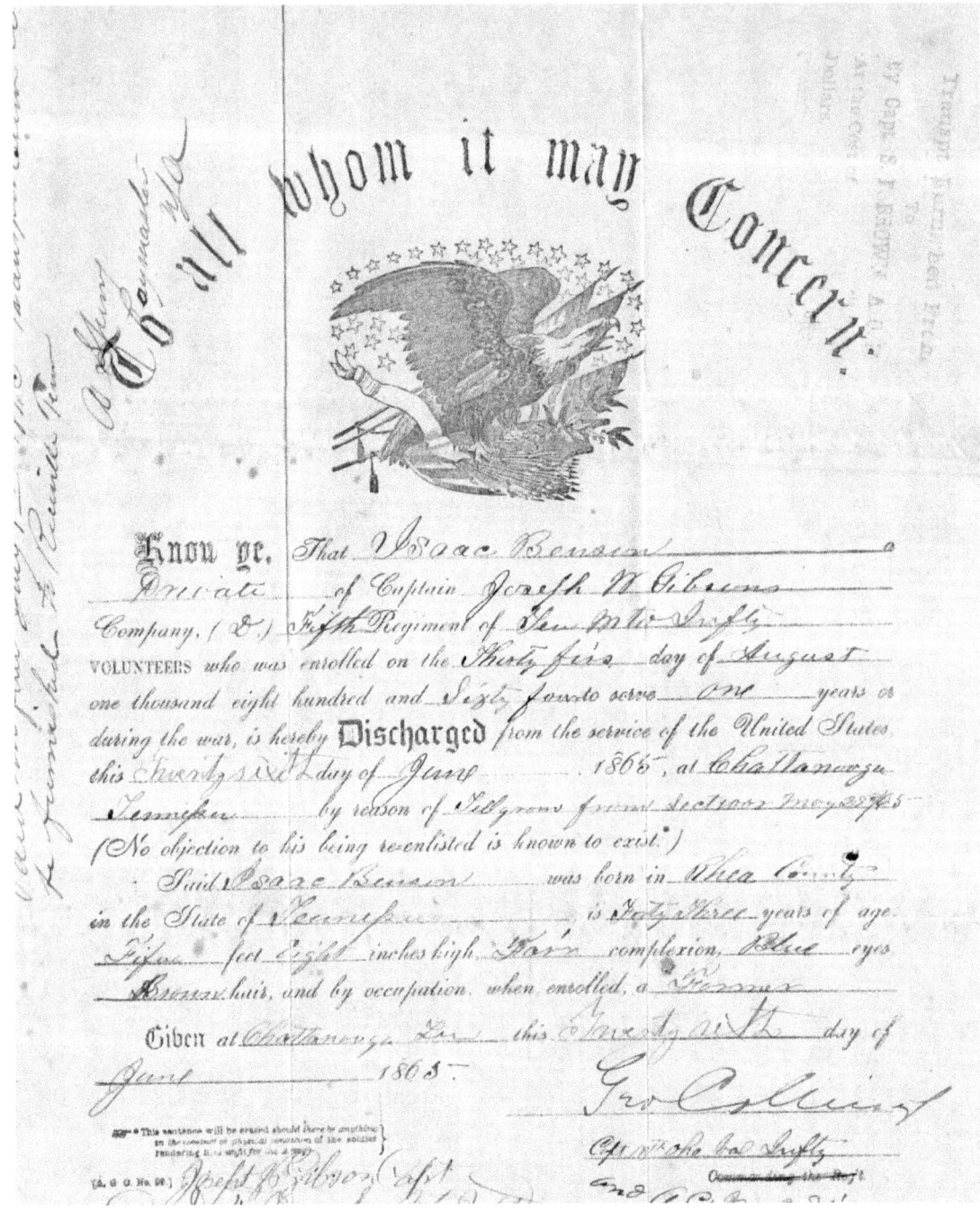

(Fig. 71) Discharge certificate from United States Army. Chattanooga, Tennessee. June 26, 1865. 8½ × 11 inches. (TN-5.65.01)

Oath of Fealty to the State of Virginia.

I do solemnly swear that I will support the Constitution of the United States, and the laws made in pursuance thereof, as the supreme law of the land, anything in the Constitution and laws of the State of Virginia, or in the ordinances of the Convention which assembled at Richmond on the 13th of February, 1861, to the contrary notwithstanding; and that I will uphold and defend the Government of Virginia, as restored by the Convention which assembled at Wheeling on the 11th of June, 1861.—So HELP ME GOD.

Robert Shanks

Sworn to and subscribed before me, a Notary Public, in the City of Petersburg, Virginia, this the 15th day of July, 1865.

Wm M Donnan
Notary Public.

(Fig. 72) Oath of Fealty to the State of Virginia. Petersburg, Virginia. July 15, 1865. 9¾ × 6¼ inches. (VA-4.65.07)

OATH OF LOYALTY.

STATE OF MISSOURI, } ss.
_____ County.

I, _____ do solemnly swear, that I am well acquainted with the terms of the third section of the second Article of the Constitution of the State of Missouri, adopted in the year eighteen hundred and sixty-five, and have carefully considered the same; that I have never, directly or indirectly, done any of the acts in said section specified; that I have always been truly and loyally on the side of the United States against all enemies thereof foreign and domestic; that I will bear true faith and allegiance to the United States, and will support the Constitution and laws thereof, as the supreme law of the land, any law or ordinance of any State to the contrary notwithstanding; that I will, to the best of my ability, protect and defend the Union of the United States, and not allow the same to be broken up and dissolved, or the Government thereof to be destroyed or overthrown, under any circumstances, if in my power to prevent it; that I will support the Constitution of the State of Missouri; and that I make this oath without any mental reservation or evasion, and hold it to be binding on me; and that I will to the best of my skill and ability, diligently and faithfully, without partiality or prejudice, discharge the duties of _____ according to the constitution and laws of this State.

_____
_____ Co. _____ Regt. M. M.

Subscribed and sworn to before me this _____ day of _____ 1866.

(Post Office address,) _____

5 Cents Revenue Stamp.

(Fig. 73) Oath of Loyalty. State of Missouri. 1866. 8½ × 11 inches. (MO-4.66.04) (blank)

both sides probably caused more destruction than the organized forces of either side against private property owners. Fraudulent claims were common, but few charges were brought and even fewer convictions were ever made.[8]

To discourage false claims, the quartermaster devised a thorough claims submission-and-verification process, complete with many forms. The submitted application, supported by evidence, statements, documents and appraisals, was sworn to under penalties of perjury.

Proof of loyalty was essential before the claims would be accepted. A local postmaster had to certify the claimant's address, length of residence and loyalty as known in the community. This then had to be verified by a clerk of a local court of record who certified the loyalty and credibility of both the claimant and his two sworn witnesses. Copies of loyalty oaths were required in Border States and were recorded in a register maintained by the regional provost.[9]

Claims accepted by the local claims board were held for review by special agents, commissioned by the secretary of war, who served as a traveling court. These agents took testimony, interpreted documentation and passed judgment on the validity of the claims submitted. At the conclusion of the local hearings, the special agents would forward their findings to the claims division in the office of the army's quartermaster general with a recommendation. That office would render an opinion on the merits and recommend allowances or rejections to the quartermaster general. He, in turn, would submit an approved-claims list to Congress for inclusion in the next appropriation bill. In practice, claims from Kentucky, Tennessee and Missouri from guerrilla raids were collectively submitted as "Morgan Raid Claims." Likewise, war claims from Pennsylvania were termed "Gettysburg Claims." As a rule, roughly 50 percent of claims submitted were allowed, except in Missouri. In that state, because of questionable documentation and doubtful loyalty in the eyes of the department, only 10 percent of claims were funded.[10] The presumption of authenticity was higher in non–Border States.

One variety of claim, only prevalent in loyal Border States, was the unique compensation permitted to former slave-owners for "a man of African descent" who enlisted with a regiment of the United States Colored Troops. Washington, D.C., claims agents specialized in submitting these claims beginning in 1866. Their work focused on claims for bounties in arrears, supplemented bounties, as well as claims for other property lost or destroyed while in the service of the United States, or property taken for use by the army. Agents fees ranged from 5 to 10 percent for a former soldier, and higher for a civilian (Figure 74). Witnesses, enlistment papers and proof of loyalty were required, even for soldiers, if from Border States.[11]

The U.S. Board of Claims, in 1864, began to consider requests submitted by owners of former slaves who were allowed to enlist in regiments in the United States Colored Troops. The former slave-owner's "proof of ownership" required sworn creditable witnesses and a signature of a local justice of the peace or clerk of court of record. By 1865, the claim for the $100 compensation to former owners also required a United States revenue stamp. The state treasurer of Maryland paid owners out of his own appropriation, granted by the Maryland General Assembly in the January session of 1864, under Chapter 15 of the act. Before payment a signature and seal of the "U.S. Board of Claims for Enlisted Slaves," 19th South Street, Baltimore, Maryland, was required. The money was paid to the owner, not the former slave. The "Colored Soldiers" had to submit separate claims for their individual enlistment bonuses (Fig. 75). All claimants had to pay costs individually, such as the U.S. Revenue tax stamp.

A similar compensation was available to former slave-owners in Missouri. These claims became active in late 1866 after the board of claims sitting at Saint Joseph, Missouri, announced that the secretary of war had issued instructions. Subsequently, the board directed that claims by former owners of slaves who had enlisted in the United States Colored Troops, including service in other states, would be considered for payment, but as a separate claim. Slave owners, as well as heirs, spouses, or joint owners, had to prove loyalty at the time of enlistment as well as continued loyalty. To joint owners, prorated payments could be made. The guidance of these rule interpretations was sent to claims attorneys in Missouri by the Washington and

Washington, D. C., August, 1866.

SIR:

We send herewith a copy of our business circular. Please post it in your place of business and bring it to the attention of persons interested.

The recent Acts, referred to therein, allowing additional Bounty Money, Extra Pay and Pensions provide for large classes of persons. We will be pleased to take charge of the prosecution of these and other claims in which you may be interested. We will send such instructions and forms for each class of claims as will enable you to prepare them with but little trouble, and our fees will be less than one-half the rates charged claimants. Upon the claims being allowed, we will send the drafts or certificates issued upon them, with full instructions for drawing the money; and our fees to be then due and payable. The drafts or certificates can be collected through any Bank or Banking House, or if they are returned to us with authority to collect the money, no charge will be made for the collection.

Our fees on claims sent by you will be as follows:

For Procuring Pensions.—$2½ if an original claim for Pension or increase of Pension, or $5 if the claim has been filed by another and suspended or rejected.

Bounty and Arrears, and Extra Pay.—Five per cent. on sums of $100 or less, or 2½ per cent. of larger claims.

Additional Bounty of $100 or $50 under Act of July 28, 1866.—$2½ for each.

Claims for Lost Horses or other Property lost or destroyed while in the service of the United States, or taken for the use of the Army.—Five per cent. on all sums of $100 or more, and ten per cent. on smaller claims.

For Procuring Full Clearance Certificates for Discharged Officers.—$15 for the first Officer's Claim, and $10 for each subsequent one.

By acting as *our Agent* in getting up these claims, and so announcing yourself to others, you will not be required to take out a license as a Claim Agent. We only will be named as the Agents for the Claims, and proof of our licenses is on file in the several offices where the claims will be examined.

We send a copy of a form of application from a discharged soldier for additional Bounty under the late Act. Printed blanks for these claims, or any others, will be forwarded when desired.

Very respectfully,

TUCKER & SELLS.

SOLDIER'S CLAIM FOR ADDITIONAL BOUNTY.

State of ――, ――County, } ss.

On this ― day of ―― 186―, before me, a ―― in and for the County and State above named, personally appeared ―― aged ― years, who being duly sworn according to law, declares that his Residence and Post Office address is ――, State of ―― and that he is the identical ―― who was a ―― of Company ――, commanded by Captain ―― in the ―― Regiment of ―― Volunteers. That he volunteered at ―― on or about the ― day of ―― 186―, for the term of ―― that he was honorably discharged from said service at ―― on or about the ― day of ―― 186―, by reason of ―― as will appear by his Certificate of Discharge herewith presented.

He further states that he has not bartered, sold, assigned, transferred, loaned, exchanged or given away his final discharge papers or any interest in the bounty provided by the Act of Congress approved July 28, 1866, or any other Act of Congress, and that he has not received and does not know that he is entitled to more than $100 Bounty under any former Act of Congress.

He makes this declaration for the purpose of obtaining the Bounty due him by reason of the services above named; and he hereby constitutes and appoints TUCKER & SELLS, of Washington, D. C., his Attorneys, to prosecute this claim, and authorizes them to receive a draft payable to this deponent's order for whatever sum may be allowed on the same, and revokes and countermands all former authority that may have been given for the above specified purpose.

In presence of

Sworn to, subscribed and acknowledged before me, the day and year first above named, and on the same day personally came ―― and ―― residents of ―― who being duly sworn according to law, declare that they are personally acquainted with ―― who has made and subscribed the foregoing declaration in their presence, that he is the identical person who performed the service therein named, and that their knowledge of his identity is derived from ――. That they are disinterested in the claim, and reside at the place above named.

Sworn to and subscribed before me, and I certify that I believe the affiants to be credible persons, and the declarant is the person he represents himself to be.

If not executed before a Judge or Clerk of a Court, the official character of the officer must be certified to by the Clerk of a Court.

The Soldier's Certificate of Discharge must be sent. It will be returned when the Draft for Bounty is forwarded.

(Fig.74) Soldier's claim for bounty. Washington, D.C. August 1866. (DC-5.66.01)

Saint Louis firm of attorneys for the collection of claims: Chipman, Hosner, Gilmore and Brown (Fig. 76).

The largest excluded class was wealthy southerners. After the war they probably numbered between 60,000 and 80,000, although, ironically, at the time a majority were worth less than the minimum $20,000. After a year, about 7,000 "wealthy Rebels" received presidential pardons. The public was angered that these were members of the "planter class." Especially

Office of the U. S. Board of Claims,

No. 19 SOUTH STREET, BALTIMORE, MD.

I hereby certify that it appears from duly authenticated muster rolls on file in this office, that Alfred Larmer *of Co.* A *9th Reg't U. S. C. T., was enlisted in the United States service, from the State of Maryland, prior to the first day of April, eighteen hundred and sixty-four,* viz on 22 October 1863 — *Witness my hand and the seal of the said Board of Claims, this* 18th *day of* April *1865.*

John L. Sears
Clerk to U. S. Board of Claims.

$100. Md., April 15th 1865.

The Treasurer of the State of Maryland, pay to the order of Joseph E. Lynch *One Hundred Dollars, appropriated under an Act of the General Assembly of Maryland, passed at January session, 1864, chapter 15, and supplements thereto, for my former slave,* Alfred Larmore, *enlisted in the service of the United States from the State of Maryland, as described in the above certificate.*

Test: Henry J. White   Marcellus W. J. Garn

(Fig. 75) Payment to former slave-owner for slave's service in the U.S. Army. Baltimore, Maryland. April 18, 1865. (MD-5.65.03)

irritating was the fact that once pardoned, some filed claims for seized estates and property. The Secretary of State processed requests for presidential pardons, often submitted in manuscript by confined prisoners (Fig. 77).

For two years, President Johnson continued to issue pardons to the dismay of many radicals in Congress (Figs. 78 and 79). Twice he vetoed funding for the Freedmen's Bureau, one of the last acts signed by the late president. This followed a pocket veto of the Wade-Davis

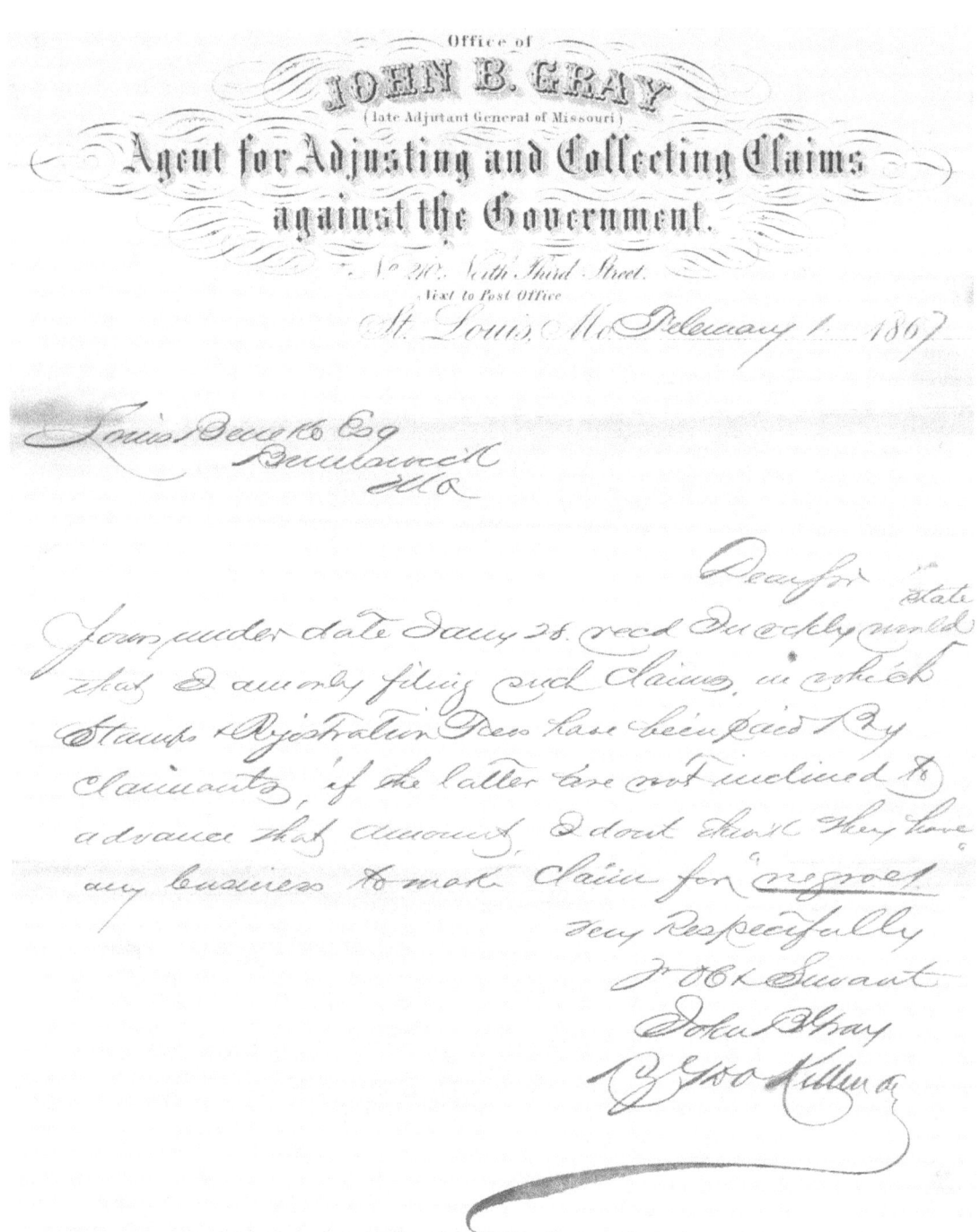

(Fig. 76) Claims adjuster's letter. Saint Louis, Missouri. February 1, 1867. (MO-5.67.01)

Bill Reconstruction bill. In retaliation Congress, repealed the amnesty provision of the Confiscation Act (Section 13, Act of July 17, 1862), and ratified the 14th Amendment, which assured full civil rights to former slaves. The "ironclad" provision of that amendment precluded Rebels from holding office even if pardoned by the president.

Included among Johnson's pardons were almost one hundred for former Confederate congressmen. Civil charges were pending against Jefferson Davis, but were postponed several times; he never requested a pardon. Davis eventually was released on $100,000 bail prior to his trial in Norfolk, Virginia. Horace Greeley, Cornelius Vanderbilt and 18 other northerners each guaranteed $5,000 of the bond (Fig. 80). After congressional Reconstruction, former Rebels generally were denied voter registration, even with a presidential pardon.

Although most disloyal citizens were released from jail, some issues were beyond reconciliation. A good example was the attempt by some in Virginia to rejoin with their brethren in the new state of West Virginia. The Virginia General Assembly resolved to "invite back and with outstretched arms [to] receive the wayward daughter," West Virginia. The people of West Virginia, led by Governor Arthur I. Boreman, had little use for their now "impoverished mother." The West Virginia governor's message to the opening 1866 session of the state legislature, instead, blasted the attempt by former Rebels to infiltrate the process of loyal government. He warned all to be ever vigilant against those still devoted to disunion.[12]

(Fig. 77) Manuscript request for presidential pardon. Fort Delaware. June 18, 1865. 10¾ × 7½ inches. (DE-4.65.01)

ANDREW JOHNSON,

PRESIDENT OF THE UNITED STATES OF AMERICA,

TO ALL TO WHOM THESE PRESENTS SHALL COME, GREETING:

Whereas, R. C. Doom of Jasper County Texas, by taking part in the late rebellion against the Government of the United States, has made himself liable to heavy pains and penalties:

And whereas, the circumstances of his case render him a proper object of Executive clemency:

Now, therefore, be it known, that I, ANDREW JOHNSON, President of the United States of America, in consideration of the premises, divers other good and sufficient reasons me thereunto moving, do hereby grant to the said R. C. Doom a full pardon and amnesty for all offences by him committed, arising from participation, direct or implied, in the said rebellion, conditioned as follows:

1st. This pardon to be of no effect until the said R. C. Doom shall take the oath prescribed in the Proclamation of the President, dated May 29th, 1865.

2d. To be void and of no effect if the said R. C. Doom shall hereafter, at any time, acquire any property whatever in slaves, or make use of slave labor.

3d. That the said R. C. Doom first pay all costs which may have accrued in any proceedings instituted or pending against his person or property, before the date of the acceptance of this warrant.

4th. That the said R. C. Doom shall not, by virtue of this warrant, claim any property or the proceeds of any property that has been sold by the order, judgment, or decree of a court under the confiscation laws of the United States.

5th. That the said R. C. Doom shall notify the Secretary of State, in writing, that he has received and accepted the foregoing pardon.

In testimony whereof, I have hereunto signed my name and caused the Seal of the United States to be affixed.

Done at the City of Washington, this Thirteenth day of April A. D. 1866, and of the Independence of the United States the Ninetieth.

Andrew Johnson

By the President:

William H. Seward, Secretary of State.

(Fig. 78) Opposite and Above: President Andrew Johnson, full pardon and amnesty. Jasper County, Texas. April 13, 1866. (DC-3.65.04)

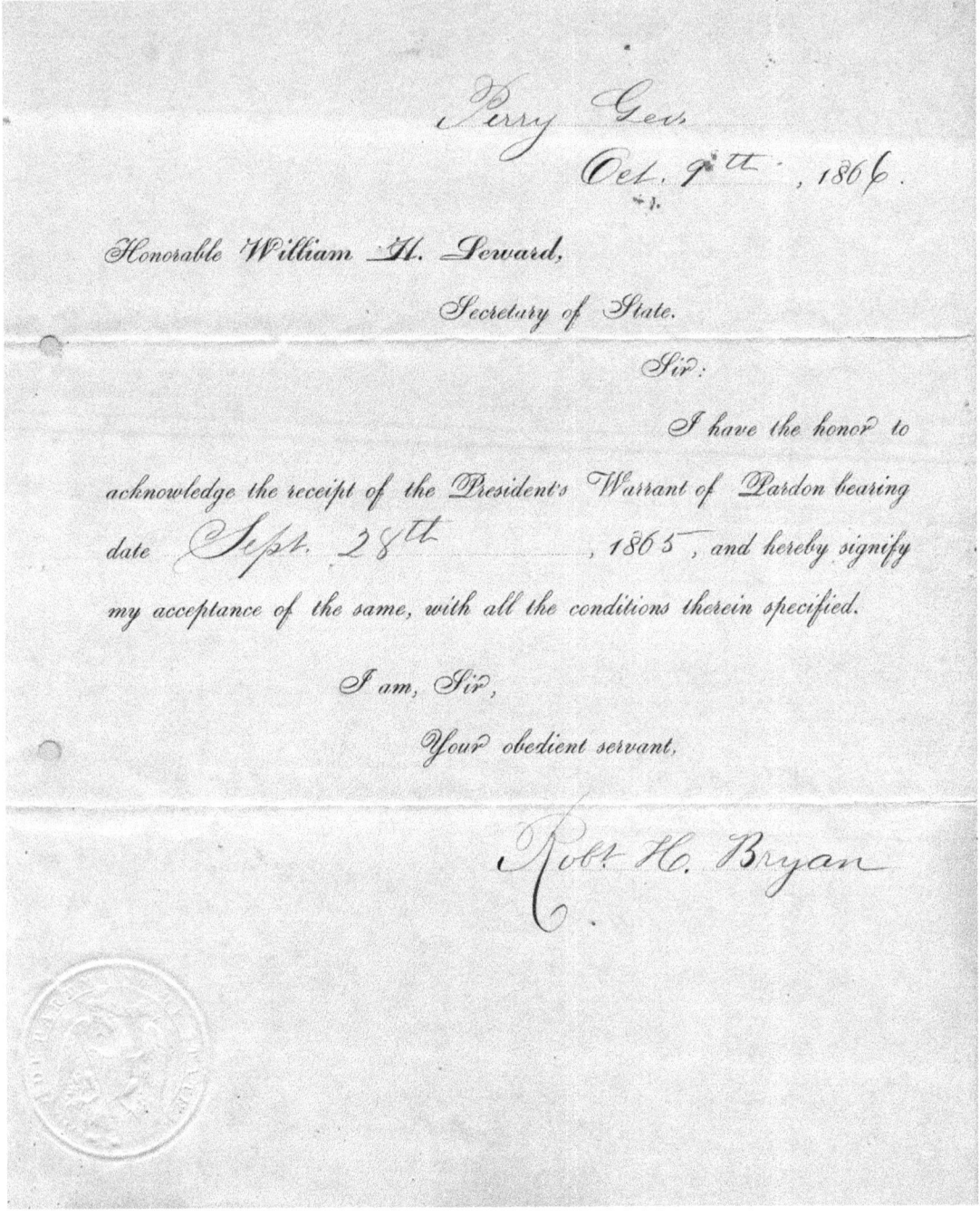

(Fig. 79) Acknowledgment of receipt of presidential pardon. Perry, Georgia. October 9, 1866. (GA-3.66.02)

Included among Confederates who surrendered with Robert E. Lee's Army of Northern Virginia were a few who had previously been released under parole by Union forces. Major W. Winthrop, in the *Digest of Opinions of the Judge Advocate General of the Army*, issued three editions of guidance through 1868. Winthrop made it clear that an amnesty did not relieve a

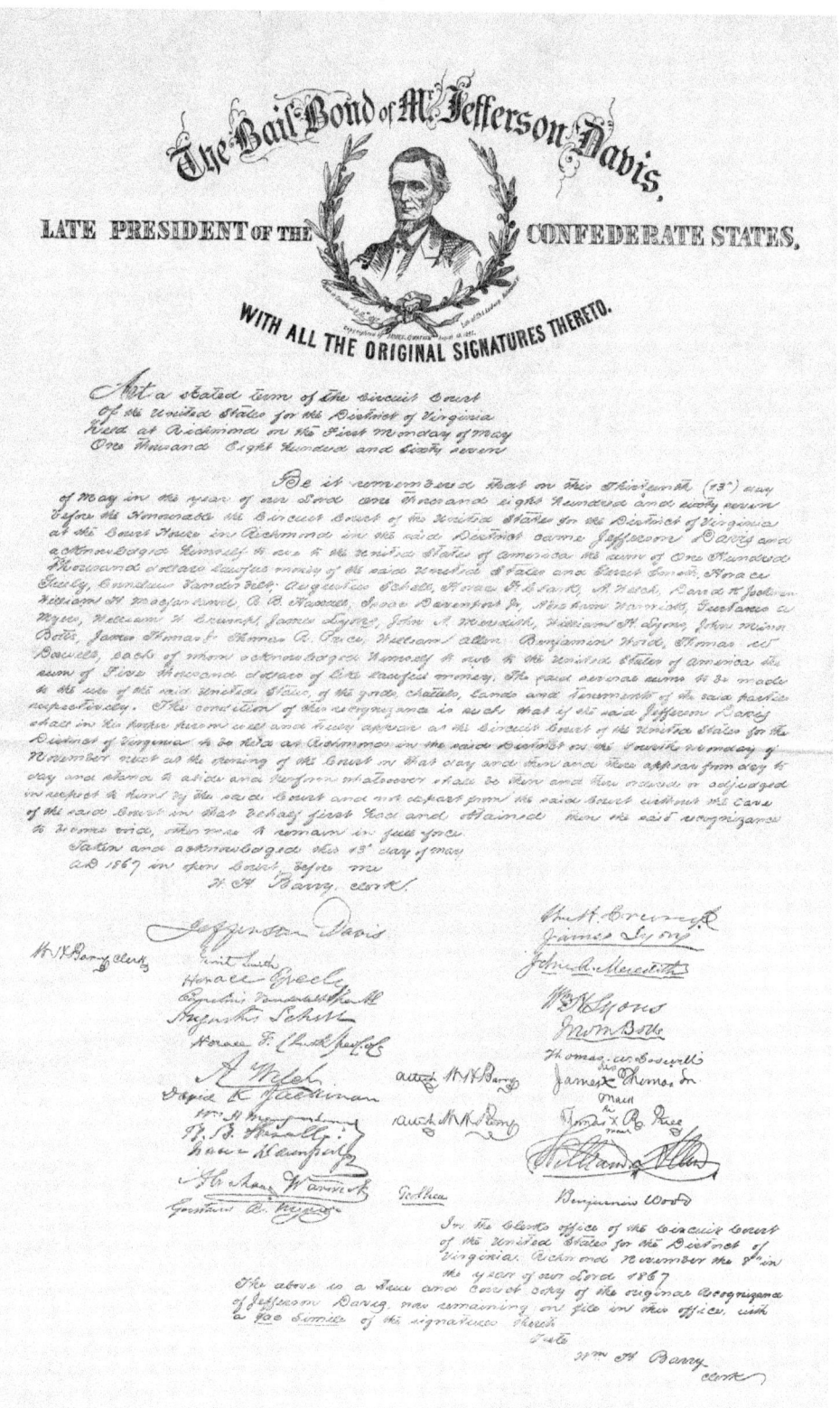

(Fig. 80) Jefferson Davis bail bond (facsimile), 20 Bondsmen for $5,000 each totaling $100,000. Richmond, Virginia. November 8, 1867. (VA-5.67.01)

HEADQUARTERS SECOND MILITARY DISTRICT,
CHARLESTON, S. C., MAY 30TH, 1867.

GENERAL ORDERS,
No. 32.

I. Any citizen, a qualified voter according to the requirements of the *"Act to provide for the more efficient government of the rebel States,"* passed March 2d, 1867, *and the Act supplementary thereto*, passed March 23rd, 1867, is eligible to office in the provisional government of North and South Carolina. All persons appointed to office will be required to take the oath prescribed by the Act aforesaid, and to file the same duly subscribed and sworn, with the Post Commander.

II. All citizens assessed for taxes and who shall have paid taxes for the current year are qualified to serve as jurors. It shall be the duty of the proper civil officers charged with providing lists of jurors, to proceed within their several jurisdictions, without delay, and ascertain the names of all qualified persons and place them on the jury lists, and from such revised lists all jurors shall be hereafter summoned and drawn in the manner required by law.

III. All citizens are eligible to follow any licensed calling employment or vocation, subject to such impartial regulations as may be prescribed by municipal or other competent authority, not inconsistent with common right and the constitution and laws of the United States. The bond required as security shall not exceed the penal sum of one hundred dollars. One or more surities, being citizens and worth in the aggregate double the amount of the bond over and above just debts will be sufficient.

IV. The mayors of cities and other municipal and town officers, and all sheriffs, magistrates and police forces are required to be vigilant and efficient in maintaining order; and in the discharge of their duties they will be expected to co-operate with the military authorities.

V. Post Commanders may summon to their aid whenever the ordinary means at their disposal shall not be sufficient to execute their orders, such of the civil officers and as many of the citizens within the territorial limits of the military post as may be necessary; and the neglect or refusal of any person to aid and assist in the execution of the orders of the commanding officer will be deemed a misdemeanor punishable by such fine and imprisonment as may be imposed by a military tribunal, approved by the Commanding General.

VI. No licence for the sale of intoxicating liquors in quantities less than one gallon or to be drank on the premises, shall be granted to any person other than an inn-keeper; the number of such licences shall be determined and the fees to be charged for each licence shall

(Fig. 81) General Order No. 32., Second Military District, Charleston, S.C. May 30, 1867. "Qualified Voter Requirements," 5 × 8 inches. (SC-5.67.01)

person of a death sentence issued by a court-martial during the war to a captured Rebel guerrilla. Pardons for treason, under both Lincoln's and Johnson's amnesty proclamations, had no effect on capital sentences, even if the Rebel escaped before the sentence was carried out.

A similar fate befell one George Butchosky, formally a Union first sergeant at Fort Bliss, Texas, before he joined the Texas Confederates after General Twiggs surrendered at San Antonio in February of 1861. After the war, while at an encampment of old comrades, Sergeant Butchosky presented himself to a colonel at Fort Bliss in hopes of completing his interrupted tour of enlistment with the Union army. Judge Advocate J. Holt was contacted by the Fort Bliss commanding officer as to the former first-sergeant's status, now that the war was over and that Mr. Butchosky was again "loyal" and in possession of an amnesty. The judge advocate, on June 12, 1866, in no uncertain terms, gave his opinion. He stated that the first sergeant had been released by a Texas state jury on a writ of habeas corpus, filed on his behalf in 1861. He further noted that the earlier Texas jury ruled that, as a citizen of Texas, Butchosky was free to follow a "paramount allegiance" to Texas and to the Rebel cause. Therefore, he must now be court-martialed for his desertion five years earlier.[13]

Congress assumed control of Reconstruction, despite the president's continued issuance of pardons. On March 2, 1867, Rebel states were divided into five military districts. Those states, excluding Tennessee, would only be ready for full participation in government after the 14th Amendment was passed by their respective legislatures. The Reconstruction Act of March 23, 1867, denied former Confederates voting rights and prohibited pardoned Rebels from holding office (Fig. 81). The third measure, enacted on July 19, 1867, allowed military

(Fig. 82) Soldier's voting certificate. McMinn County, Tennessee. June 5, 1867. 5½ × 8½ inches. (TN-5.67.01)

commissioners to remove from office any official considered a hindrance to Reconstruction. The most active southern voters in the former Rebel states were citizens who had served in the Union army (Fig. 82). Finally, on March 11, 1868, Congress, over the president's veto, defined majority voting to exclude southerners who refused to vote, thereby voiding elections because of too few ballots. Under the earlier law, staying away from the polls could control the outcome (Fig. 83). Two classes of voters soon assumed greater significance: naturalized citizens (Fig. 84) and freedmen (Fig. 85). Former slaves gained majorities in a number of southern counties. Both classes were well represented in the first Texas State Convention after the war.

The president retaliated against congressional encroachments by announcing a second amnesty on September 7, 1867. Now only persons "legally held to bail either before or after convictions" were excluded. About three hundred Rebels, remained unpardonable including Davis, Vice President Stephens, department heads, governors, foreign agents and high-ranking military officers. So enraged was Congress that, after Johnson dismissed his secretary of war, the House brought impeachment charges against him.

The president ultimately was cleared of the charges by the Senate in May 1868. President Johnson then issued a third amnesty. After much debate within his cabinet, the proclamation, dated July 4, 1868, excluded only persons under indictment for treason or other felonies. Jefferson Davis and John C. Breckinridge from Kentucky, who was in Cuba, were among the few beyond amnesty. A difference between this and previous amnesties was the omission of an oath of allegiance. The Reconstruction Acts had required oaths as a requisite to clemency and claim petitions, and to restate this qualification was redundant.

(Fig. 83) Commission for registration of "Unconditional Union Man." Monroe County, Tennessee. November 2, 1868. (TN-5.68.02))

United States of America,
STATE OF TEXAS

ORIGINAL NO. 1671   2d DISTRICT.

REGISTER'S OFFICE,

Washington County.

This 25d day of June Anno Domini, 1867.

I, L. E. Edward, Register of the Names and Residence of qualified Electors of Washington County, for the 2d District, duly commissioned and sworn, do hereby certify that John Brophy was this day duly registered as a qualified Elector of said County, on the Original Registry of this District under No. 1671 as a naturalized citizen of the United States, and residing at Brenham

That the evidence of his naturalization as exhibited in this Office shows that he was naturalized at Brenham on the eleventh day of June in the year 1857 by the County Court of Washington County

Witness my hand, the day and date above mentioned.

L. E. Edward
Register.

(Fig. 84) Certificate of naturalization of foreign born qualified elector. Register's Office. Washington County, Texas. June 25, 1867. (TX-4.67.03)

United States of America,
STATE OF TEXAS.

Original No. _18_

REGISTER'S OFFICE,

Travis _____ County.

OATH.

"I, _Ruffin Grudenton (Col'd)_ do solemnly swear, or affirm, in the presence of Almighty God, that I am a citizen of the State of _Texas_____, that I have resided in said State for ___12___ months next preceding this day, and now reside in the County of ___Travis___, or the parish of _____, in said State, as case may be; that I am twenty-one years old; that I have not been disfranchised for participation in any rebellion or civil war against the United States, nor for felony committed against laws of any of the United States; that I have never been a member of any State Legislature, nor held any executive or judicial office in any State, and afterwards engaged in insurrection or rebellion against the United States, and given aid or comfort to the enemies thereof; that I have never taken an oath as a member of Congress of the United States, or as an officer of the United States, or as a member of any State Legislature, or as an executive or judicial officer of any State, to support the Constitution of the United States, and afterwards engaged in insurrection and rebellion against the United States, or given aid or comfort to the enemies of; that I will faithfully support the Constitution and obey the laws of the United States; and will, to the best of my ability, encourage others so to do. So help me God."

Attest _S. N. Collins_   Ruffin X Grudenton
                                     his mark

I do hereby certify that on this ___1st___ day of ___July___ 1867 appeared before me _Ruffin Grudenton (Col'd)_ who subscribed to the foregoing oath.

W. C. Philips
Register.

ORIGINAL.

(Peter O'Donnell, Stationer, 16 Camp St., N. O.)

(Fig. 85) Oath of "Colored" elector as qualified to register. Register's Office. Travis County, Texas. July 1, 1867. 8½ × 11 inches. (TX-4.67.02)

President Johnson issued his last clemency proclamation just prior to his party's July convention in hopes of helping his chances for the nomination. As his presidency came to an end, Johnson hoped to end the issue of treason. He stated in his December message to Congress that "the authority of the Federal Government" had been established throughout the States." He reassured the country that "universal amnesty and pardon for participation in the Rebellion" would help "secure permanent peace, order, and prosperity throughout the land, and to renew and fully restore confidence and fraternal feeling among the whole people, and their respect

(Fig. 86) Planter's oath. Lavaca County, Texas. October 12, 1865. (TX-4.65.08)

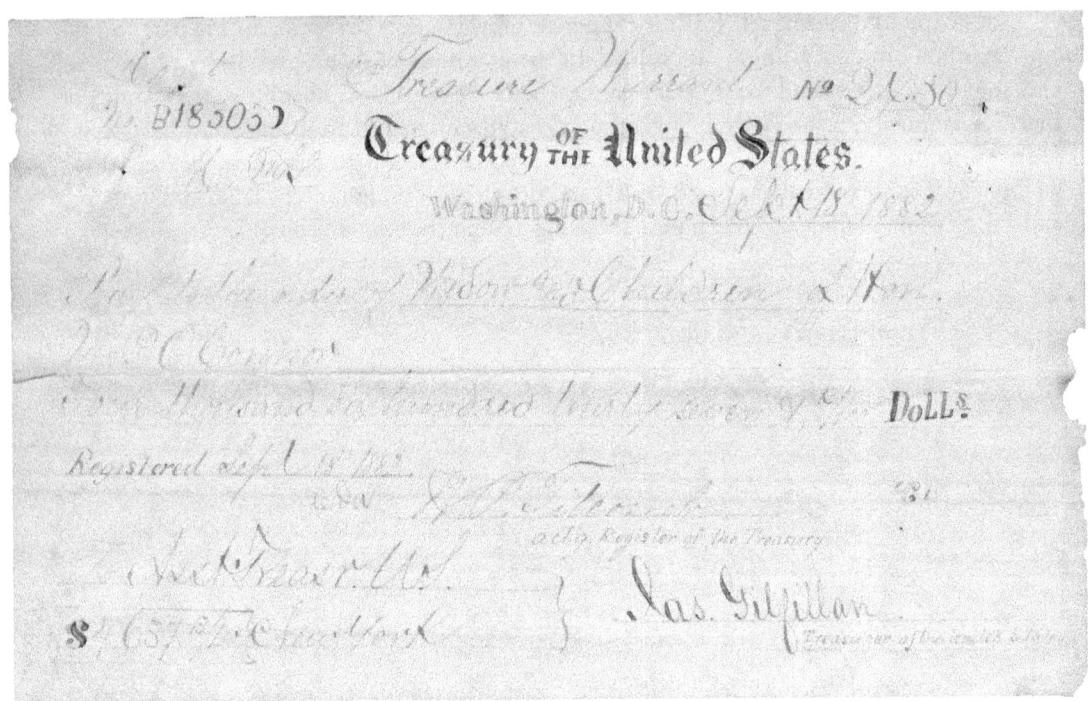

(Fig. 87) Treasury Warrant, $4,637.13. Payable for claim due for confiscated property in Beaufort, South Carolina during war. "Widow and Children" of W. P. O'Connor. Washington. September 18, 1882. 5 × 8 inches. (DC-5.82.01))

for and attachment to the National Government." Treason was now more a political than criminal issue for former Rebels.

The most significant financial benefit of a pardon was the removal of impediments to compensation for confiscated or destroyed property. Military commanders during reconstruction were flooded with claims for the return of real estate, livestock and cotton. Cotton was at the forefront of all claims, having been seized by Federal troops upon occupation and sold at auction by Treasury agents. In Texas, owners filed "Planters' Oaths" to establish private rather than government ownership of their cotton. Claims for cotton extended into the next century (Fig. 86). Another group of claimants were those losing property through tax foreclosures under the U.S. Direct Tax Act. Some former Rebels received compensation from the U.S. Treasury by establishing loyalty (Fig. 87).

Johnson's last amnesty, dated Christmas Day, 1868, was called "universal" because it covered the "offense of treason." Earlier amnesties had substituted the word "Rebellion" for "treason." This final clemency included all but 37 individuals, such as President Davis, General Robert E. Lee and the most senior military officers. Six amnesty proclamations, beginning with President Lincoln on December 8, 1863, and ending with Johnson on December 25, 1868, had provided for the "restoration of all rights, privileges and immunities under the Constitution." Jefferson Davis never had his civil rights restored because of the Reconstruction Acts of Congress. Only by a two-thirds vote of Congress could an excluded Rebel's voting rights be returned. The "ironclad" oath was required for every federal office after March 2, 1867.

In 1869, the U.S. Supreme Court in *Texas v. White* sustained congressional Reconstruction. The court ruled that the rebellious states, although never seceding from the union, did fail to represent their respective citizens within the government of the United States. Congress, the court ruled, had authority to establish a workable relationship between those rebellious states and their illegitimate governments and the federal government. That year, Virginia, Georgia, Texas, and Mississippi, after complying with conditions imposed by Congress, were allowed representation. Tennessee, Arkansas, Louisiana and the Carolinas were already in compliance. Not until July 15, 1870, did Georgia ratify the 15th Amendment to the U.S. Constitution and revoke the so-called "Black Codes" of the "Jim Crow" period.

New York newspaper editor Horace Greeley long advocated complete amnesty for all former Confederate officials and officers. For years such efforts were blocked by Radical Republicans angered by continued discrimination in the South by hotels and common carriers. Democrats seized the opportunity to remove impediments still hampering former disloyal citizens at the opening of the 42nd Congress, on December 4, 1871. On May 22, 1872, Congress passed another amnesty provision that removed restrictions against most of the remaining former Rebels, except for those U.S. congressmen, judicial officers, military officers, ministers and cabinet members who left office to join the Confederate government.

Twice during the Civil War the president offered clemency to army and navy deserters if only they would return to serve out their enlistment terms. If the unauthorized absentees returned before April 1, 1863, they would be freed of punishment, except for the loss of pay during their absence. On March 11, 1865, one month prior to Lincoln's death, he offered full amnesty to all deserters returning within 60 days, providing they remained to the end of their enlistments. President U. S. Grant, on October 10, 1873, promised a full pardon to all remaining deserters if they would only surrender to officials before July 1, 1874, and complete their enlistment contracts. Deserters, like former Rebels who refused to take advantage of the amnesty provisions of the several presidential proclamations, were not entitled to vote, hold public office, receive public assistance or do business requiring a license.

President U. S. Grant, during his second term, oversaw implementation of voting rights after passage of the 15th Amendment in 1876. General Order No. 85, Headquarters of the Army, dated August 17, 1876, threatened punishment to all who would "attempt by force, fraud, terror, intimidation or otherwise, to prevent the free exercise of the right of suffrage." Despite the law of the land, states continued to deny voting rights to former slaves through "Jim Crow" laws, poll taxes and literacy tests. In the end, the need for congressional Reconstruction had some basis in fact.

The language of the loyalty oath continued to evolve. On June 25, 1868, the ironclad oath was again modified. By July 11, the oath only required a pledge "to support and defend the Constitution against all enemies, foreign and domestic" while faithfully discharging the duties of office. On February 1, 1871, Congress allowed persons who had taken an oath to the Confederacy to pledge allegiance to the U.S. Constitution in order to be restored. Up to 18,000 individuals had been affected by the disability clause of the 14th Amendment. Only after May 23, 1872, was every congressional district fully represented by members from the former Rebel states.

Congress required every federal juror to swear they had never given aid to rebellion. In April 1871, the requirement was lessened by being applied only to cases covered under the 14th Amendment. Not until May 24, 1884, were federal jurors no longer required to swear they had never aided the Rebellion. The new oath simply required that they would support the Constitution and perform their duties faithfully. At the same time military officers who had resigned their commissions to join the Rebellion were allowed to be recommissioned into the U.S. Army.[14]

Of the 750 former Rebels excepted from the general amnesty act of 1872, about two hundred were allowed to register to vote by special acts of Congress. Not until war with Spain, did Congress pass its final amnesty act on June 8, 1898. Jefferson Davis had died nine years earlier — he was neither tried for treason nor pardoned for disloyalty. Treason remains one of the rarest crimes charged under the Federal Code. "Death to Traitors" is simpler to threaten than accomplish in the United States, even during times of war.

Introduction to the Appendices

Ending a war is as complex as the issues that cause it. American wars are declared by Congress and end after the approval of a peace treaty by the Senate. The Civil War was different since a rebellion is not a declared war but involves belligerents from the same country. The charge of treason was normally reserved for enemies of the state during times of war. Rebellion created state enemies and disloyal citizens. However, "State" or political enemies were not charged with crimes for their political views. Traitors during the Rebellion were identified, questioned and restricted. A disloyal citizen's activities and movements were controlled by the president through the State Department or War Office. If the disloyal individual was considered a clear and present danger, he could be confined in a state (political) prison beyond appeal to the courts. Suspected disloyal citizens, not confined, were subject to loss of the rights of assembly, speech and movement.

Even with the United States' tradition of clemency to enemies of the state, few appreciate the historic necessity of this executive privilege. During times of national urgency, politics and emotions control the debate concerning loyalty and persons presenting a danger to the nation. Reunion with Rebels was measured in decades rather than years. Peace and reconciliation with enemies, both domestic and foreign, were long and hard in coming, and were possible only after such a demonstration of national clemency and personal forgiveness.

The following examples of documentary evidence in the form of passes, paroles, pardons and oaths used by both sides during the Civil War show the evolution of a divided nation's struggle between the extreme emotions of threats to traitors and forgiveness to prodigal sons.

Appendix 1: Paroles

State prisoners and captured enemy soldiers could not be released by court order. Only the president could grant freedom, and release was secured through an executive parole. Paroles were granted if the applicant was considered worthy, no longer a danger, and promised not to return to combat until exchanged as a prisoner of war. Parole violators were subject to capital punishment if recaptured. Paroled enemy prisoners were allowed to switch their allegiance to the Union. If a Rebel captive swore to support the United States, remain loyal and abandon the Rebel cause, he could resettle in the North and accept civilian employment. Confederate officials offered similar terms to captured Federal soldiers.

AL-1.65.01 Gainesville, AL, parole and pass

Head Quarters Dist. East. Ark.

Helena, Arkansas _Mch 23"_ 1865.

Parole _Rosecrans_

Countersign _Missouri_

By command of Maj. Gen'l. A. McD. McCOOK.

O. O. McIntyre

Assistant Adjutant General.

AR-1.65.01 Helena, AR, parole

Certificate of Parole.

Augusta, _May 15_ 1865.

Amory Coffin 2nd Lieut of Co. _Adjt S.C._ Regiment _Cadets_ having been this day surrendered by _Parole_

in compliance with a Military Convention made on April 26th, 1865, at Bennett's House, near Durham's Station, North Carolina, between General JOSEPH E. JOHNSTON, of the Confederate Army, and Major-General W. T. SHERMAN, U. S. A., and having given his individual obligation and parole, in writing, not to take up arms against the United States Government, nor to do any act hostile thereto, until properly released from the effect of this obligation in such manner as shall be mutually approved by the respective authorities, he is hereby permitted to return to his home in _Barnwell Dist. S.C._ He will not be disturbed by the United States authorities so long as he observes his obligation and the laws in force where he may reside.

Fred Wilkinson _Amory Coffin_
Capt 128 N.Y.V. _Lt_
Parole Officer

GA-1.65.02 Augusta, GA, parole

Above: GA-1.65.03 Macon, GA, parole and oath

Left: KY-1.62.02 Cynthiana, KY, CSA-issued parole (front)

List of Home Guards and Citizens paroled by Morgan at Cynthiana Ky July 18th 1862.

Luther VanHook — Home Guard   John Kilmartin — citizen
J. D. Ward   "   "
James F. Ware   "   "
Joseph M. Wood   "   "
J. I. Stephens   "   "
M. Kaufman   "   "
G. H. Givens   "   "
John Bruce   "   "
J. B. Nichols — 1st Lieut Wilson's Co.
H. Cox — Home Guards
J. J. Parish   "   "
E. D. McAdams

W. A. Stewart
C. Reakle   "   "
John Frohleg   "   "
F. Grey   "   "
James J. Tebbs   "   "
Adam Renaker — citizen
Samuel Renaker   "
Abraham Renaker   "
Robt. Renaker   "
Geo. W. Dunn   "
R. C. Wherritt   "
John Riedy   "
Oliver N. Marston — Home Guards
William Kimbro   "
John Douglass
W. M. McMillin — Citizen
Alpheus Conner — Citizen

Above: LA-1.63.01 Brashear City, LA, CSA parole of honor

Left: MD-1.62.01 Antietam, MD, parole

> VICKSBURG, MISSISSIPPI, July 6 A. D. 1863.
>
> TO ALL WHOM IT MAY CONCERN, KNOW YE THAT:
>
> J. W. Roby a City Employee of Reg't ACSD&c Vols. C. S. A., being a Prisoner of War, in the hands of the United States Forces, in virtue of the capitulation of the City of Vicksburg and its garrison, by Lieut. Gen John C. Pemberton, C. S. A., Commanding, on the 4th day of July, 1863, do in pursuance of the terms of said capitulation, give this my solemn parole under oath——
>
> That I will not take up arms again against the United States, nor serve in any military, police, or constabulary force, in any Fort, Garrison or field work, held by the Confederate States of America, against the United States of America, nor as guard of prisons, depots or stores, nor discharge any duties usually performed by Officers or soldiers against the United States of America, until duly exchanged by the proper authorities.
>
> Jas. W. Roby
>
> Sworn to and subscribed before me at Vicksburg, Miss., this 6 day of July, 1863.
>
> C. A. Carthis Capt. 101 Reg't Ills Vols.
>
> AND PAROLLING OFFICER.
>
> Witness
> A. H. Anderson
> Maj. & ACS

MS-1.63.01 Vicksburg, MS, parole

> Hd. Cav. Div. Dist. E. Tenn.
> Ashville N. C.
> April 28th 1865—
>
> A. H. Pretts Capt. & A.A.G. C.S.A. has given his word of honor that he will not take up arms against the United States Govt. nor in any way assist the cause of the Confederate States Govt. until regularly exchanged.
>
> W. J. Patterson
> Capt & A.A.G.

NC-1.65.04 Ashville, NC, parole

Appendix 2: Passes

One of the first rights suspended during the Civil War was the right to travel. Travel passes were civil- and military-regulated controls over individual movement. Consequently, travel during wartime was viewed as a privilege rather than an unfettered right. Under martial rule, denials of travel requests were not reviewable by the courts.

Applications for travel required disclosure of the reason for the trip, destination, and length of stay. Domestic travel permission typically was approved by local military administrators, usually provost marshals, while the State Department was charged with international passport control. Applicants were required to give loyalty oaths and promise not to reveal strategic information to the enemy. Even disloyal citizens were given travel passes. If released, a disloyal individual was granted safe passage under the safeguard provision of the Articles of War and was protected as long as conditions of release were not violated.

(Fig. 1) AL-2.64.01 Stevenson, AL, pass

(Fig. 2) AR-2.63.01 Helena, AR, pass

(Fig. 3) AR-2.63.02 Little Rock, AR, pass

(Fig. 4) AR-2.64.p01 Helena, AR, pass

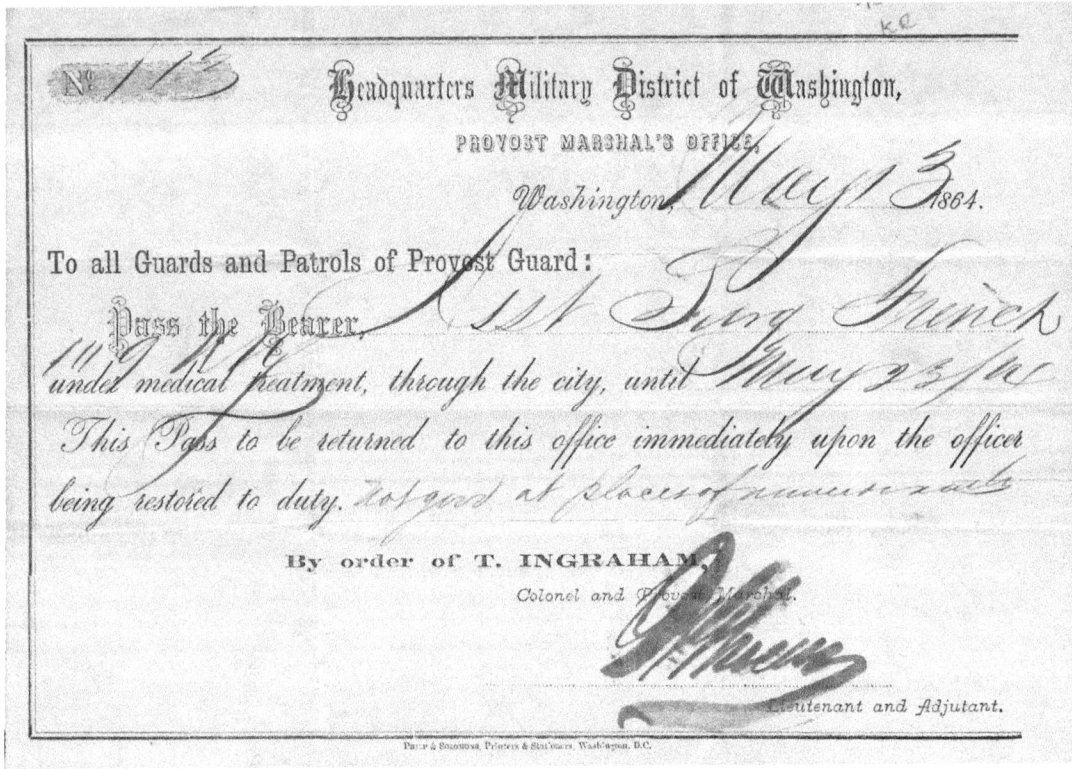

(Fig. 5) DC-2.64.01 Washington, DC, medical pass

(Fig. 6) DC-2.64.02 U.S. War Department pass

(Fig. 7) GA-2.62.01 Savannah, GA, pass

(Fig. 8) GA-2.62.02 Atlanta, GA, Confederate provost pass

(Fig. 9) GA-2.63.02 Milledgeville, GA, pass

(Fig. 10) GA-2.63.03 Resaca-Calhoun, GA, post pass

(Fig. 11) GA-2.64.02 LaGrange, GA, hospital pass

(Fig. 12) IL-2.62.01 Cairo, IL, pass

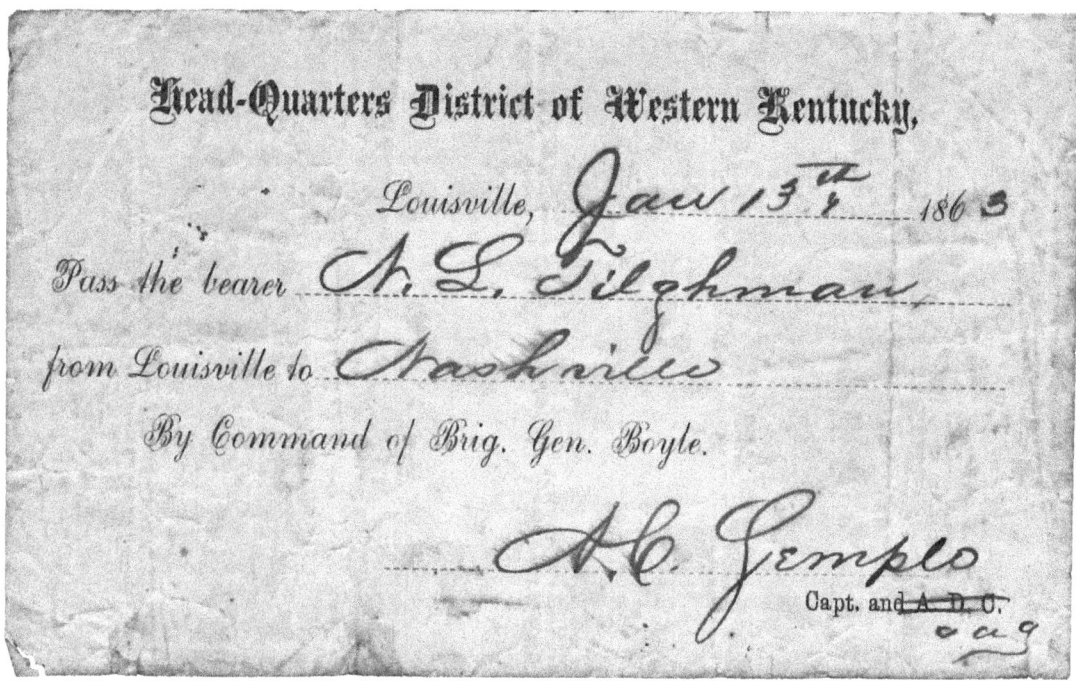

(Fig. 13) KY-2.63.01 Louisville, KY, pass

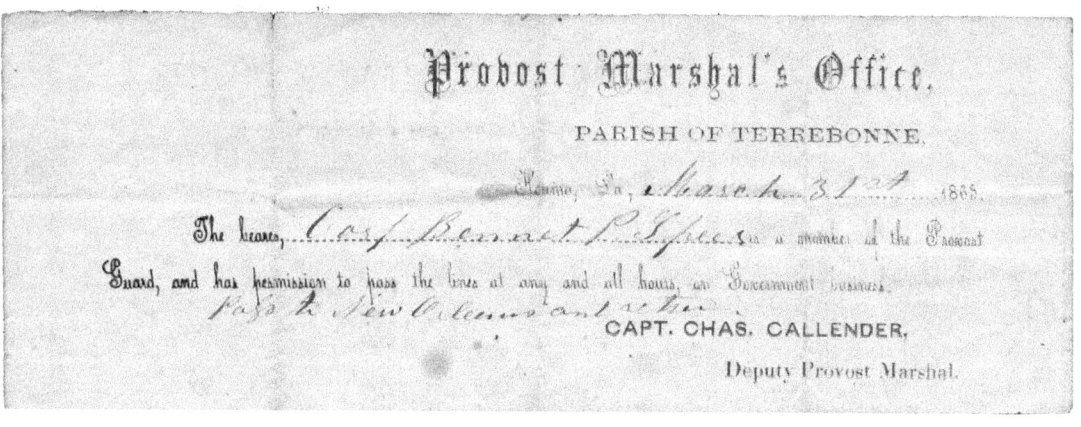

(Fig. 14) LA-2.63.01 Houma, LA, pass

PASS (Copy)   No. _____
OFFICE PROVOST MARSHAL GENERAL—Department of the Gulf.

Military Pass for Crew of Vessels.

New Orleans, Nov 23ᵈ 1863

Pass A C Goddin Master _____
if necessary _____ Crew of Steamer Mittie Stephens
from New Orleans to Port Hudson & return
                                   for one month

This Pass is given upon the Parole of Honor of the holders, that they will in no way give information, countenance, aid or support to the so-called Confederate Government or States.

James Bowen
Brig. Gen. & Provost Marshal General.

Pickets and guards, will stop all vessels or skiffs not having the above pass attached to the Customhouse Clearance, and will be careful to note that the names correspond.

(Fig. 15) LA-2.63.02 New Orleans, LA, naval pass

No. 55

Head Quarters, Hookers Division
Camp Baker Lower Potomac Md
March 13th, 1862.

To all officers commanding guards and patrols on the route from Washington to Leonardtown, and from Washington to Port Tobacco:

The bearer Saml N. Thayer, having furnished satisfactory evidence of his loyalty _____ to the Government of the United States, will be permitted to pass from Camp Baker to Washington D.C.; person and baggage being subject to the inspection of the guards.

Age 20
Height 5 ft 6 in
Complexion Fair
Hair Light
Eyes Brown
Build Medium
Whiskers None

{ This Pass is only for one trip, and for the requisite time to make the same, and shall be taken up by the

Expires not until farther orders

By command of Joseph Hooker, Brig. Gen'l U.S.A.
Wm H Lawrence 1st Lieut & Aide-de-Camp.

(Fig. 16) MD-2.63.02 Camp Baker, MD, pass

(Fig. 17) MS-2.63.01 Vicksburg, MS, steamer pass

(Fig. 18) NC-2.62.02 Charlotte, NC, railroad pass

(Fig. 19) NC-2.63.01 Raleigh, NC, pass

(Fig. 20) NC-2.63.02 Goldsboro, NC, Confederate passport office pass

(Fig. 21) NC-2.64.01 Goldsboro, NC, medical pass

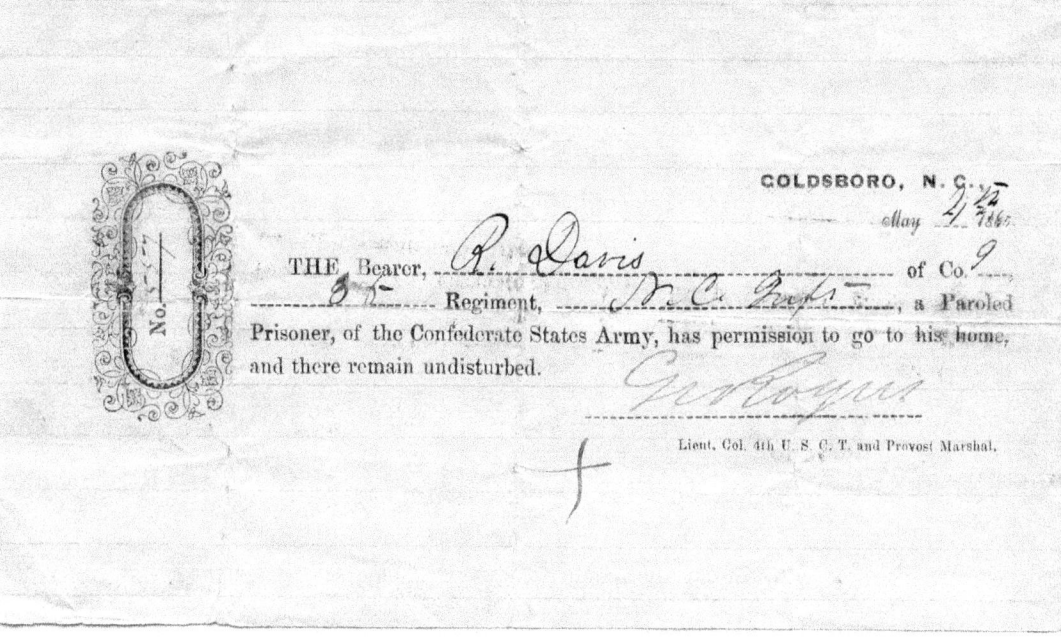

(Fig. 22) NC-2.65.03 Coldsboro (Goldsboro), NC, paroled prisoner pass

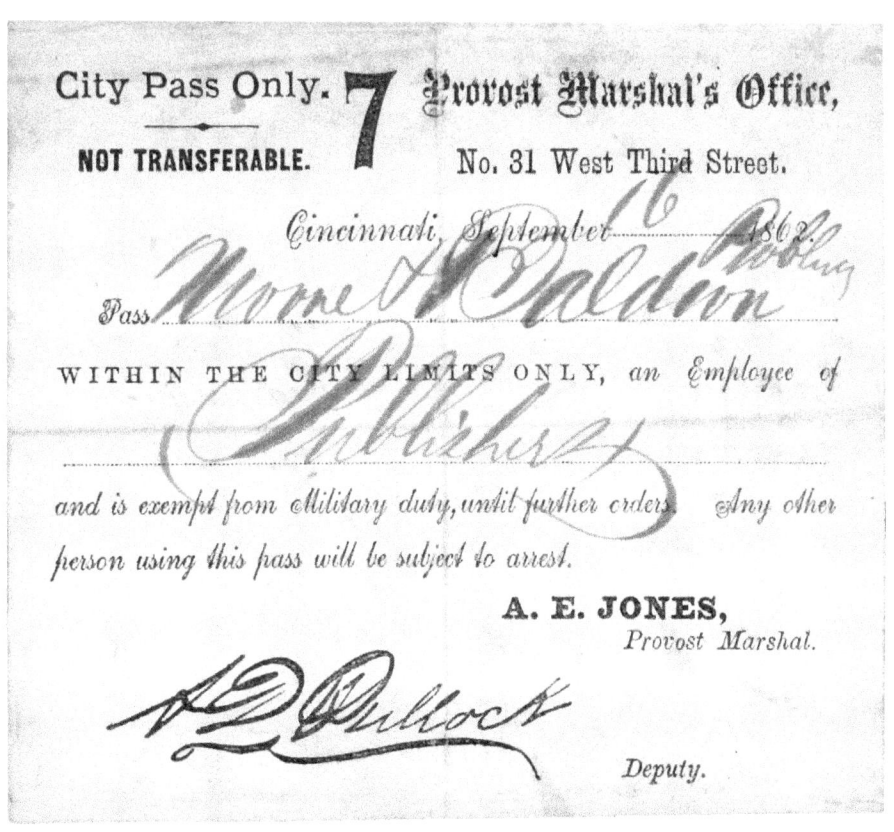

(Fig. 23) OH-2.62.01 Cincinnati, OH, city pass

HEADQUARTERS, U. S. FORCES,
St. Helena Island, S. C., *25th March* 1863.

The bearer *Private Buchanan – 24th Mass –*

has permission to pass *to Hilton Head*

and return *to-day*

By order of
BRIG. GEN. O. S. FERRY.

Capt. & Asst. Adjt. Gen.

(Fig. 24) SC-2.63.01 St. Helena Island, SC, pass

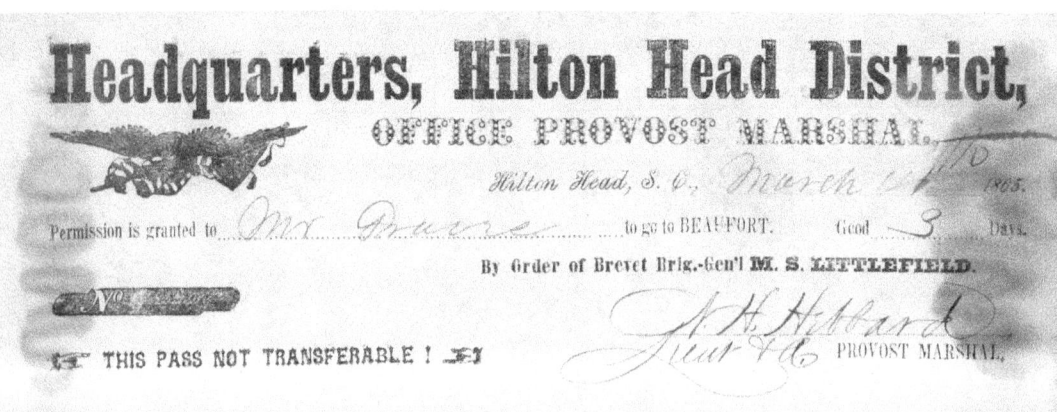

(Fig. 25) Hilton Head, SC, pass

(Fig. 26) TN-2.63.07 Memphis, TN, Union pass

(Fig. 27) TN-2.64.01 Chattanooga, TN, pass

(Fig. 28) TN-2.64.02 Clarksville, TN, pass

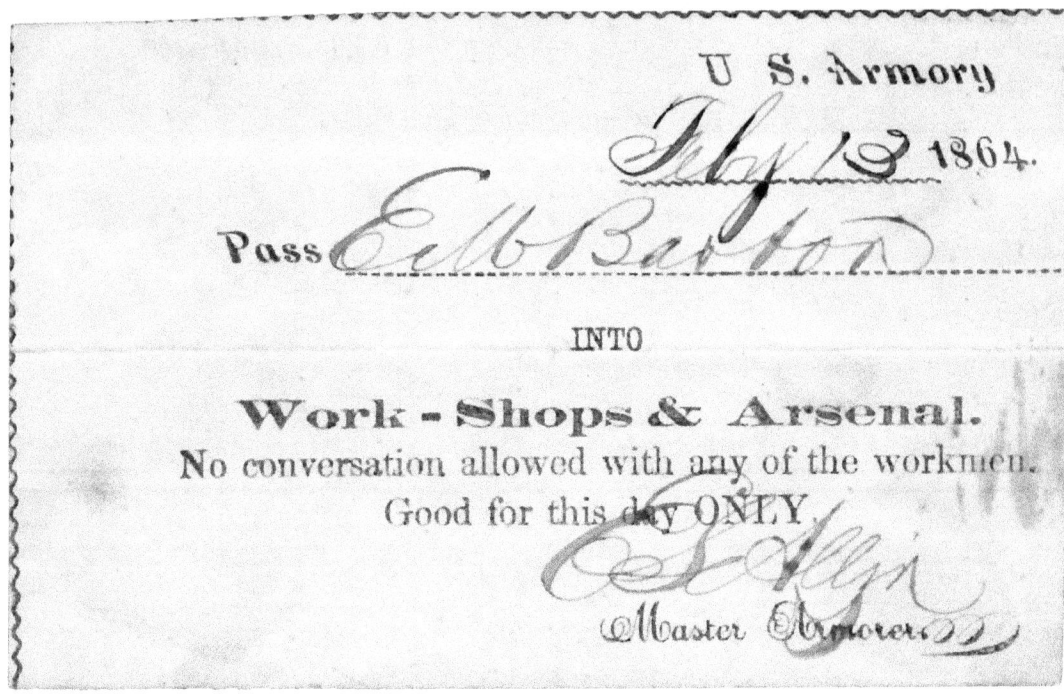

(Fig. 29) UNK-2.64.01 Pass, U.S. armory, unknown location

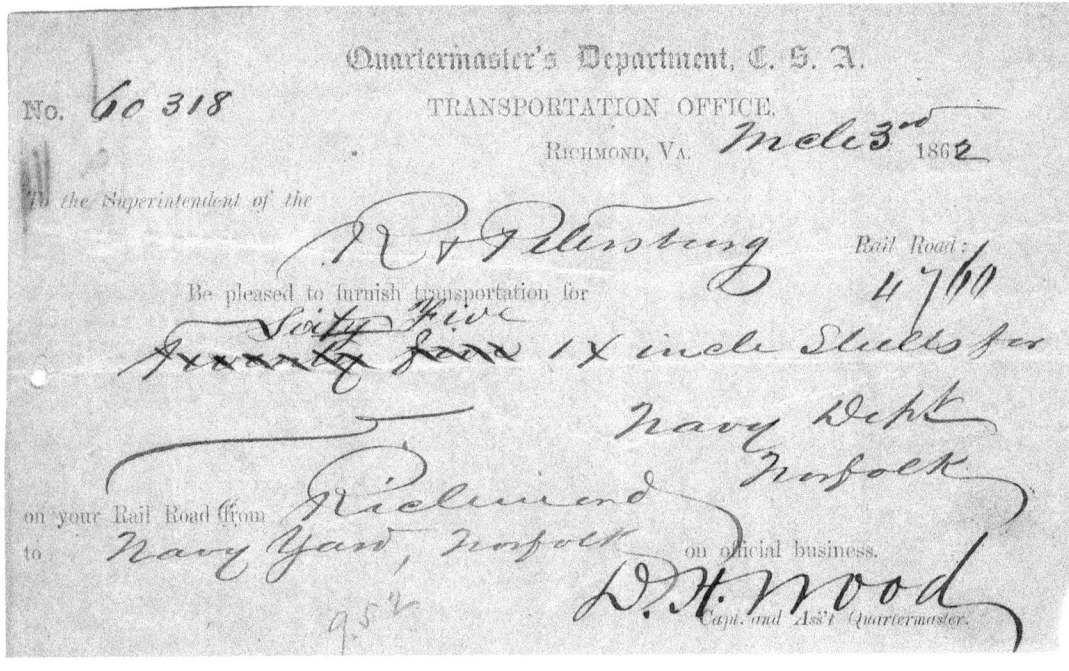

(Fig. 30) VA-2.62.06 Richmond, VA, railroad pass (Note: Transportation to Norfolk Navy Yard for 14-inch Naval artillery shells.)

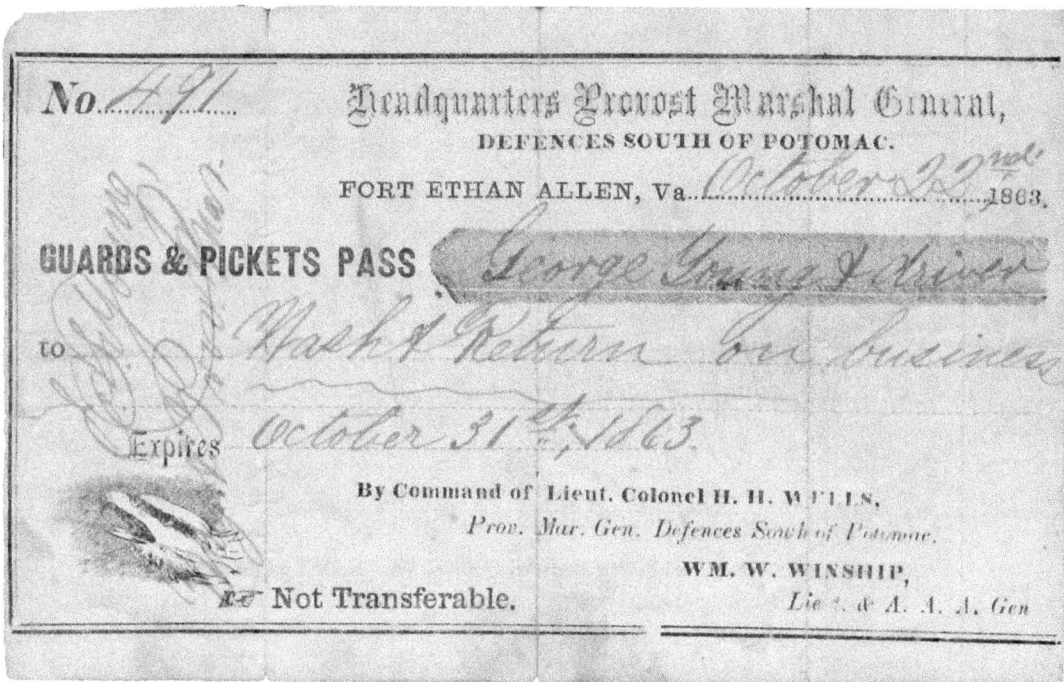

(Fig. 31) VA-2.63.09 Fort Ethan Allen, VA, pass

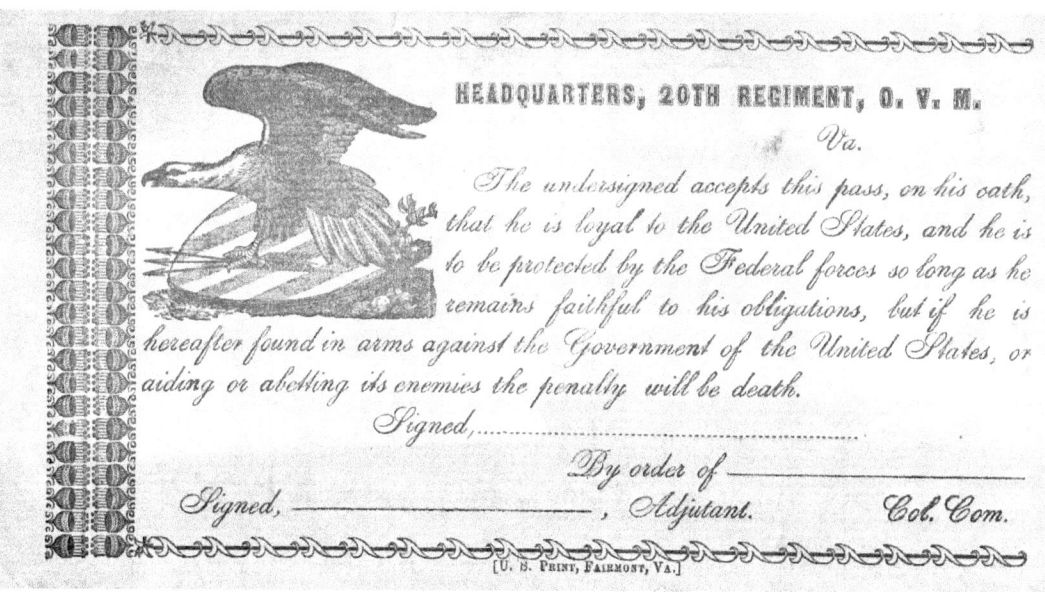

(Fig. 32) VA-2.65.09 20th O.V.M. Reg. blank pass and oath

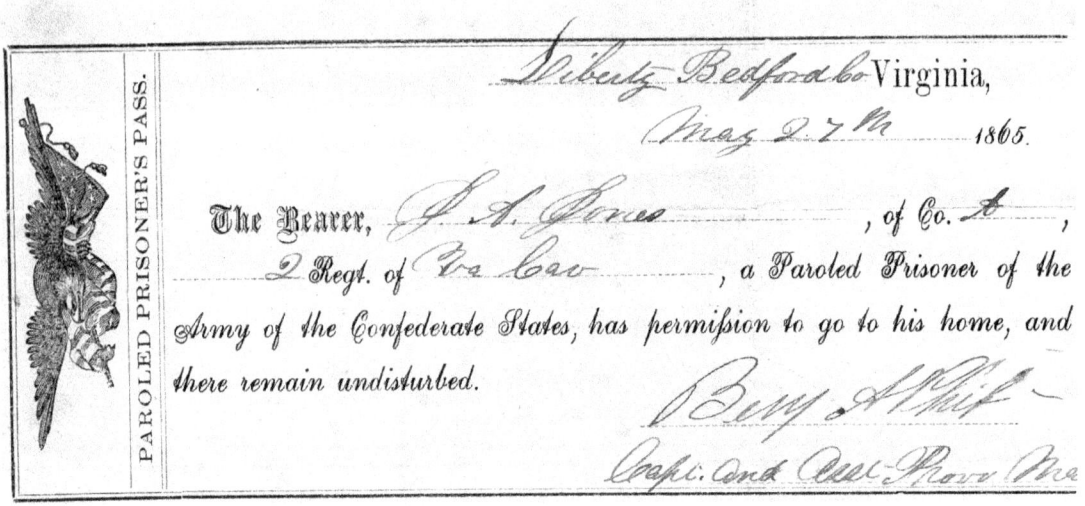

(Fig. 33) VA-2.65.15 Liberty, Bedford County, VA, paroled prisoner pass

Appendix 3: Pardons

Political clemency was offered to Rebels and disloyal citizens as a common inducement to hasten the return to national unity. Under the Constitution, the President had the power to pardon crimes, both charged and uncharged. If pardoned, the offender was forever cleared of all crimes as disclosed in the pardon application and was fully restored to all rights of citizenship, as if the acts had never occurred. Once granted, pardons were beyond judicial review.

Pardon applications included all acts in need of forgiveness and proof of sincerity and loyalty. When extended to groups, pardons were termed grants of amnesty and were just as binding and final as a pardon. During Reconstruction, the United States Congress assumed administration over amnesty applications made by former high-ranking Rebel officials and wealthy planters.

United States of America.

DEPARTMENT OF STATE.

To all to whom these presents shall come, Greeting:

I Certify, That the document hereunto annexed is a true Copy of the original on file in this Department.

In testimony whereof, I, William H. Seward, Secretary of State of the United States, have hereunto subscribed my name and caused the Seal of the Department of State to be affixed.

Done at the City of Washington, this twentieth day of September A. D. 1865 and of the Independence of the United States of America the Ninetieth.

William H. Seward

(Fig. 1) DC-3.65.01 Washington, DC, true copy of pardon issued by State Department, signed by Secretary of State William H. Seward, 1865, page 1 (Black ribbon and seal indicated national mourning after Lincoln's recent death.)

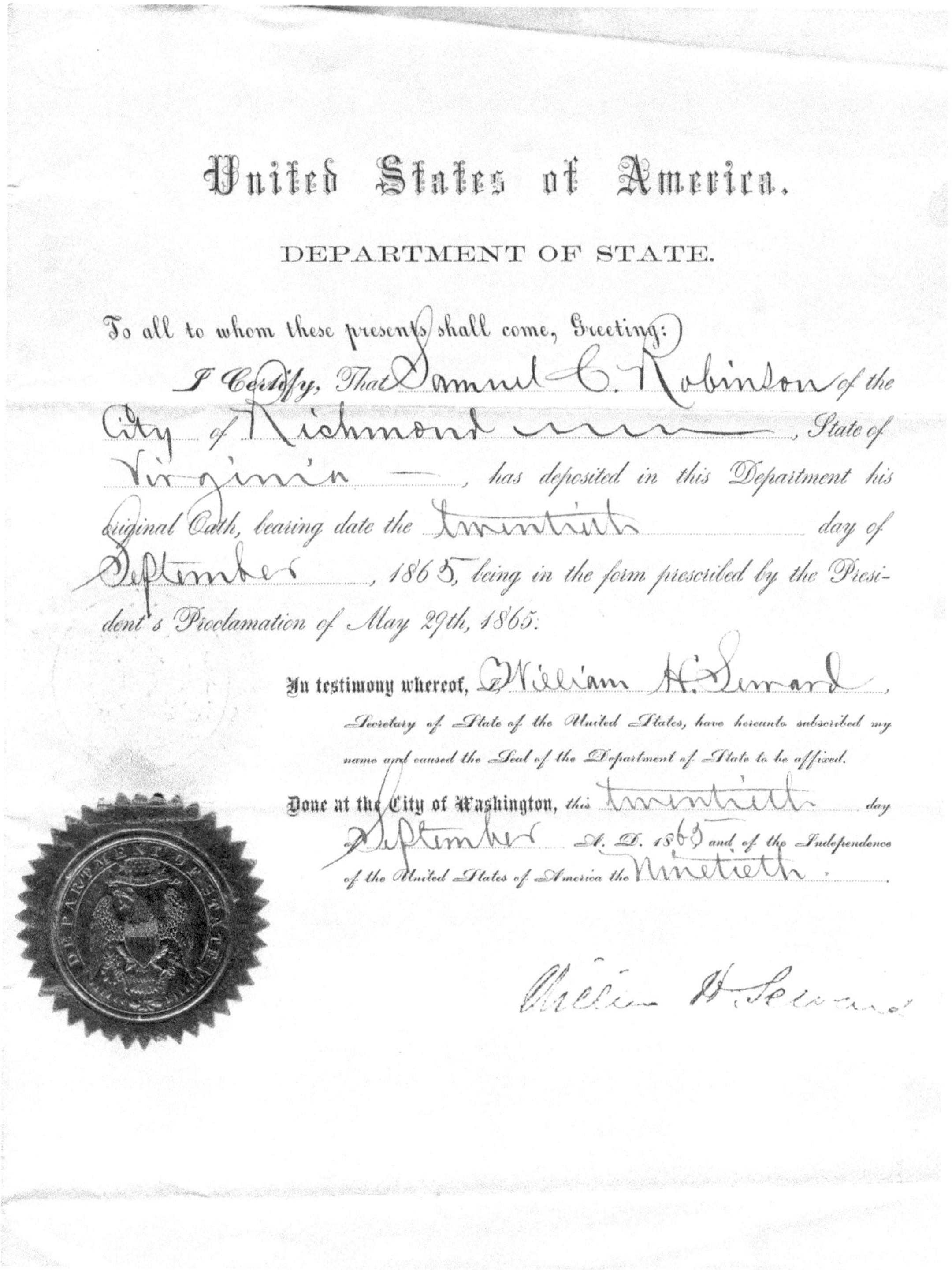

United States of America.

DEPARTMENT OF STATE.

To all to whom these presents shall come, Greeting:

I Certify, That Samuel C. Robinson of the City of Richmond, State of Virginia, has deposited in this Department his original Oath, bearing date the twentieth day of September, 1865, being in the form prescribed by the President's Proclamation of May 29th, 1865.

In testimony whereof, William H. Seward, Secretary of State of the United States, have hereunto subscribed my name and caused the Seal of the Department of State to be affixed.

Done at the City of Washington, this twentieth day of September A. D. 1865 and of the Independence of the United States of America the Ninetieth.

William H Seward

(Fig. 2) DC-3.65.01 Washington, DC, true copy of pardon issued by State Department, signed by Secretary of State William H. Seward, 1865, page 2 (Black seal indicated national mourning after Lincoln's recent death.)

(Fig. 3) DC-3.65.03 Washington, DC, acknowledgment of receipt of pardon, 1865

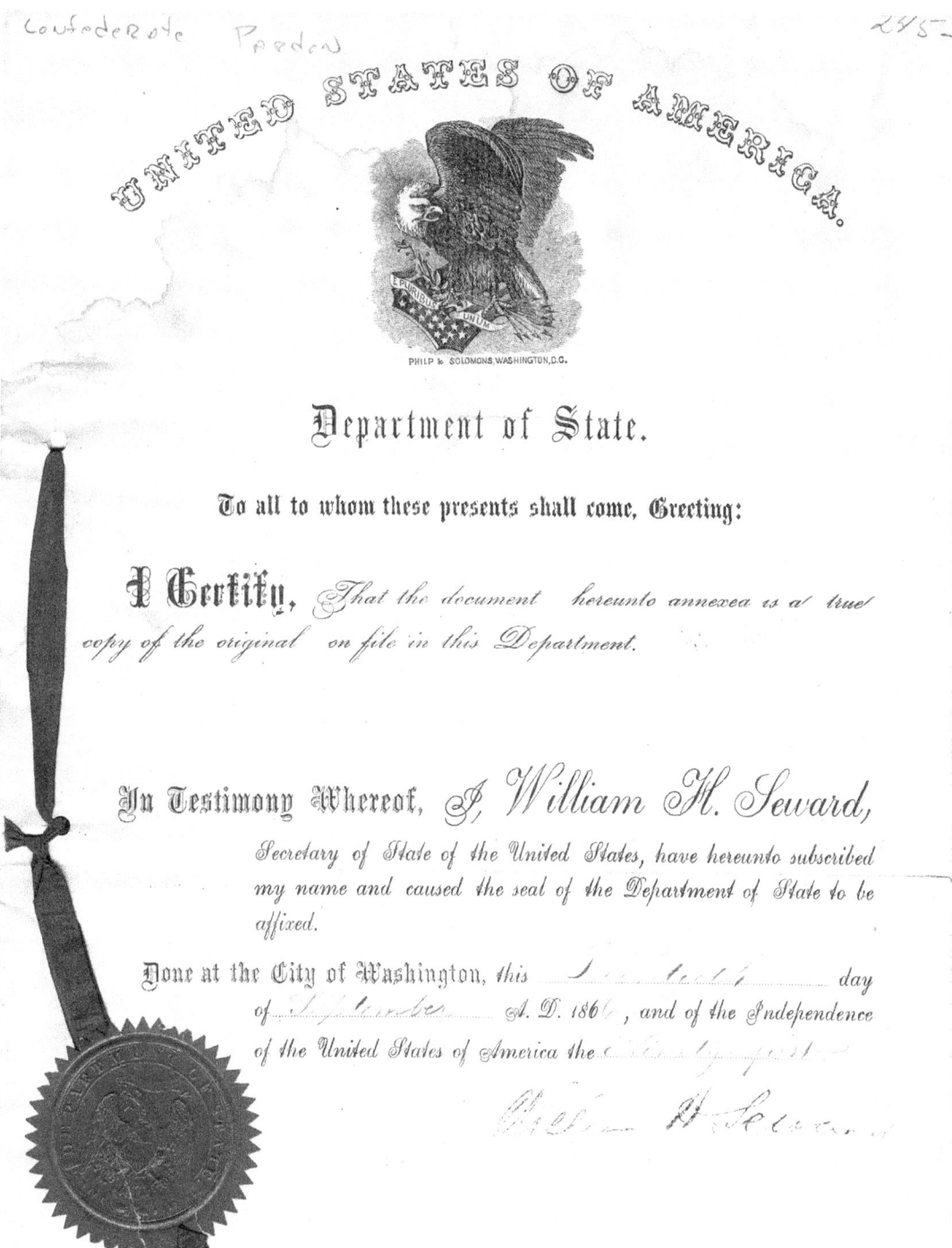

(Fig. 4) DC-3.66.01 Washington, DC, true copy of pardon issued by State Department, signed by Secretary of State William H. Seward, 1866. The period of national mourning was over by this date in 1866 and the seal was now its usual red color.

Appendix 4: Promises of Loyalty

Once restricted, a disloyal citizen could not have his civil constraints removed until allegiance was restored. Proof of loyalty was the universal standard for removal from the state enemies' list. This proof required an oath, witnesses and evidence of sincerity. Typically, political prisoners were quick to swear future loyalty and to promise no further threat of harm in order to secure their release. If an oath of fealty was violated, the released state prisoner could be subjected to dire consequences. Suspected public officials or persons of trust were forced to pledge loyalty to retain their positions of office. Violations of the loyalty oath by a state prisoner or public official were considered as an act against the state and, consequently, they were charged and prosecuted as felons. During times of national threat, the public, as a whole, accepted the necessity of political prisoners and loyalty oaths.

The Oath of Registration.

THE STATE OF ALABAMA: *Madison* COUNTY.

I, *Robert Garven*, do solemnly swear, that I will henceforth faithfully support, protect, and defend the Constitution of the United States, and the Union States thereunder; and that I will, in like manner, abide by and support all Laws and Proclamations which have been made during the existing rebellion with reference to the Emancipation of Slaves.— So help me God.

Robert H. Gar[ven]

SWORN TO and subscribed before me, this ... day of ... 1865. / 1872

R. W. White

(Fig. 1) AL-4.72.01 Madison County, AL, loyalty oath

Amnesty Oath, under Proclamation of the President of the United States, dated May 29, 1865.

STATE OF ARKANSAS, *Columbia* County, ss.

I, *William Olin* of *Columbia* County, State of Arkansas, do solemnly swear, in the presence of Almighty God, that I will henceforth faithfully support, protect and defend the Constitution of the United States, and the Union of States thereunder: and that I will in like manner, abide by and faithfully support all laws and proclamations which have been made during the existing rebellion with reference to the emancipation of slaves--so help me God.

William Olin

Sworn to, and subscribed, before me, this 3rd day of Jany 1866.

W. B. McThill

[IN DUPLICATE.]   Clerk of the Circuit Court *Columbia* County.

(Fig. 2) AR-4.65.02 Columbia County, AR, amnesty oath

OATH PRESCRIBED BY ACT OF JULY 2, 1862.

[This oath must be taken and subscribed by every person elected or appointed to office in any of the five Military Districts, before a notary public or some magistrate authorized by law to administer oaths, before entering upon the duties of his office. (See Section 9, Act of July 19, 1867.)

I,..., of..
County of..............................., and State of........................ ...., do solemnly..that I have never voluntarily borne arms against the United States since I have been a citizen thereof; that I have voluntarily given no aid, countenance, counsel, or encouragement to persons engaged in armed hostility thereto; that I have neither sought, nor accepted, nor attempted to exercise the functions of any office whatever, under any authority, or pretended authority, in hostility to the United States; that I have not yielded a voluntary support to any pretended government, authority, power, or constitution, within the United States hostile or inimical thereto. And I do further............................that, to the best of my knowledge and ability, I will support and defend the Constitution of the United States against all enemies, foreign and domestic; that I will bear true faith and allegiance to the same; that I take this obligation freely, without any mental reservation, or purpose of evasion; and that I will well and faithfully discharge the duties of the office on which I am about to enter: So help me God.

John M. Donaldson

Sworn........ and subscribed before me,
this 15th day of December A. D. 1868.

Ira Fugate N.P.

(Fig. 3) DC-4.68.01 Washington, DC, civilian loyalty oath

Provost Marshals Office.

Barrancas July 24 1865

Upon the Order of Brig. General Asboth Commanding District of West Florida, duly endorsed upon petition of A. McNally on file in my office, and Numbered 589 I hereby certify, that the said petitioner has this day taken the oath prescribed by the President's Proclamation, and the Orders in relation thereto, and that he is entitled to Amnesty for the treasonable acts set forth by him in the petition above referred to, and for none other.—

J. M. Adams
Lt & Act Provost Marshal.

Filed and numbered in my Office, No 589

Signature of the Applicant: Amasiah McNally
In my presence: J. M. Adams, Provost Marshal.

(Fig. 4) FL-4.65.01 Barrancas, FL, amnesty oath

UNITED STATES OF AMERICA.

I, ... of the County of .... State of ...., do solemnly swear, or affirm, in presence of Almighty God, that I will henceforth faithfully support and defend the Constitution of the United States and the Union of the States thereunder, and that I will in like manner abide by and faithfully support all laws and proclamations which have been made during the existing rebellion with reference to the emancipation of slaves.—SO HELP ME GOD.

Subscribed and sworn to before me at ...., this .... day of ....
A. D. 1865.

Ordinary of .... County.

The above named has .... complexion .... hair, and .... eyes; is .... feet .... inches high, aged .... years; by profession a ....

(Fig. 5) GA-4.65.03 White County, GA, loyalty oath

STATE OF GEORGIA, ORDINARY'S OFFICE, CHATHAM COUNTY.

No. ....

I, W. Robert Gignilliat, of the County of Chatham, State Georgia, do solemnly affirm in the presence of Almighty God, that I will henceforth faithfully support and defend the Constitution of the United States, and the Union of the States thereunder, and that I will, in like manner, abide by and faithfully support all Laws and Proclamations which have been made during the existing Rebellion with reference to the Emancipation of Slaves—So Help Me God.

(Signed,) W. Robt Gignilliat

I certify that the above is a true copy.
September 25th 1865.

D. A. Byrne
Ordinary of Chatham County.

The above named has Dark complexion, Dark hair, and Hazel eyes; is 5 feet 11 inches high, aged 26 years; by profession a Attorney at Law

(Fig. 6) GA-4.65.05 Chatham County, GA, loyalty oath

UNITED STATES OF AMERICA,

State of Georgia,

County of Jasper

I, Wily H. Lynch of the County of Jasper and State of Georgia, do solemnly swear or affirm, in the presence of Almighty God, that I will henceforth faithfully support, protect and defend the Constitution of the United States and the Union of the States thereunder, and that I will, in like manner, abide by and faithfully support all laws and proclamations which have been made during the existing rebellion, with reference to the emancipation of slaves. So help me God.

W. H. Lynch

Subscribed and sworn to before me this 25 day of October 1865.

M. J. Hutcheson
Ordinary.

I hereby certify that the above is a true copy of an oath taken and subcribed before me by Wily H. Lynch this the 25 day of Oct. 1865.

M. J. Hutcheson
Ordinary.

(Fig. 7) GA-4.65.11 Jasper County, GA, loyalty oath

UNITED STATES OF AMERICA.

I, C. S. Hargrove, of the County of Oglethorpe, State of Georgia, do solemnly swear, in the presence of Almighty God, that I will henceforth faithfully support, protect and defend the Constitution of the United States, and the Union of the States thereunder, and that I will, in like manner, abide by, and faithfully support, all Acts of Congress passed during the existing rebellion with reference to slaves, so long and so far as not repealed, modified or held void by Congress, or by decision of the Supreme Court; and that I will, in like manner, abide by and faithfully support all proclamations of the President made during the existing rebellion having reference to slaves, so long and so far as not modified and declared void by decision of the Supreme Court—So HELP ME GOD.

C. S. Hargrove

Subscribed and sworn to before me, at Augusta, Ga., this 3d day of May A. D., 1865.

Capt 31 nysovaa and Provost Marshal.

The above named has Dark complexion, Dark hair, and Blue eyes; is 5 feet 9 inches high; aged 30 years; by profession a Rail Road Gun 1040

P. C. Crawford

(Fig. 8) GA-4.65.12 Oglethorpe County, GA, loyalty oath

OATH.

I, David Jewell, duly elected as 2nd Lieutenant of Company _____, _____ regiment, Iowa State Militia, do solemnly swear that I will support the Constitution of the United States, and of this State, and bear true and faithful allegiance to the same; that I will promptly obey all orders coming to me from the Governor of this State, and in every respect faithfully discharge the duties of my said office according to law, and obey the orders and commands of my superior officers to the best of my ability; and I do further swear that I do not belong to any organization, either secret or otherwise, which has for its object opposition to the present war against the States in rebellion, or opposition to the Federal Administration in its efforts to prosecute said war; that I have no sympathy whatever with those in rebellion and that my desire is to see said war prosecuted with vigor until the rebellion is crushed and an honorable peace is restored; and to this end I will faithfully exert my influence and endeavor to sustain those in power. To all this without reservation I fully and cheerfully agree.

David Jewell

Subscribed and sworn to by the said David Jewell, on this 30th day of November, 1864.

Iowa Ready?s

Homer Butler
Justice of the Peace
Clerk of District Court of Clayton County, Iowa.

(Fig. 9) IA-4.64.01 Iowa State Militia, ironclad oath

UNITED STATES OF AMERICA.

I, Anthony Thomas, of the County of Owen, State of Kentucky, do solemnly swear that I will support, protect, and defend the Constitution and Government of the United States against all enemies, whether domestic or foreign; that I will bear true faith, allegiance, and loyalty to the same, any ordinance, resolution, or laws of any State, Convention, or Legislature, to the contrary notwithstanding; and further, that I will faithfully perform all the duties which may be required of me by the laws of the United States; and I take this oath freely and voluntarily, without any mental reservation or evasion whatever.

Subscribed and sworn to before me this ___ day of ___ 1865.

Anthony Thomas

Provost Marshal General, Dept. Cumberland.

The above-named has Dark complexion, Dark hair, and Blue eyes; and is 5 feet 11 inches high. Was formerly a Pvt in Co. 6, 1st Ky Regiment Cav in Rebel army.

(Fig. 10) KY-4.65.02 Owen County, KY, loyalty oath

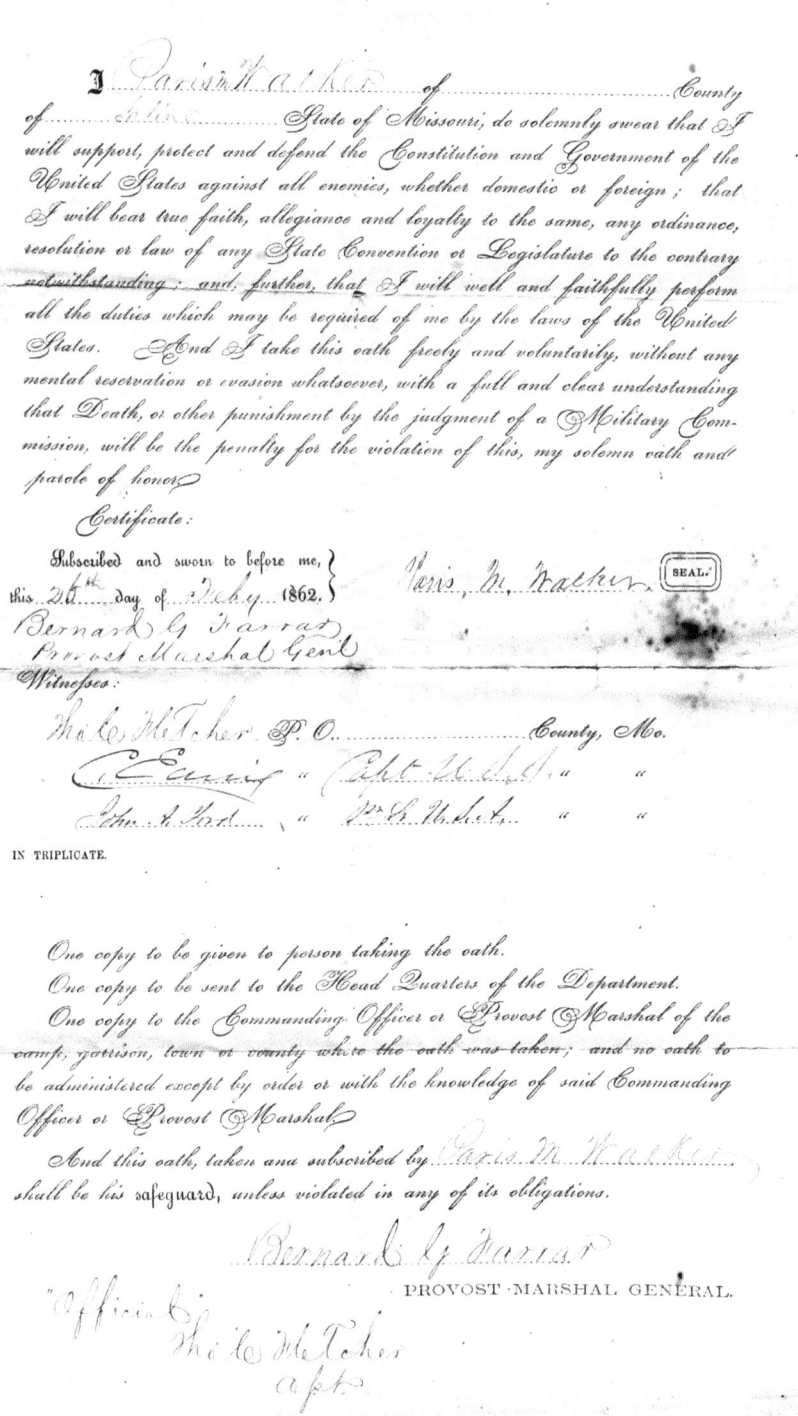

(Fig. 11) MO-4.62.02 Saline, MO, loyalty oath

DESCRIPTION OF PERSON.

Name, *Geo. H. Howard*
Age, *32* Height, *5 — 11¾*
Color of Eyes, *Blue*
Color of Hair, *Black*
Nativity, *N. J.*
Residence, *Jeff City, Mo*
Peculiarities, *Path Master*

I hereby acknowledge that I accept this Pass upon my word of honor, solemnly pledged, that I will ever bear true faith and allegiance to the United States of America, and that I will consider such allegiance as paramount to that due to any other power, sovereignty or State whatsoever; that I will never take arms against the United States, or those acting under its authority, or give aid, information or comfort to its enemies; and that I will do all in my power, as a citizen, to discourage the present rebellion, and preserve the Federal Union.

Geo. H. Howard

(Fig. 12) MO-4.64.03 Jefferson City, MO, pass and oath

STATE OF MISSISSIPPI----Attala County.

I, Samuel G. Peeler, do solemnly swear in the presence of Almighty God that I will hereafter faithfully protect and defend the Constitution of the United States, and the Union of the States thereunder, and that I will in like manner abide by and faithfully support all laws and proclamations which have been made during the existing rebellion with reference to the emancipation of slaves. So help me God.

S. G. Peeler

Sworn to and subscribed before me this the 2 day of October 1865.

I certify that the above is a true copy of an oath sworn to and subscribed before me this the 2 day of October A. D. 1865.

(Fig. 13) MS-4.65.01 Attala County, MS, loyalty oath

I, R of A Teague, of Davidson County, State of North-Carolina, do solemnly swear or affirm in presence of Almighty God, that I will henceforth faithfully support, protect and defend the Constitution of the United States and the Union of the States thereunder; and that I will, in like manner, abide by and faithfully support all laws and proclamations which have been made during the existing rebellion with reference to the emancipation of slaves. So help me God.

R B A Teague

Sworn and subscribed to this the 15 day of Sept, A. D., 1865, before M. Evans, J. P.

It is hereby certified that the above is a true copy of the original oath taken and subscribed by R of A Teague

E G Burton, J. P.
M. Evans, J. P.
_____, J. P.

(Fig. 14) NC-4.65.04 Davidson County, NC, loyalty oath

[OATH PRESCRIBED BY SEC. 4, ART. VI. OF THE CONSTITUTION AND SEC. 4 OF "AN ACT TO PROVIDE FOR THE REGISTRATION OF VOTERS," RATIFIED THE 24TH DAY OF AUGUST, 1868.]

I, L T Smith, do solemnly swear, [or, affirm,] that I will support and maintain the Constitution and laws of the United States, and the Constitution and laws of North Carolina not inconsistent therewith. So HELP ME GOD.

L Turner Smith

Sworn and subscribed before me this 26 day of Oct, 1868.

W Estes J P

(Fig. 15) NC-4.68.01 NC voter's loyalty oath

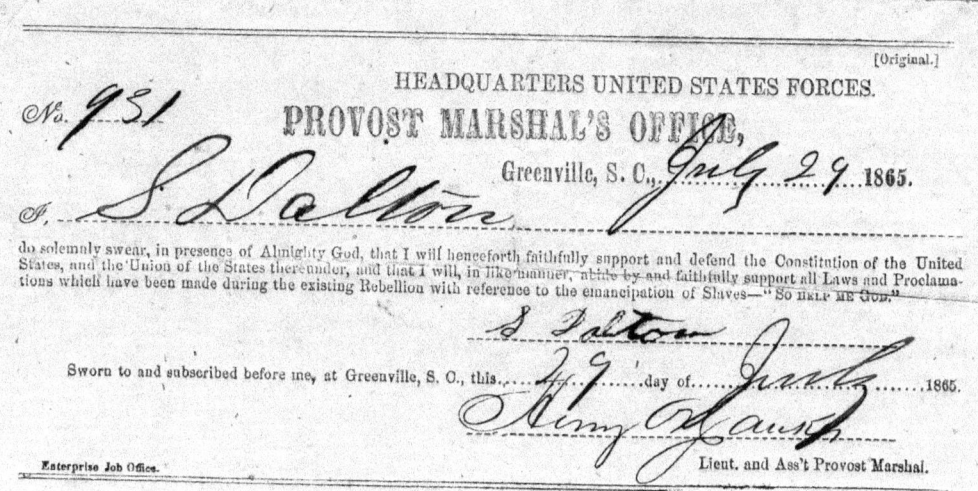

(Fig. 16) SC-4.65.01 Greenville, SC, loyalty oath

To Brig. Genl. H. W. Orme
          General
                    Your petitioner
Wm T Avery a loyal citizen of Shelby County Tennessee having on the third day of June 1865 taken and subscribed the amnesty oath herein filed and marked Exhibit A. and also having been especially pardoned by the President, a certified Copy of which pardon is herewith filed would respectfully represent that he is lawfully seized and possessed of the following described property to wit. a four story brick store house situated on the West side of Main Street in the City of Memphis between Court and Jefferson Streets being No 287½ and occupied as a Saddlery and harness establishment by N. H. Ford the title to which said property is evidenced by the certified Copy of the Deed thereto herein filed and marked Exhibit B

Your petitioner would also represent that he is also seized and possessed of a certain lot or parcel of ground in Shelby County Tennessee adjacent to the City of Memphis lying on what is known as the Germantown plank road on the north side thereof adjoining and lying immediately West of the premises of Mr B Walker containing three acres more or less the title to which lot or parcel of ground is evidenced by a Certified Copy of the deed thereto herein filed and marked Exhibit C.

Your petitioner would further represent that the first mentioned piece of property to wit the store house aforesaid

(Fig. 17) TN-4.62.01 Memphis, TN, property oath (front)

was on the 1st day of September 1862 taken possession of by the United States Government as abandoned property, and rented out on behalf of said Government by Capt. H. J. Fitch, Quarter Master, and continues so to be rented by first one Quarter Master and then another until the 1st day of December 1864 when it fell under the control and management of the 2nd Agency Treasury Department at Memphis Tenn. and by that agency rented out to the present occupant W. H. Ford and that the said rental office still remain in the government and control of said property.

Your petitioner would also represent that the second mentioned piece of property above described to wit the Country lot containing three acres more or less was likewise seized by the U. S. Government as abandoned property and rented out by the aforesaid rental office to one Mrs. J. Tipping who still remains in possession thereof.

Your petitioner therefore most respectfully and earnestly prays, that, in view of the fact that he is now a loyal Citizen of the United States, having been made so by the special pardon of the President, and by him restored to the full possession of his right of property as such,

(Fig. 18) TN-4.62.01 Memphis, TN, property oath (back)

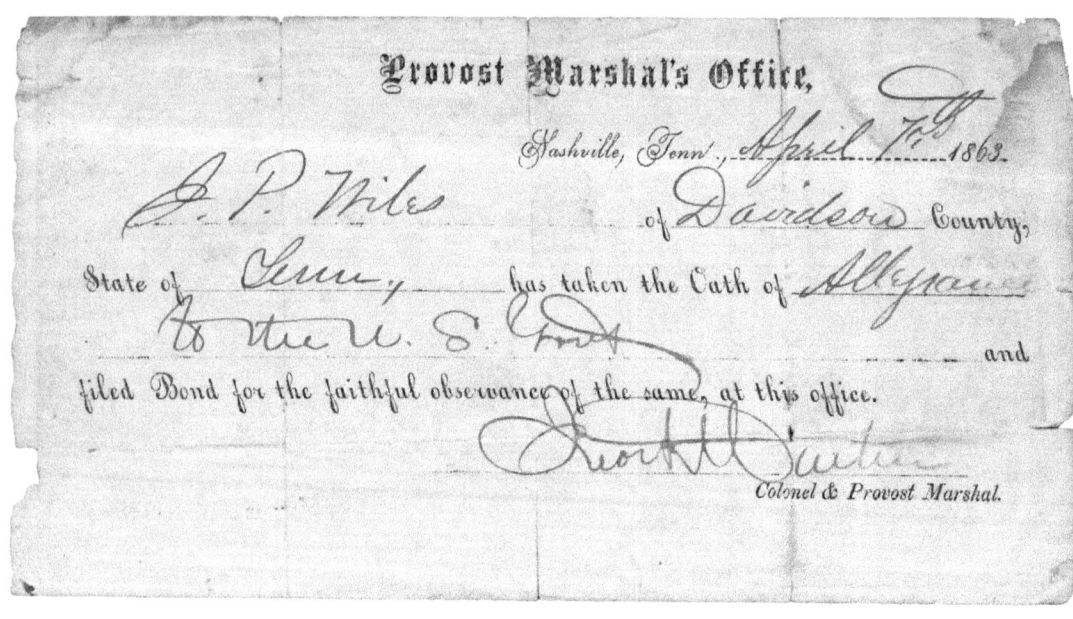

(Fig. 19) TN-4.63.01 Nashville, TN, oath of allegiance

(Fig. 20) TN-5.67.01 McMinn County, TN, Union soldier's voter registration certificate

278

UNITED STATES OF AMERICA.

THE STATE OF TEXAS,

COUNTY OF CORYELL.

TO ALL WHOM IT MAY CONCERN--

KNOW YE: That *G. J. Buck* ....of the County of Coryell, and State of Texas, has this day, *Nov. 7th*......, A. D. 1865, before me, taken the Oath of Amnesty, prescribed by Andrew Johnson President of the United States and his name is placed on the Register of said county as a Voter

To which facts, I certify.

F. W. Maberry., Chief Justice Coryell County.

ATTEST;

R. G. Pidcock...Clerk County Court.

(Fig. 21) TX-4.65.06 Coryell County, TX, amnesty oath

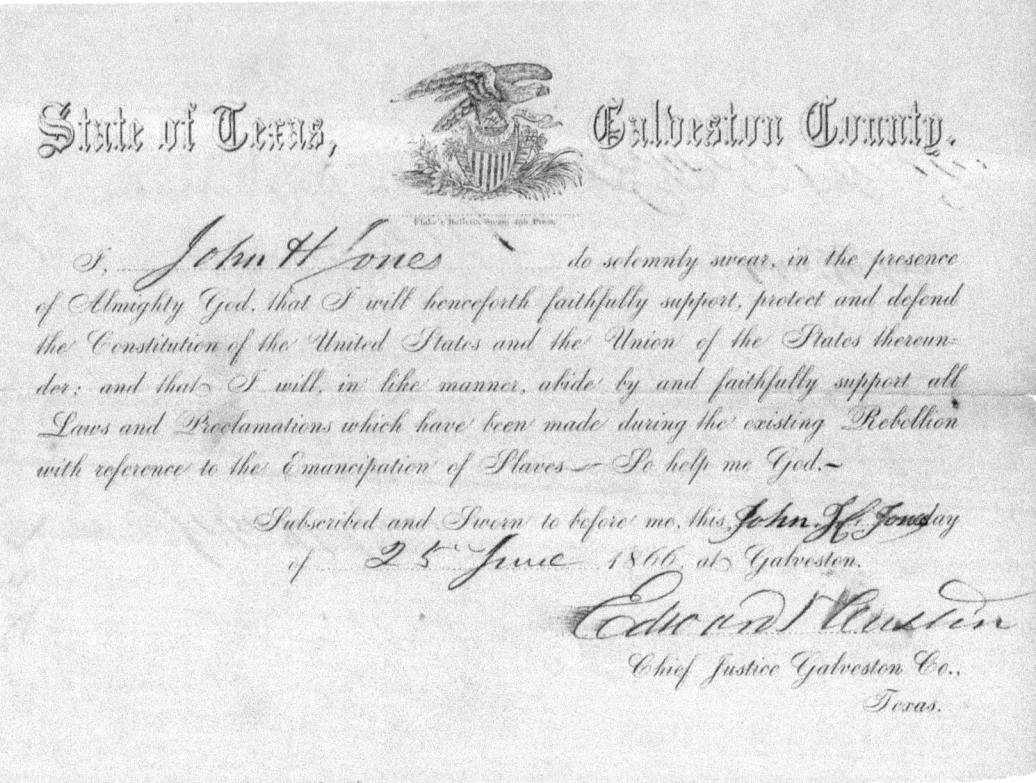

(Fig. 22) TX-4.66.01 Galveston, TX, loyalty oath

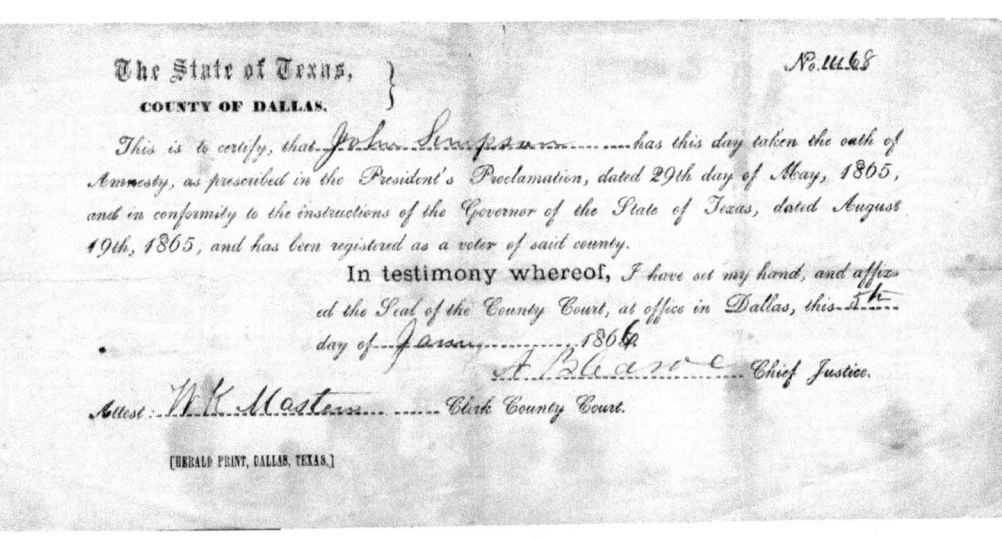

(Fig. 23) TX-4.66.02 Dallas, TX, amnesty oath

> I solemnly swear that I will support the Constitution of the United States, and the Laws made in pursuance thereof, as the Supreme Law of the land, any thing in the Constitution and Laws of the State of Virginia, or in the Ordinance of the Convention, which assembled at Richmond on the 13th February, 1861, to the contrary notwithstanding; and that I will uphold and defend the Government of Virginia, as vindicated and restored by the Convention, which assembled at Wheeling, on the 11th day of June, 1861.
>
> (Signed)
>
> VIRGINIA: WYTHE COUNTY, TO WIT:
>
> The above Oath was subscribed and sworn to before me, by _____, this ___ day of _____, 1865.
>
> Given under my hand, this day and year aforesaid.

(Fig. 24) VA-4.65.07 Wythe County, VA, oath

> OFFICE OF PROVOST MARSHAL,
> RICHMOND, VA., _____ 19 1865.
>
> I, _____ of _____, do solemnly swear, or affirm, in presence of Almighty God, that I will henceforth faithfully support and defend the Constitution of the United States, and the Union of the States thereunder; and that I will, in like manner, abide by and faithfully support all laws and proclamations which have been made during the existing rebellion with reference to the emancipation of slaves, so HELP ME GOD.
>
> Sworn and subscribed to before me, this ___ day of _____ 1865, at _____.
>
> Provost Marshal.

(Fig. 25) VA-4.65.08 Richmond, VA, loyalty oath

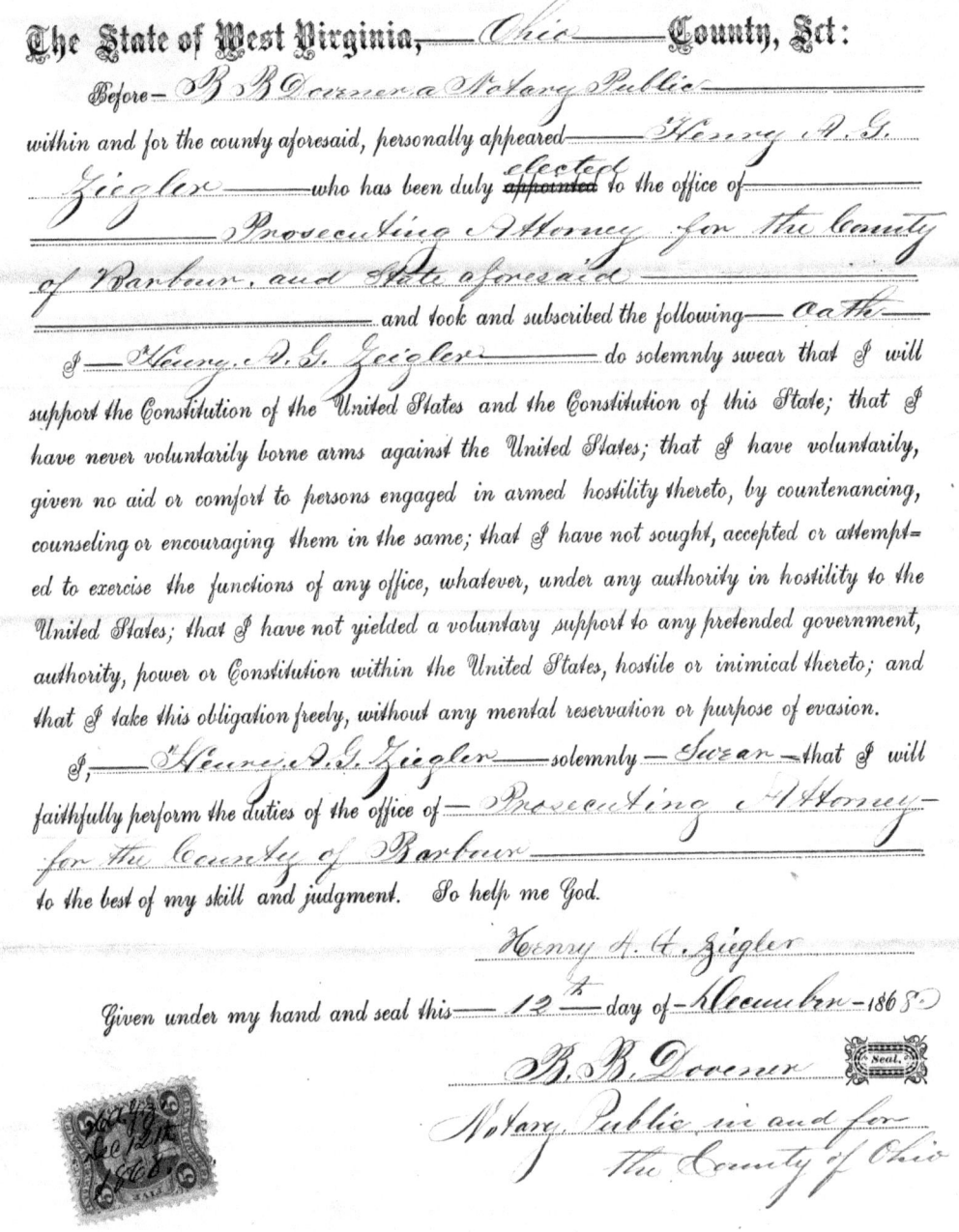

The State of West Virginia, Ohio County, Sct:

Before B. B. Dovener a Notary Public within and for the county aforesaid, personally appeared Henry A. G. Ziegler who has been duly elected to the office of Prosecuting Attorney for the County of Barbour, and State aforesaid and took and subscribed the following Oath

I, Henry A. G. Ziegler do solemnly swear that I will support the Constitution of the United States and the Constitution of this State; that I have never voluntarily borne arms against the United States; that I have voluntarily, given no aid or comfort to persons engaged in armed hostility thereto, by countenancing, counseling or encouraging them in the same; that I have not sought, accepted or attempted to exercise the functions of any office, whatever, under any authority in hostility to the United States; that I have not yielded a voluntary support to any pretended government, authority, power or Constitution within the United States, hostile or inimical thereto; and that I take this obligation freely, without any mental reservation or purpose of evasion.

I, Henry A. G. Ziegler solemnly swear that I will faithfully perform the duties of the office of Prosecuting Attorney for the County of Barbour to the best of my skill and judgment. So help me God.

Henry A. G. Ziegler

Given under my hand and seal this 12th day of December 1865

B. B. Dovener [Seal]

Notary Public in and for the County of Ohio

(Fig. 26) WV-4.68.01 Barbour County, WV, oath of office and allegiance

Notes

Introduction

1. Caroline Thomas Harnsberger, *Treasury of Presidential Quotations* (Chicago: Follett, 1964), 338.
2. *Ibid.*, 287.
3. *Ibid.*, 338.

Chapter 1

1. *Appleton's American Annual Cyclopedia*, Vol. 1, 1861, 358.
2. *Ibid.*, 359.
3. Frances Bellamy, "The Story of the Pledge of Allegiance to the Flag," *University of Rochester Library Bulletin*, Vol. VIII, Winter 1953; Title 4, Chapter 1, U.S. Code; Harold Melvin Hyman, *Era of the Oath: Northern Loyalty Tests During the Civil War and Reconstruction* (Philadelphia: University of Pennsylvania Press, 1954).

Chapter 2

1. *Ex parte E. Milligan* 71 US 2 (1866); *Ex parte Merryman* 17F. Cas. 144.
2. Circular No. 2, Headquarters, Department of the South, Provost Marshal, Hilton Head Island, South Carolina, [1864].
3. Hyman, *Era of the Oath*. 7; 13–20.
4. *The New South*, Sept. 6, 1862.
5. *Appleton's American Annual Cyclopedia*, Vol. 3, 1863, 469–491.
6. *Ibid.*, 606–608.
7. *Appleton's American Annual Cyclopedia*, Vol. 4, 1864, 423; 453.
8. *Appleton's American Annual Cyclopedia*, Vol. 5, 1865, 414, 421.
9. Opinion of the Attorney General, May 1, 1865, Report to the Provost Marshal General, Part I, Appendix to the Report of the Secretary of War, Accompanying Message of the President, 39th Congress, First Session (Washington: GPO, 1866), 256–261.

Chapter 3

1. War of the Rebellion: A Compilation of the Official Records of the Union and Confederate Armies (Washington: GPO, 1900), Hereafter cited "*O.R.R.*," Series II, Vol. 1, 567.
2. *Appleton's American Annual Cyclopedia*, Vol. 1, 1861, 419.
3. *Ibid.*
4. *Appleton Williams American Annual Cyclopedia*, Vol. 1, 51; 440.
5. *Appleton's American Annual Cyclopedia*, Vol. 1, 1861, 361–362.
6. *Appleton's American Annual Cyclopedia*, Vol. 2, 1862, 560.
7. *O.R.R.*, Series II, Vol. 1, 689.
8. *Ibid.*, 733; "American Historical Manuscripts," William Reese Cmpany Bulletin 18.
9. *Appleton's American Annual Cyclopedia*, Vol.2, 1862, 589–595.
10. *Appleton's American Annual Cyclopedia*, Vol. 3, 1863, 561.
11. *O.R.R.*, Series I, Vol. 2, 48.
12. *Appleton's American Annual Cyclopedia*, Vol. 1, 1861, 74–744.
13. *O.R.R.*, Series I, Vol. 5, 577.
14. *Ibid.*, 638–9.
15. *O.R.R.*, Series II, Vol. 2, 1380–1.
16. *Appleton's American Annual Cyclopedia*, Vol. 2, 1862, 342.
17. *O.R.R.*, Series I, Vol. 4, 275–6.
18. *Appleton's American Annual Cyclopedia*, Vol. 2, 1862, 342.
19. *Ibid.*
20. John S. C. Abbott, *The History of the Civil War in America*, Vol. 1 (New York: Henry Bell, 1863), 489–491.
21. *Appleton's American Annual Cyclopedia*, Vol. 2, 1862, 596–597.
22. *Ibid.*, 765–768.
23. *O.R.R.*, Series II, Vol.5, 24, 339.
24. *Appleton's American Annual Cyclopedia*, Vol. 2, 1862, 567–569.
25. Memphis *Appeal*, May 26, 1863.
26. *O.R.R.*, Series II, Vol. 2, 56.
27. *Ibid.*, 63.
28. *The New South*, Sept. 13, 1862.
29. *O.R.R.*, Series II, Vol. 5, 174.
30. *Ibid.*, 56, 80.

31. *Ibid.*, 117–119.
32. B. M. Palmer. *The Oath of Allegiance to the United States Discussed in Its Moral and Political Bearings...* (Richmond: Macfarlane and Ferguson, 1863).

Chapter 4

1. *Appleton's American Annual Cyclopedia*, Vol. 2, 1862, 509.
2. *O.R.R.*, Series II, Vol. 3, 525.
3. *Appleton's American Annual Cyclopedia*, Vol. 2, 1862, 561.
4. *Ibid.*, 516.
5. *O.R.R.*, Series II, Vol. 4, 393.
6. *Ibid.*, 652.
7. *Appleton's American Annual Cyclopedia*, Vol. 2, 1862, 516.
8. *O.R.R.*, Series II, Vol. 5, 174, 312–315.
9. *Appleton's American Annual Cyclopedia*, Vol. 3, 1863, 610–621.
10. *Ibid.*, 334–337.
11. *Ibid.*, 811–817.
12. *Ibid.*, 486.
13. *O.R.R.*, Series II, Vol. 7, 898–899.
14. *O.R.R.*, Series II, Vol. 6, 802–803.
15. *O.R.R.*, Series II, Vol. 6, 175, 186, 212, 868, 942, 1057.
16. *O.R.R.*, Series II, Vol. 5, 546.
17. *O.R.R.*, Series III, Vol. 4, 46.
18. *Appleton's American Annual Cyclopedia*, Vol. 3, 1863, 828.
19. *Appleton's American Annual Cyclopedia*, Vol. 4, 1864, 765–769.
20. *Appleton's American Annual Cyclopedia*, Vol. 3, 1863, 14–15.
21. *Appleton's American Annual Cyclopedia*, Vol. 5, 1865, 28–29.
22. *Brownsville Journal*, July 1864.
23. *Appleton's American Annual Cyclopedia*, Vol. 3, 1863, 563–570.
24. *Ibid.*, 845.
25. *Ibid.*, 652–657.
26. *Appleton's American Annual Cyclopedia*, Vol. 4, 1864, 551–554.
27. *Appleton's American Annual Cyclopedia*, Vol. 2, 1865, 587–593.
28. *Appleton's American Annual Cyclopedia*, Vol. 4, 1864, 497–507.
29. *Appleton's American Annual Cyclopedia*, Vol. 5, 1865, 464–466.
30. *Appleton's American Annual Cyclopedia*, Vol. 4, 1864, 438; Vol. 5, 1864, 438.
31. *O.R.R.*, Series II, Vol. 7, 714.
32. *Ibid.*, 930–953, 1214–1217.
33. *O.R.R.*, Series II, Vol. 8, 255–257.
34. *O.R.R.*, Series II, Vol. 4, 152; Vol. 8, 986–1004.
35. *Appleton's American Annual Cyclopedia*, Vol. 5, 1865, 202–203.

Chapter 5

1. *O.R.R.*, Series II, Vol. 3, 9–10.
2. *Ibid.*
3. *Ibid.*, 51–52.
4. *Ibid.*, 163–164, 263.
5. *Ibid.*, 9–10, 52.
6. *O.R.R.*, Series I, Vol. 3, 473.
7. *Appleton's American Annual Cyclopedia*, Vol. 1, 1861, 591.
8. *Ibid.*
9. *O.R.R.*, Series II, Vol. 3, 264.
10. *Ibid.*, 256.
11. *Ibid.*, 782, 840.
12. *O.R.R.*, Series II, Vol. 4, 94, 242, 246, 356, 490.
13. *O.R.R.*, Series II, Vol. 3, 698.
14. *O.R.R.*, Series II, Vol. 4, 417, 522, 569, 598.
15. *O.R.R.*, Series II, Vol. 5, 113–114.
16. *O.R.R.*, Series II, Vol. 4, 150; *O.R.R.*, Series I, Vol. 20, Part 2, 4–5; *O.R.R.*, Series II, Vol. 5, 299.
17. *O.R.R.*, Series II, Vol. 5, 169.
18. *Ibid.*, 306–307, 679–680.
19. *Appleton's American Annual Cyclopedia*, Vol. 3, 1863, 762.
20. *O.R.R.*, Series II, Vol. 6, 14, 38, 103, 111, 177, 178.
21. *Appleton's American Annual Cyclopedia*, Vol. 3, 1863, 164.
22. *O.R.R.*, Series II, Vol. 7, 144–145.
23. *O.R.R.*, Series II, Vol. 8, 239–240; 266.

Chapter 6

1. William G. Nine and Ronald G. Wilson, *Appomattox Paroles, April 9–15, 1865* (Lynchburg: H. E. Howard, 1989), 4–26.

Chapter 7

1. *Appleton's American Annual Cyclopedia*, Vol.5, 1865, 136.
2. *Ibid.*, 568–576.
3. *O.R.R.*, Series II, Vol. 8, 585, 654–656, 658, 709–710, 929.
4. *Ibid.*, 711, 986, 1004.
5. *Ex parte Garland*, 4 Wallace 333 (1867).
6. Wiley Britton, *The Aftermath of the Civil War: Based on the Investigation of War Claims* (Kansas City: Smith-Grieves,1924) 45, 179.
7. *Ibid.*, 25–26.
8. *Ibid.*, 26–27, 146, 149.
9. *Ibid.*, 46–47, 50–51.
10. *Ibid.*, 52–53.
11. *Ibid.*, 53–55.
12. *Appleton's American Annual Cyclopedia*, Vol. 5, 1865, 819–820.
13. *O.R.R.*, Series II, Vol. 1, 88.
14. *U. S. Statutes at Large*, XVIII, 152, Sec. 822.

Bibliography

Abbott, John S.C. *The History of the Civil War in America*. Vol. 1. New York: Henry Bell, 1863.

Alotta, Robert I. *Civil War Justice: Union Army Executions Under Lincoln*. Shippensburg, PA: White Mane, 1989.

The American Annual Cyclopedia and Register of Important Events of the Year 1861–1865. Vols. I–V New York: D. Appleton, 1870.

Britton, Wiley. *The Aftermath of the Civil War Based on the Investigation of War Claims*.
Kansas City: Smith-Grieves, 1924.

Cooper, Thomas V. and Hector T. Fenton. *American Politics (Non-Partisan) from the Beginning to Date... Federal Blue Book*. Philadelphia: Fireside, 1862.

Cox, Samuel S. *Union-Disunion-Reunion: Three Decades of Federal Legislation, 1855 to 1885 ... etc.* Providence, R.I.: J.A. and R.A. Reid, 1885.

Dorris, Jonathan Truman. *Pardon and Amnesty Under Lincoln and Johnson: The Restoration of the Confederates to their Rights and Privileges, 1861–1898*. Chapel Hill: University of North Carolina Press, 1953.

Hall, Clifton R. *Andrew Johnson: Military Governor of Tennessee*. Princeton: Princeton University Press, 1916.

Hesseltine, William Best. *Civil War Prisons: A Study in War Psychology*. American Classic Series. New York: Frederick Ungar, 1930.

Holberton, William B. *Homeward Bound: The Demobilization of the Union and Confederate Armies, 1865–1866*. Mechanicsburg, PA; Stackpole, 2001.

Hyman, Melvin Howard. *Era of the Oath: Northern Loyalty Test During the Civil War and Reconstruction*. Philadelphia: University of Pennsylvania Press, 1954.

Lonn, Ella *Desertion During the Civil War*. Gloucester, MA; Peter Smith, 1966.

McKitrick, Eric L. *Andrew Johnson and Reconstruction*. Chicago: University of Chicago Press, 1960.

Palmer, B. M. *The Oath of Allegiance to the United States, Discussed in its Moral and Political Bearings*. Richmond: Macfarlane & Fergusson, 1863.

Nine, William G., and Ronald G. Wilson. *Appomattox Paroles, April 9–15, 1865*. Lynchburg: H. E. Howard, 1989.

Thomas, W. Stephen. *Fort Davis and the Texas Frontier*. College Station: Texas A & M University Press, 1976.

Tillotson, Lee A. *The Articles of War Annotated* Harrisburg, PA; The Military Service Publishing Co., 1943.

War of the Rebellion: A Compilation of the Official Records of the Union and Confederate Armies. 128 vols. Washington, D.C.: Government Printing Office, 1900.

Willis, Anson. *Our Rules and Rights: or Outlines of the United States Government, Its Origin, Branches, Departments, Institutions, Offices and Modes of Operation*. New York: C.L. Van Allen, 1870.

Index

Adjutant General of the US Army 31, 50, 68, 75, 77, 79, 82, 84, 91
amnesty: definition 19; offers 6, 21, 22, 40, 53, 103, 108; post war 13, 110–117, 121, 131–132, 135–138; qualifications 6, 86, 91, 92; terms 53, 56, 60, 124
Anderson, Robert A. (U.S. general) 36
Appomattox Court House, Virginia 92, 96–97
Army (U.S.) Regulations 12
Articles (Rules) of War 23, 56, 59, 78, 103, 146, 187
Atlanta, Georgia 68, 149
Attorney General of the United States 17, 22, 112, 185

Baltimore, Maryland 11, 15–17, 21, 24–26, 42, 49, 60, 121, 123
Banks, Nathan P. (U.S. general) 25, 42–43, 89
border states 2, 6–7, 15, 19, 24–25, 35, 41, 43, 49–50, 65, 77, 91, 116, 121
Boston, Massachusetts 11, 17, 25, 27, 49, 50, 52, 110
Breckinridge, John C. (U.S. senator) 14, 132
Bright, Jesse D. (U.S. senator) 14, 81
Brown, Joseph E. (governor of Georgia) 114–115
Butler, Benjamin (U.S. general) 15, 24–25, 42–43, 47, 89

Cairo, Illinois 42, 150
Camp Chase, Ohio 36, 68, 79, 81, 113
Camp Lew Wallace, Ohio 81
Charleston, South Carolina 1, 25, 42, 67, 69–70, 77, 89, 98, 130

claims 20, 32, 65, 70, 116, 120–124, 136, 186–187
Colored Troops 65, 121
Commissary General of Prisoners 67–68, 81, 83–84, 108, 114
Confederate Congress 77, 82, 116
Confederate Constitution 11, 43
Confederate Passport Office 154
Confiscation Act 14, 21–22, 62, 124
Conscription Act 52
Constitutional Convention: Missouri 65; Tennessee 60; West Virginia 62
court cases: *Alderman v. Booth* 52; *Norris v. Dompleon* 62; *Texas v. White* 136
Crittenden, John J. (U.S. senator) 36

Davis, Jefferson (CS president) 13, 22, 37, 42, 77, 82, 110, 112, 114–115, 124, 129, 132, 136, 138
District of Columbia 4, 21, 49–50, 68, 114
Dix, John A. (U.S. general) 17, 22, 80–81, 83–84, 89

Emancipation Proclamation 63, 67

Fort Bliss, Texas 131
Fort Delaware, Delaware 49, 52, 114
Fort Hamilton, New York 25, 43
Fort Lafayette, New York 15, 17, 25, 77, 114
Fort McHenry, Maryland 17, 25, 52, 68, 75
Fort (Fortress) Monroe, Virginia 41, 74, 77, 89, 110, 114–115
Fort Pulaski, Georgia 68, 114
Fort Warren, Massachusetts 17, 25, 27, 49–50, 110, 114

Frank Leslie's Journal/Frank Leslie's Illustrated Newspaper 57, 69–70
Frémont, John C. (U.S. general) 15, 22, 27, 33, 75
Fry, James B. (U.S. provost marshal general) 16

Garfield, James A. (U.S. general and future U.S. president) 7
Goldsborough, Louis M. (U.S. admiral, flag officer of the North Atlantic Blockading Squadron) 76, 78–79
Grant, U.S. (U.S. general) 37, 41, 78, 83, 86, 91–92, 95, 98, 102
Grant, U.S. (U.S. president) 137

Halleck. Henry W. (U.S. general) 77, 81, 83, 91
Harper's Weekly 69, 95
Hill, D.H. (CS general) 22, 80–81, 83–84, 89
Holt, Joseph (U.S. judge advocate general) 56–57, 86, 131
Huger, Benjamin (CS general) 76, 78–79

"Ironclad" Oath 7, 11, 18–19, 112, 115–116, 124, 136–137, 172

Johnson, Andrew (military governor) 37, 39–41, 57–60
Johnson, Andrew (U.S. president) 7, 11, 13, 21–22, 67, 108, 110, 112, 114–115, 123, 127, 132, 135–136, 187

Kentucky 7, 21, 24, 27, 33, 35–37, 40, 58, 60, 62–63, 65, 67, 75–76, 79, 81, 84, 93, 102, 115–116, 121, 132

Lee, Arthur T. (Western artist and U.S. captain) 71–73
Lee, Robert E. (CS general) 92, 95, 98, 101, 136
Letcher, John (Virginia governor) 33
Lincoln, Abraham (U.S. president) 5, 7, 13–15, 20–22, 24, 29, 37, 41, 43, 46, 50–52, 56, 62, 68, 77–78, 83, 97, 110, 112–113, 116, 136, 187
Little Rock, Arkansas 60–61, 68, 102, 104, 147
Louisville, Kentucky 35–37, 68, 151
loyalty oaths 6, 26, 51, 57, 60, 62–63, 67, 69, 81, 92–93, 116, 137, 166–168, 170–173, 175–177, 182–183

Magoffin, Beriah (Kentucky governor) 36
Maryland 24–26, 49–51, 65, 79, 99, 109, 112–116, 121, 123
McClellan, George B. (U.S. general) 32, 74–75
Memphis, Tennessee 37, 40–41, 68, 91, 157, 178–179, 185
Missouri 7, 15, 21–22, 24, 27–32, 36, 50, 63, 65–67, 71, 75, 77–79, 84, 102, 107, 109, 115–116, 120–121, 124
Mitchel, Ormsby (U.S. general) 36–37
Montgomery, Alabama 38, 74, 102
Morgan, John Hunt (CS colonel) 121

Nashville, Tennessee 37, 39–40, 59, 68, 91, 109, 180
New Orleans, Louisiana 22, 42–44, 46–48, 103, 107, 152
New York Herald 49

Official Records of the War of the Rebellion 185, 187
Old Capitol Prison, D.C. 17, 46, 51, 114
Ould, Robert (CS prisoner exchange agent) 83, 91

Paducah, Kentucky 36

Palmer, Benjamin M. (Presbyterian bishop of New Orleans) 47–48, 186–187
Pardons: definition 19; parole of honor 20, 49, 71–72, 79, 92, 96, 98, 102, 105, 108, 144; presidential 6, 11, 13, 17, 20, 22, 24, 49, 51, 53, 57, 59, 61–63, 65, 67, 69, 92, 110, 113, 115–116, 122–123, 125, 128, 137, 185
paroles (field test) 7
passes (safeguard) 30–31, 56, 59, 61, 73–74, 96–97, 100, 102, 104–105, 107–108, 114, 146
Payment Act of July 4, 1864 116
Perry (U.S. brig) 77
Pledge of Allegiance 6–7, 10–11, 185
political (state) prisoners 5–6, 11, 13, 15, 17, 19–21, 25, 36, 40, 43, 50–52, 67–68, 114–115, 166
Potter, John F. (U.S. representative) 17
presidential proclamations 115, 137
prisoner exchange 22, 52, 56, 71, 79–80, 82

Quantrill, William (CS colonel) 32

Richmond, Virginia 18, 21, 32–33, 35, 47, 70, 74–75, 79, 81, 83, 87, 89–91, 110, 115, 129, 158, 183, 187–187
Rosecrans, W.S. (U.S. general) 33, 39, 63, 79

St. Louis, Missouri 89
San Francisco, California 110
Savannah (CS privateer) 77–78
Savannah, Georgia 42, 68–69, 89, 98, 100, 114, 149
Schofield, J.M. (U.S. general) 32, 63
Scott, Winfield (U.S. General of the Army) 74
secession conventions: Kentucky 35–36; Missouri 30–32; Virginia 35
Sherman, William T. (U.S. general) 41, 62, 67–69, 98, 100

South Carolina 1–2, 6–7, 11, 16, 21, 25, 37, 41, 50, 60, 69–70, 77, 98, 114–115, 136, 185
Stanton, Edwin M. (U.S. secretary of state) 46, 78, 91, 97–98
suspension clause 15

Taney, Roger B. (U.S. chief justice) 15, 52
"Ten Percent" Plan 11, 57, 59–60, 112
Tennessee 14, 21, 24, 33, 36–41, 56–60, 62, 65, 81–93, 85, 92, 102, 109, 112, 115–116, 118, 121, 131–132, 137, 187
treason 6–7, 9–11, 13–15, 19–20, 22, 27, 38, 40, 56, 67, 77, 110, 112, 114, 131–132, 135–136, 138–139

United States Congress 7, 9, 13–14, 16–22, 24, 35–36, 41, 43, 47, 49–51, 53, 60, 74, 77–78, 84, 92, 112, 115–116, 121, 123–124, 131–132, 135–139, 161, 185
United States Constitution 1, 5–7, 9–11, 14–19, 22, 27, 29, 35–36, 42–43, 49, 62, 66–67, 75, 92, 110, 113, 136–137, 161
United States Passport Office 15, 36
United States State Department 6, 15, 17, 25, 43, 46, 49, 57, 139, 146, 163, 165
United States Supreme Court 11, 15, 20, 21, 52, 67, 70, 112, 116, 136
United States War Department 6, 13, 17, 19, 20, 36, 49, 55, 82, 84, 86, 102, 110–111, 114, 148

Wallace, Lew (U.S. general) 81
Washington, D.C. 6, 11, 14–15, 17, 21–22, 24–26, 30, 33, 36–37, 52, 55, 71, 75, 81, 92, 109, 111, 121–122, 133, 136, 148, 162–165, 168, 185, 187
West Virginia 33–35, 62, 116, 125
Wheeling, West Virginia 32–35, 62, 68, 79, 116

www.ingramcontent.com/pod-product-compliance
Lightning Source LLC
Chambersburg PA
CBHW081559300426
44116CB00015B/2938